Topical Song Cycles
of the Early
Nineteenth Century

Recent Researches in Music

A-R Editions publishes seven series of critical editions, spanning the history of Western music, American music, and oral traditions.

Recent Researches in the Music of the Middle Ages and Early Renaissance
  Charles M. Atkinson, general editor

Recent Researches in the Music of the Renaissance
  James Haar, general editor

Recent Researches in the Music of the Baroque Era
  Christoph Wolff, general editor

Recent Researches in the Music of the Classical Era
  Eugene K. Wolf†, general editor

Recent Researches in the Music of the Nineteenth and Early Twentieth Centuries
  Rufus Hallmark, general editor

Recent Researches in American Music
  John M. Graziano, general editor

Recent Researches in the Oral Traditions of Music
  Philip V. Bohlman, general editor

Each edition in *Recent Researches* is devoted to works by a single composer or to a single genre. The content is chosen for its high quality and historical importance, and each edition includes a substantial introduction and critical report. The music is engraved according to the highest standards of production using the proprietary software MusE, owned by MusicNotes, Inc.

For information on establishing a standing order to any of our series, or for editorial guidelines on submitting proposals, please contact:

A-R Editions, Inc.
Middleton, Wisconsin

800 736-0070 (U.S. book orders)
608 836-9000 (phone)
608 831-8200 (fax)
http://www.areditions.com

Recent Researches in the Music of the Nineteenth and Early Twentieth Centuries, 37

Topical Song Cycles of the Early Nineteenth Century

Edited by Ruth O. Bingham

A-R Editions, Inc.
Middleton, Wisconsin

To the impetus, Christopher Hill

A-R Editions, Inc., Middleton, Wisconsin
© 2003 by A-R Editions, Inc.

All rights reserved. No part of this book may be reproduced or transmitted in any form by any electronic or mechanical means (including photocopying, recording, or information storage and retrieval) without permission in writing from the publisher.

The purchase of this edition does not convey the right to perform it in public, nor to make a recording of it for any purpose. Such permission must be obtained in advance from the publisher.

A-R Editions is pleased to support scholars and performers in their use of *Recent Researches* material for study or performance. Subscribers to any of the *Recent Researches* series, as well as patrons of subscribing institutions, are invited to apply for information about our "Copyright Sharing Policy."

Printed in the United States of America

ISBN 0-89579-526-4
ISSN 0193-5364

∞ The paper used in this publication meets the minimum requirements of the American National Standard for Information Sciences—Permanence of Paper for Printed Library Materials, ANSI Z39.48-1984.

Contents

Abbreviations   viii

Acknowledgments   x

Introduction   xi
  Coherence and Shape in Topical Song Cycles   xi
  Poets, Composers, Publishers, and Cycles   xvii
  Notes   xxvi

Texts and Translations   xxix
  The Poems   xxix
  Glossary of Deities and Characters   lxi

Plates   lxiii

Die zwölf Monate
Text by Ignaz Vincenz Franz Castelli
Music by Johann Heinrich Karl Bornhardt

  [1.] Januar: Den ersten Monat heiße füglich   3
  [2.] Februar: Gott Komus führet jetzt das Zepter   5
  [3.] Maerz: Noch wehen rauh und kalte Lüfte   7
  [4.] April: Das ist der Mann   10
  [5.] Mai: Du herrlichster von deinen Brüdern   12
  [6.] Junius: Ihr holden Frauen!   14
  [7.] Julius: Der heiße Strahl der Morgensonne   16
  [8.] August: Das Jahr steht nun auf seiner Spitze   18
  [9.] September: Durch Wald und Flur, im Tal, auf Bergen   20
  [10.] October: Die Rebe schwillt   23
  [11.] November: Die rauhen kalten Winde wehen   25
  [12.] December: Erreicht hat nun das Jahr sein Ende   28

Die Jahreszeiten
Text by T. L. A. Heinroth
Music by Friedrich Schneider

  I. Winter
    1. Winters Ankunft: Welch Tosen da draußen!   33
    2. Winterruhe: Die Sonne weicht nach kurzem Lauf   36
    3. Winternachtleben: Fachet zum Feuer die glimmende Kohle!   37
  II. Frühling
    1. Frühlingshimmel: Es schauet vom Himmel   39
    2. Frühlingserde: Willkommen, trautes Baches Rieseln   40
    3. Frühlingsleben: Unter blauem Himmelsbogen   41

III. Sommer
    1. Im Walde: Es treibt uns die Glut   43
    2. Auf dem Flusse: Die Sonne sinkt   44
    3. In der Laube: Lieblich weht die duft'ge Kühle   45

IV. Herbst
    1. Garten: Die holden Rosen sind erbleicht   46
    2. Weinberg: Lustig den Hügel hinan!   47
    3. Herbstöde: Durch Herbsteslüfte, durch Nebeldüfte   50

Die Farben
Text by Karl Friedrich Müchler
Music by Friedrich Franz Hůrka (nos. 1–5, 7) and Friedrich Heinrich Himmel (no. 6)

    1. Lob der weißen Farbe: Zartes Weiß, die Feier meiner Lieder   53
    2. Lob der roten Farbe: Dir gebühren meine Huldigungen   54
    3. Lob der blauen Farbe: Von allen Farben auf der Welt   56
    4. Lob der gelben Farbe: Der gelben Farbe bin ich hold   58
    5. Lob der grünen Farbe: Singt rot und blau und gelb und grau   59
    [6.] Lob der violetten Farbe: Farbe, die Cytherens Götterhand   61
    [7.] Lob der schwarzen Farbe: Schwarz der Nacht, von dir umgeben   62

Sechszehn Blumen
Text by Joseph Scholz
Music by Paul Anton Wineberger

    [1.] Das Stiefmütterchen: Es blühet auf Hügel und Auen   67
    [2.] Die Sonnenblume: Blume, die von Phöbus Glanz umflogen   68
    [3.] Das Vergissmeinnicht: In feuchten Schatten-Gründen   70
    [4.] Die Nelke: Gepflanzet durch des Gärtners Hand   72
    [5.] Die Nachtviole: Es sinkt Asträa von den Bergen nieder   73
    [6.] Die Lilie: Dir sing' ich, holde Lilie   74
    [7.] Die Kamille: Ich kenn' ein Blümlein klein und zart   76
    [8.] Die Rose: Wenn prangend sich die Rose Kelch entfaltet   78
    [9.] Das Gänseblümchen: Dir, kleine Blume, weih' ich ein Gedicht   79
    [10.] Die Kornblume: Wer kennt sie nicht   80
    [11.] Die Wasser-Lilie: Aus den Fluten keimt ein Blumen-Leben   82
    [12.] Die Hyazinthe: In des Winters trüben Stunden   84
    [13.] Die Mohn-Blume: Kennt ihr die Zeit   86
    [14.] Das Veilchen: Holdes Blümlein, sei willkommen   88
    [15.] Die Tulpe: Die Schönheit bleibt auch ohne Seele schön   90
    [16.] Der Lavendel: Ein Liedchen dir zu singen   96

Die Blumen und der Schmetterling
Text by Karl Friedrich Müchler
Music by Friedrich Heinrich Himmel

    [1.] Zueignung an Deutschlands Töchter: Euch ihr Guten, Euch ihr Schönen   101
    [2.] Das Schneeglöckchen: Wenn noch Eis die Fluren drückt   104
    [3.] Das Veilchen: Von dunklem Laub umschlossen   106

[4.] Die Myrte: Dir Myrtenreis, gebührt der Preis   108
[5.] Die Narzisse: Horch, was tönt vom Felsenhange   110
[6.] Das Vergissmeinnicht: Freundlich glänzt an stiller Quelle   111
[7.] Die Palme: Es mag der Held den Lorbeer preisen   112
[8.] Die Rose: Bild der jungfräulichen Tugend   114
[9.] Wechselgesang der Blumen: Wir Kinder des Lenzen   116
[10.] Der Schmetterling: Von Knosp' auf Knospe schwebend   126

Die Temperamente bei dem Verluste der Geliebten
Text by Wilhelm Gubitz
Music by Carl Maria von Weber

[1.] Der Leichtmütige: Lust entfloh und hin ist hin!   131
[2.] Der Schwermütige: Sel'ge Zeiten sah ich prangen   138
[3.] Der Liebewütige: Verraten! Verschmähet!   141
[4.] Der Gleichmütige: Nun, ich bin befreit   148

Critical Report   149

Editorial Methods   149
Critical Notes and Commentary   151
Notes to Performers   156

Abbreviations

ADB — *Allgemeine deutsche Biographie.* Auf Veranlassung und mit Unterstützung seiner Majestaet des Königs von Bayern Maximilian II. Herausgegeben durch die historische Commission bei der Königl. Akademie der Wissenschaften. Reprint of the 1st ed. of 1876. Berlin: Duncker & Humblot, 1968.

Eitner — Robert Eitner. *Biographisch-bibliographisches Quellen-Lexikon der Musiker und Musikgelehrten der christlichen Zeitrechnung bis zur Mitte des neunzehnten Jahrhunderts.* 1st ed., Leipzig: Breitkopf und Härtel, 1900–1904. 2d ed., revised, 1959–60.

Fétis — François-Joseph Fétis. *Biographie universelle des musiciens et bibliographie générale de la musique.* 2d ed. Paris: Librairie de Firmin Didot et Cie., 1883.

Gerber — Ernst Ludwig Gerber. *Historisch-biographisches Lexikon der Tonkünstler (1790–1792) und Neues Historisch-biographisches Lexikon der Tonkünstler (1812–1814) mit den in den Jahren 1792 bis 1834 veröffentlichten Ergänzungen sowie der Erstveröffentlichung handschriftlicher Berichtungen und Nachträge.* Edited by Othmar Wesseley. Graz, Austria: Akademische Druck- und Verlagsanstalt, 1969.

GGGDD — *Goedekes Grundriß zur Geschichte der deutschen Dichtung.* Neue Folge: Fortführung von 1830 bis 1880. Herausgegeben von der Deutschen Akademie der Wissenschaften zu Berlin unter Leitung von Leopold Magon. 17 vols. Berlin: Akademie Verlag, in Arbeitsgemeinschaft mit dem Verlag L. Ehlermann in Düsseldorf, 1955.

Kosch-2 — Wilhelm Kosch. *Deutsches Literatur-Lexikon: biographisches und bibliographisches Handbuch.* 2d ed., enlarged. Bern: A. Francke AG Verlag, 1956.

Kosch-3 — Wilhelm Kosch. *Deutsches Literatur-Lexikon: biographisches und bibliographisches Handbuch.* Edited by Heinz Rupp and Carl Ludwig Lang. 3d ed. Bern: K. G. Saur, 1994.

NG — *The New Grove Dictionary of Music and Musicians.* Edited by Stanley Sadie. 20 vols. London: Macmillan, 1980.

NG2 — *The New Grove Dictionary of Music and Musicians.* Edited by Stanley Sadie; executive editor, John Tyrrell. 29 vols. 2d ed. London: Macmillan, 2001.

NG-MPP — *Music Printing and Publishing: The Norton New Grove Handbooks in Music.* Edited by Donald William Krummel and Stanley Sadie. New York: W. W. Norton, 1990.

HRML — *Hugo Riemanns Musik Lexikon.* Edited by Alfred Einstein. 11th ed. Berlin: M. Hesse, 1929.

Whistling   Carl Friedrich Whistling and Friedrich Hofmeister Catalogues. *I. Handbuch der musikalischen Literatur.* Vol. 1, 1816. Ten supplements, 1818–27. 2d ed., 1828. Three supplements, 1829, 1834, 1839. 3d ed., 1844/45. Supplements, 1852–1933. *II. Jahresverzeichnis der deutschen Musikalien und Musikschriften* compiled from the Monatsberichte. *III. Musikalisch-Literarischer Monatsbericht,* now known as *Deutsche Musikbibliographie,* 1929–33.

Acknowledgments

Works such as this cannot honestly list a single author: too many people have contributed their assistance and expertise. Although there is not room to name every one here, I would like to extend my heartfelt gratitude to all, including those now lost to history who have supported the arts, created universities and libraries, and made research possible. Their unsung contributions continue to enrich our lives.

Christopher Hill first suggested this project and opened the gates that set me on the path, offering guidance and encouragement along the way, as did Rufus Hallmark and Susan Youens. Jurgen Thym and William F. Scherer generously read translations and offered suggestions on two particularly thorny spots. Don W. Krummel assisted with details of dating; most importantly, he helped me accept that there can be an end to chasing details, even when questions remain.

I am indebted to Dr. Helmut Hell, Director of the Musikabteilung mit Mendelssohn-Archiv, and Dr. Ina Köhn at the Staatsbibliothek zu Berlin; Director Dr. Hartmut Schaefer, Dr. Uta Schaumberg, and Dr. Ute Roth at the Bayerische Staatsbibliothek in Munich; Dr. Günther Brosche, Director of the Österreichische Nationalbibliothek in Vienna; and Dr. Otto Biba, Director of the Gesellschaft der Musikfreunde in Vienna—and their staffs—for their timely assistance with matters large and small and for permission to publish critical editions of works in their collections. The staff at Stanford University's Music Library and Cecil H. Greene Library also proved to be an invaluable resource.

I am particularly grateful to the music librarians at the University of Hawai'i, Mānoa, Gregg Geary and Barbara Kudo, who provided assistance at every stage, and to the interlibrary loan office, which was able to obtain obscure sources when I needed them.

The editors at A-R Editions, whose expertise shines on every page, deserve special thanks for ushering this work down its long and winding path. Any errors that remain are assuredly my own.

Finally, no project reaches closure without the immeasurable support of family. My father, Carl W. Otto, never doubted (or never let on, if he did doubt) that something would eventually be produced. My mother, Gloria W. Otto, graciously donated weeks of her life to give me time to complete major sections. My children, Dustin and Michael, amiably endured the neglect and mess concomitant to a research project. And my husband, Tom, assisted me in every way imaginable every step of the way.

Introduction

Coherence and Shape in Topical Song Cycles

Lexica of the latter half of the nineteenth century and early twentieth century frequently addressed the ideal song cycle, enumerating its characteristics at great length. The most frequently cited characteristics include the presence of a title such as "Liederkreis" or "Liedercyclus"; one central theme, idea, or mood in the poetry; a text that is a lyric cycle (as opposed to a collection of poems) or that exhibits a progression of some sort; an overall key scheme; thematic return; motivic and textual connections between songs; and so on. In short, Beethoven's *An die ferne Geliebte,* and some authors say as much, for Beethoven's cycle is not uncommonly cited as the first piece entitled "Liederkreis," the first true cycle, and the best example of the genre.[1] This appraisal neatly encapsulates the history of the genre in a single work: earlier sets, being different from Beethoven's, are not true cycles; later cycles, being similar, are emulations. As long as Beethoven's cycle embodies the ideal, Beethoven's primacy is secure: any new "firsts" will simply be seen as forerunners.

Discovering earlier cycles, however, is contingent upon establishing criteria for identifying such works, for choosing song cycles from among the hundreds of song sets and collections published each year in the early nineteenth century. Unfortunately, a working definition of "song cycle" does not yet exist. Each of a wide variety of distinguishing characteristics seems to exclude some work that is generally accepted as belonging to the genre: "written for solo voice" excludes Berger's *Schöne Müllerin;* "text by a single poet" excludes Schumann's *Myrthen und Rosen;* "individual songs in closed forms" excludes Schumann's *Dichterliebe;* "lyric cycle as text" excludes Mahler's *Kindertodtenlieder;* "presence of a textual progression" excludes Neefe's *Bilder und Träume;* the list could go on. In order to include as many cycles as possible, recent dictionaries have taken refuge in a general definition modified by "usually," "sometimes," and "may," as does this entry from *The New Harvard Dictionary of Music:*

> A group of songs, usually for solo voice and piano, constituting a literary and musical unit. . . .
> The poems of a song cycle are usually by a single poet and often exist as a poetic cycle, taken over in whole or in part by the composer. The poems may be related in general theme . . . and sometimes suggest a narrative outline. . . . In other cases, the song texts are the composer's selection and arrangement of poems by a single poet . . . , from a single source . . . , or, less commonly, from different poets. . . .
> The songs in a cycle are sometimes drawn together by musical means. . . . Songs may also be related by common musical motives. However, Schubert's cycles, for example, manifest none of these traits.[2]

Without the qualifications, the only concrete part of the definition is "a group of songs constituting a unit." Unfortunately, that alone fails to distinguish cycles from collections of songs, and it is that distinction that justifies instantiating the song cycle as a genre.

In contrast to current lexica, nineteenth-century sources rarely defined song cycles, and the few that did entered the definition under a wide variety of terms, including "Liederzyklus," "Liederkreis," "Kreislieder," "Liederreihe," "Liederkranz," "ciclica," "cyklus," "cyclique," and "song cycle." The defintions all were published in the latter half of the century and all are remarkably similar. The earliest definition seems to be in Arrey von Dommer's expanded edition of *H. Ch. Koch's Musikalisches Lexicon*, published in 1865:

> *Liederkreis, Liedercyclus.* A unified complex of different lyric poems. Each of the poems is in closed form, but can also differ outwardly from the others in terms of meter and verse structure; all, however, have an inner relationship to one another, because one and the same basic idea runs through all of them; the individual poems display ever differing expressions of it [the basic idea], presenting it in various and often also contrasting likenesses and from different viewpoints, so that the basic feeling is delivered in fairly comprehensive completeness.[3]

Even Dommer's definition, however, is hardly contemporary: cycles were common long before mid-century, and even counting Beethoven's 1816 cycle as the first, almost fifty years seem to have elapsed between the appearance of the genre and the appearance of its definition. The usual explanation for this gap is that lexica are inherently conservative and tend to lag behind current practice.[4] There is undeniably a time lag between event and lexicographical documentation, but a lag of over fifty years is suspect.

Perhaps an explanation for this gap lies in Dommer's lexicon. It may be significant that the term "Cyclische Formen" (cyclic forms) also appears for the first time in

Dommer's lexicon; thereafter, "cyclic form," "song cycle," or "cycle" appear regularly in all the major lexica. Of the three terms, "cyclic form" is defined and discussed most often, most regularly, and at greater length, which seems to suggest that it was the form, the cyclic concept, that was most important. The focus of this new concept was on instrumental forms, specifically multi-movement sonatas and symphonies; the song cycle was presented as simply the vocal counterpart. This may explain in part why the definition appeared almost unchanged in lexica throughout the nineteenth century. It also seems significant that definitions of sonatas and symphonies acquired the "cyclic form" designation at the same time song cycle definitions appear. And it is doubtless not coincidence that the earliest definition of song cycle, written to reflect the new aesthetics of cyclic theory, both perfectly exemplified the theory and tacitly excluded cycles that did not fit the theory. The result was an enduring conflict between definition and repertoire. The gap is not just between the appearance of cycles and the appearance of a definition; it is more fundamentally between the actual music and the stated ideal.

Following the dictates of later nineteenth-century definitions, recent researchers have found that many early song sets were, quite simply, not cycles; if they tried to include these works, they had to alter the accepted definition. Reluctance to tamper with the only contemporary "Liederkreis" definition is understandable, but the sheer size of the time lag (1790s to 1865) suggests that its cause was not sluggish lexicography but a changing aesthetic. Beginning with late nineteenth-century definitions ensures that the results will affirm the premise upon which the definition was built: it all began with Beethoven. To break out of this circular reasoning, we need to know more about early nineteenth-century concepts of "cycle" and the types of forms and compositional techniques used.

General dictionaries, encyclopedias, and even some music dictionaries between 1780 and 1840 occasionally define the term "cycle," but in terms of abstract concepts, not of music, but not of poetry, either. The 1824 *Allgemeine deutsche Real-Encyclopaedie*, for example, gives several different meanings for "cycle," each suggesting a different conceptual shape. The first shape, and perhaps most familiar to us, is the periphery of a circle:

Two definitions from the *Allgemeine deutsche Real-Encyclopaedie* are relevant here:

> In terms of shape, *Kreis* means any return to the point at which one began.

> *Cyklus*, literally translated, means the *Kreis;* thus any uniform, recurring series of the same events.[5]

These definitions include examples such as the calendar, the lunar and solar periods, and circle dances.[6] This definition is fundamental to the type of song sets published in the late eighteenth and early nineteenth centuries; in fact, non-musical cycles often served as central themes.

In his 1796 *Musikalischer Almanach,* for example, Friedrich Reichardt published reviews of lieder alongside his own settings of twelve poems depicting the year's cycle; each explicates the other. In his review of songs by Haydn, Mozart, and three lesser-known composers, he describes what a lied should be and determines that their songs are not lieder, however well delivered:

> The lied should be the simple and comprehensible musical expression of a distinct sentiment, so that it permits participation by those voices suited to natural song as well as being a small artwork easily taken in at a glance, and must even more essentially be a *correct* [and] complete whole, whose real worth lies in the unity of the song, and whose instrumental accompaniment, while not dispensable, yet should be there only for the support of the song. If this theory of lied is correct, then all the lieder mentioned above are no lieder . . .[7]

In short, Reichardt upheld the time-honored aesthetics espoused by Gluck, Goethe, and the composers of Berlin lieder for nearly two generations. In fact, the only German-speaking region that resisted these views centered around Vienna, so it is not surprising that lieder by Haydn and Mozart did not meet Reichardt's criteria.

Reichardt's music in the same volume demonstrated "correct": in twelve songs, there is hardly a note of prelude, interlude, or postlude; rhythms are virtually identical to the poetry's meter and accent; melodies are folklike and rarely employ melisma; accompaniments are light and straightforward, reserving chromatics to respond to the text. Coherence in the twelve poems lies in the topic: Reichardt assembled the texts in a variety of styles from a variety of poets, including five by Voß, two by Fr. von Köpken, and one each by Herklots, Goethe, Herder, Gleim, and Schiller. Nevertheless, each poem effectively represents a step in the sequence of months, the final poem returning to the opening and even looking beyond to continuing cycles of months, of new giving way to old, giving way to new again: i.e., a circular cycle, not of similarity, but of variety. Music's role is primarily to support the text.

Calendar cycles remained popular well into the 1820s and are represented in this edition by Friedrich Schneider's *Die Jahreszeiten* and Johann Bornhardt's *Die zwölf Monate*. In each of these, as in Reichardt's cycle, the keys, meters, and tempos seem to provide minimal connections between songs (see table 1). Although Bornhardt's cycle begins and ends in C and roughly follows the circle of fifths, and although Schneider's cycle has some internal groupings (the Summer and Fall groups, for example, each use closely related keys, and the Winter group uses metric return and a fast-slow-fast pattern), it is difficult to find tonal, metric, or temporal patterns for

TABLE 1
Keys, Meters, and Tempos of Calendar Song Cycles

1. Johann F. Reichardt, *Musikalischer Almanach*, 1796

[1.] Januar: "Skolie zum Winterabend"	C	3/8	Nicht langsam (Solo & Chor)
[2.] Februar: "Winterlied"	E♭	3/4	Edel gesungen
[3.] März: "Der Federschmuck"	C	2/4	Leicht
[4.] April: "An die Nachtigall"	B♭	2/4	———
[5.] May: "An der Quelle"	C	6/8	Sanft (Chorgesang)
[6.] Junius: "Die Rosenfeier"	B♭	6/8	Innig
[7.] Julius: "Die Linde"	D	3/8	Sanft
[8.] August: "Skolie im Abendroth"	B♭	2/2	Mässig (Solo & Chor)
[9.] September: "Dithyrambe"	A	6/4	Feurig
[10.] October: "Der Herbsttag"	A	2/4	Mässig & mild (Dreistimmig)
[11.] November: "An die Freude"	C	4/4	Feierlich froh (Solo & Chor)
[12.] December: "Beim Rheinwein"	D	4/4	Froh (Chorgesang)

2. Friedrich Schneider, *Die Jahreszeiten*, between 1821 and 1828

I. Winter

1. Winters Ankunft	D	6/8	Lebhaft (Solo & Chor)
2. Winterruhe	E	3/4	Mit ruhigem Vortrag (Solo)
3. Winternachtleben	C	6/8	Fröhlich (Männergesang)

II. Frühling

1. Frühlingshimmel	E	3/8	Sanft (Solo)
2. Frühlingserde	G	9/8	Mit innigem Vortrag (Solo)
3. Frühlingsleben	D	3/4	Fröhlich und leicht (Solo)

III. Sommer

1. Im Walde	B♭	4/4	Mit leichter Bewegung (Chor)
2. Auf dem Flusse	E♭	2/4	Sanft, schwebend (Chor)
3. In der Laube	A♭	6/8	Sehr sanft (Chor)

IV. Herbst

1. Garten	C–a	4/4	In mässiger Bewegung (Bass solo)
2. Weinberg	E	6/4	Kräftig und schnell (Bass & Chor)
3. Herbstöde	A	3/4	Langsam, mit vielem Gefühl (Solo)

3. Johann Bornhardt, *Die zwölf Monate*, 1828–29

[1.] Januar	C	4/4	Andante
[2.] Februar	F	3/4	Allegretto
[3.] Maerz	g–B♭	4/4	Allegro
[4.] April	C	4/4	Allegretto scherzoso
[5.] Mai	E♭	4/4	Andante grazioso
[6.] Junius	A♭	3/4	Andantino
[7.] Julius	E	4/4	Andante
[8.] August	A	4/4	Andantino
[9.] September	D	6/8	Vivace—Andantino grazioso
[10.] October	G	4/4	Andantino con moto
[11.] November	a–A	4/4	Allegro agitato—Un poco lento
[12.] December	C	4/4	Andantino—Andantino
"Erreicht hat nun das Jahr sein Ende…"			

each work as a whole. Attempts to identify such patterns primarily generate patterns accompanied by numerous exceptions that tolerate little scepticism. Furthermore, there are no obvious motivic or thematic returns and two of the sets are not even for solo voice. According to most definitions, these works are little more than collections; at most, they are primitive forerunners of the "true" song cycle. They were, however, all published as sets (in Reichardt's case, as an integral part of a book) and the months and seasons follow in order and reveal the expected external and internal progressions. Notice, for example, the titles of Schneider's songs: "Winters *Ankunft*" (onset), "Winter*ruhe*" (peace), "Winternacht*leben*" (life); "Frühlings*himmel*" (heaven), "Frühlings*erde*" (earth), "Frühlings*leben*" (life, as in the last song of the winter group). Each of these songs could be extracted and sung alone; but together they reveal closer connections and more structure than most collections do.

xiii

A second conceptual shape cited in contemporary lexica is based on the mathematical definition of "circle":

> *Cyklus:* In Geometry, *Kreis* is the location of all points in a plane that are equidistant from a given point in the same plane.[8]

This shape resembles a spoked wheel, in that each point of the circle relates directly only to the central point, not to other points around the circle, yielding a versatile form that provides both "unity" (to the central point) and "variety" (to the other points):

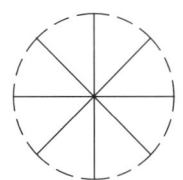

The spoked wheel shape readily lends itself to poetic and musical analogies: a series of individual poems or songs on a central idea, image, or mood. Like the points of a circle, the number of possible poems or songs in these sets is infinite and, as Helen Mustard points out in *The Lyric Cycle in German Literature*,[9] infinite cycles are quintessentially Romantic. Not surprisingly, song sets that correspond to this shape are the most common type of cycle during the bloom of Romanticism in Germany, from as early as the 1790s through the first few decades of the 1800s. Examples of such cycles abound: *Wanderlieder, Frühlingslieder, Blumensträuße, Lieder der Liebe*, etc.

One of the earliest examples of this type was *Die Farben*, written by Karl Müchler, set by Friedrich Hůrka, and first published in Berlin in 1795. The cycle proved to be popular, appearing in at least three different versions and published by several different houses, yet the piece is not recognized today as a cycle. First, the settings are not all by one composer—"Lob der violetten Farbe," added to later editions, is by Friedrich Himmel—and the final poem, "Lob der schwarzen Farbe," may not have been written by Müchler. Also, like the calendar cycles, the keys, meters, and tempos reveal no clear pattern (see table 2). There seems to be no progression either in the titles or in the texts, yet these songs are clearly related. Notice, for example, the variation style of the titles, in which only the color changes. Müchler seems to have approached one central idea—color—from different perspectives. He presented these poems as a group, but their coherence does not depend on their order; "white-red-blue-yellow-green-violet" is no more cohesive than "white-yellow-green-blue-violet-red." They are a set of variations on a topic, or a topical cycle.

Perhaps the most popular topic for early cycles of this type was flowers: *Blumensträuße, Blumenkreise, Blumenkränze*, and the like abounded. Flower cycles remained popular well into the nineteenth century, but were eclipsed by the more intrinsically Romantic topics of wandering and love in the 1810s. The popularity of flow-

TABLE 2
Keys, Meters, and Tempos of *Die Farben*

Friedrich Hůrka and Friedrich Himmel, *Die Farben*, 1795
1. Lob der weissen Farbe	C	2/2	Adagio non tanto
2. Lob der rothen Farbe	E♭	2/2	Andante grazioso
3. Lob der blauen Farbe	A	3/4	Alla Polacca
4. Lob der gelben Farbe	D	2/2	Allegro maestoso
5. Lob der grünen Farbe	F	6/8	Allegro

Added in later editions:
[6.] Lob der violetten Farbe	F	2/2	Gemässigt
[7.] Lob der schwarzen Farbe	A♭	4/4	Adagio

ers was deeply rooted in eighteenth-century culture: the return to "nature" in the pastoral movement (however tamed and stylized that nature was); the intricate games of social intercourse conducted through the "language of flowers," in which each flower meant something and in which bouquets held "secret" messages; the genteel occupation of "gardening" (performed by the gardeners, of course) and the owners' consequent pride in their flower, and especially rose, gardens. In short, love of flowers was a sign of refined tastes: through flowers, gentlemen displayed their cultivated interests in botany, in landscaping, and in the cultured appreciation of (subdued) nature, while ladies displayed their femininity in rapt adoration, in arranging and displaying, and in private pageants and entertainments, in which they not so subtly underscored the analogy between themselves and the delicate, unfolding beauty of blossoms. Perhaps the degree to which flowers permeated eighteenth-century culture should not surprise: they provided a medium through which men and women could play out their roles.

Flowers also provided an infinite source of "unified variety" and a particularly pliant and rich source of allegory: they were a natural topic for cycles. Like many topical cycles of the "spoked wheel" variety, Paul Wineberger's *Sechszehn Blumen*, a setting of Joseph Scholz's lyric cycle *Die Blumen*, reveals few internal connections, whether tonal, metric, or textual. Each song presents another variation of the topic, independent of the others (see table 3).

Lexica and encyclopedias occasionally included definitions that yield a third conceptual shape. This third definition, however, appeared only rarely, perhaps because it is an imprecise use of the term "cycle." Nonetheless, the third definition seems to have been accepted and in common use. In 1792, for example, Georg Friedrich Wolf defined "Rondo" as a "Zirkelstück" (circle piece) and the *Allgemeine deutsche Real-Encyclopaedie* described Greek literature of Homer's era as epic cycles and cyclic poetry:

> Under *Cyklos*, one understands not only the circle of tales and fables concerning the events of the Trojan war; cyclic poetry permeates all mythology . . .[10]

In both of these examples, there is clearly a central point, or idea, but the number of individual units is no longer

TABLE 3
Keys, Meters, and Tempos of *Sechszehn Blumen*

Paul Wineberger, *Sechszehn Blumen*, between 1799 and 1816			
[1.] Das Stiefmütterchen	D	6/8	Andante moderato
[2.] Die Sonnenblume	A	4/4	Andante
[3.] Das Vergissmeinnicht	B♭	6/8	Andante
[4.] Die Nelke	E	3/8	Allegretto
[5.] Die Nachtviole	E♭	2/4	Larghetto
[6.] Die Lilie	D	2/2	Adagio
[7.] Die Kamille	F	2/4	Allegretto vivace
[8.] Die Rose	B♭	2/4	Adagio
[9.] Das Gänseblümchen	C	6/8	Vivace
[10.] Die Kornblume	a–A	2/4	Un poco adagio
[11.] Die Wasser-Lilie	D	3/8	Allegretto
[12.] Die Hyacinthe	A	3/8	Andante moderato
[13.] Die Mohn-Blume	B♭	2/4	Adagio
[14.] Das Veilchen	G	2/4	Allegretto
[15.] Die Tülpe	A♭	2/2	Adagio
[16.] Der Lavendel	B♭	2/4	Andante con moto

TABLE 4
Keys, Meters, and Tempos of
Die Blumen und der Schmetterling

Friedrich Himmel, *Die Blumen und der Schmetterling*, 1803			
[1.] Zueignung an Deutschlands Töchter	E♭	4/4	Froh, tändelnd
[2.] Das Schneeglöckchen	B♭	4/4	Mit ruhigem Vortrag
[3.] Das Veilchen	A♭	6/8	Ruhig und sanft
[4.] Die Myrthe	A	3/4	Leicht
[5.] Die Narzisse	f	6/8	Schwermütig, doch nicht zu langsam
[6.] Das Vergissmeinnicht	F	4/4	Leise und wogend
[7.] Die Palme	B♭	4/4	Feurig, doch nicht zu geschwind
[8.] Die Rose	E	4/4	Gemässigt, doch heiter
[9.] Wechselgesang der Blumen	B♭	6/8	Fröhlich, doch nicht zu geschwind
[10.] Der Schmetterling	F	6/8	Leicht

infinite or random; internal progressions and relationships set the order and a general structure emerges that adds a linear aspect to the cycle, creating a conceptual paradox—a circle that closes in a different place than where it began. It would be difficult, for example, to maintain that the sections within a rondo could be rearranged without damaging the whole or that the piece lacks structural closure by ending where it began. The third shape, then, is a "sprung" circle:

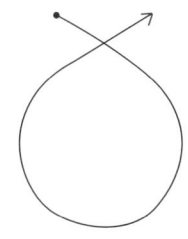

An early example of this type of cycle is Friedrich Himmel's 1803 cycle, *Die Blumen und der Schmetterling* (see table 4). As with Hůrka's set, the ten songs are variations on a central idea (flowers once again); also, music and text seem to form no progression. On closer examination, however, a general structure emerges in which the outer songs frame an inner wreath and one in which the final song provides structural closure. The first song, "Zueignung an Deutschlands Töchter," sets up the rest of the cycle, dedicating the ensuing wreath of flowers ("Blumenkranz") to German girls, "zart wie Blüthen." The next seven songs are the wreath of flowers, each song describing a particular flower: snow-drop, violet, myrtle, narcissus, forget-me-not, palm, and rose. These seven are not without a certain order: the snow-drop, the harbinger of spring, leads the four flowers that bloom in early spring; the next two, the forget-me-not and the palm, represent summer; and the final, culminating flower is, of course, the rose, which blooms from early spring through fall. These songs seem to be written for a variety of singers—they vary in tessitura and difficulty—perhaps for seven girls who represent the German maidens introduced in the opening song and who sing the part of the chorus in the following "Wechselgesang der Blumen." This "Wechselgesang" seems to tie the previous songs together: it is longer than most; choral verses alternate with solo verses; and the style is on a larger, less intimate scale. In many ways, this song sums up the previous songs and provides both climax and close. The four flowers that sing solos in the middle verses of "Wechselgesang" reprise their earlier songs. That those reprises remain in their original keys argues strongly in favor or the keys having been chosen for the melody's tessituras rather than for long-range harmonic function. The seven verses yield the following tonal scheme, the B-flat sections belonging to the choruses and the other keys to the reprises: B♭–B♭–A♭–F–A–E–B♭. Those same four flowers—violet, forget-me-not, myrtle, and rose—are also prominent in the opening song, and three of them—violet, myrtle, and rose—return in the final song, as well. That final song, "Der Schmetterling" (The Butterfly), seems to stand outside the inner wreath of songs, although it refers back to the rest and brings the presentation to a close by "flitting from bud to bud." That "butterfly" is male in German, and "flower" female, should not be overlooked.

The reviewer for the Leipzig *Allgemeine musikalische Zeitung* in May 1808 also found the linear structure (closure) and the inner connections of this cycle noteworthy. He opens his article with a phrase that later dominated German definitions of "song cycle": "Diese in Zusammenhang stehende kleine Liedersammlung . . ." (This small, coherent collection of songs . . .), and he dwells on the staging and significance of the final two songs for two paragraphs.

Next follows a longer *Wechselgesang der Blumen*, in which, after a short, merry, three-part *Tutti*, several flowers (entering one after the other) reprise their appropriately and well arranged solos from the previous songs; finally, they unite once again in the *Tutti* (with a few changes)....

The set would best end with this movement; it is written as though that should happen. But still to enter, somewhat isolated, is the butterfly, or rather the poet, who, in the guise of the singer, expresses with inner feeling much that is good and true about the butterfly. In general, the composer has rendered this song commendably....[11]

Finally, note that the unusual "tonal scheme," including tritone moves from B-flat major to E major between songs 7, 8, and 9 and between the reprises within song 9, disturbed neither composer nor critic.

The three conceptual shapes outlined above suggest general structures and possible categories of cycles that are not based on the techniques Beethoven used to create cycles. In the past, analysis of cycles has focused on techniques that promote coherence, but topical cycles are striking more for their contrast than for their unity. Unfortunately, although "Einheit und Vielfältigkeit" (unity and variety) was a fundamental aesthetic criterion of early nineteenth-century reviews, theories of creating a coherent work by balancing "unity and variety" are scarce: controversy reigns in explaining how individual sections of theme and variations movements connect, how sections of operas interact, how movements of sonatas or symphonies relate. But if topical cycles are indeed cycles and not collections, the songs must somehow relate as a unit and contrast must have some role in that relationship.

Carl Maria von Weber's opus 46, *Die Temperamente bei dem Verluste der Geliebten* (1816), a setting of four poems by Friedrich Wilhelm Gubitz, may suggest ways in which contrast creates relationships. The titles of the poems alone imply contrasting variations: all four have a male persona ending in "-mütige" or the closely rhymed "-wütige," yet encompass opposites, pairing light with heavy, raging with even-temperedness:

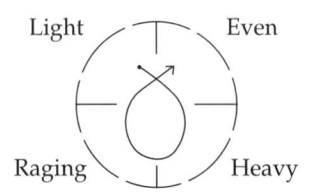

Not surprisingly, the music emphasizes contrast: "Der Leichtmütige" is characterized by sixteenth-note runs and staccato chords, while "Der Schwermütige" has sigh motives and legato arpeggios; "Der Liebewütige" is characterized by sudden fortissimo-pianissimo contrasts and driving triplets, while "Der Gleichmütige" is confined to an extremely narrow melodic range and static eighth notes. In light of these contrasts, the choice of keys begins to appear less random. The music drops from a brighter D major for "Der Leichtmütige" down a semitone into a darker, more melancholy D-flat major for "Der Schwermütige," then down another semitone into C minor (the only minor key) for "Der Liebewütige's" raging, finally breaking away to a mild F major for "Der Gleichmütige."

In each of these cases, the order of the songs emphasizes the contrast, and the contrast sets the order. D-flat major would not seem so "flat," so "sweetly melancholy" if it followed C minor rather than D major, and C minor would not seem nearly so dark if it did not follow two semitone drops in key. Similarly, the sudden contrasts and activity of "Der Liebewütige" would not seem so raging if it were not between the legato sighs of "Der Schwermütige" and the monotony of "Der Gleichmütige."

Conversely, Weber used similar material to emphasize contrast. Compare, for example, the phrases in measures 25–27 of "Der Leichtmütige" and in measures 7–9 of "Der Schwermütige." The first uses staccato leaps, while the second uses legato sighs; the first breaks out of the overall stepwise ascent, while the second sighs on each and every step. Weber also connects the songs structurally. Both "Der Leichtmütige" and "Der Gleichmütige," for example, include a musical return within a strophic form, a long middle section suspended on the dominant, and a distinctive harmony (marked by an asterisk) in the B section of each strophe (see table 5). Such structural similarity may reflect the personae's similar situations: both credos are threatened by marriage. Once again, however, similarity only underscores differences. "Der Leichtmütige" is enamored of love and chases women, right to the brink of marriage—the brink being the fermata on a striking harmony (mm. 14–15)—but, protected by God (and by Weber—there is no modulation), he slips down a semitone onto the dominant of tonic and says good-bye solidly in tonic before beginning the next wild adventure with the musical return. "Der Gleichmütige," on the other hand, is more in love with puddings than people and really only wants to lead a quiet, comfortable life. The dissonance in measure 8 disturbs his diatonic life almost by accident, as the bass meanders around the dominant, suggesting his inability to experience any emotion at all. That one dissonance summarizes the fleeting inconvenience of his entire marriage.

Weber seems to have used the musical contrast unifying this cycle as a symbolic counterpart of the textual extremes and exaggeration typical for satire, but his use of contrast on several different levels suggests that it has a structural significance. At least, the connections created by contrast and the contrast created by similarities are much stronger than connections created by recurring material, the material usually offered as proof of a work's unity.

TABLE 5
Harmonic Progressions in *Die Temperamente*, nos. 1 and 4

"Der Leichtmütige"

A	B ⌒	C	A	
I...V^7–I	V...V/iii*–V^7–I	I...V^7–I	I...V^7–I	Coda

"Der Gleichmütige"

A	B		A	
I...V^7–I	V...♭5*...		I...V^7–I	Codetta

Traditionally, topical cycles have been dismissed either as collections, as "primitive" cycles that lack unity, or as forerunners of "true" cycles. In fact, they and their history have simply been overshadowed by the types of cycles that became prominent later in the nineteenth century, i.e., by internal-plot cycles, such as Schubert's, which narrate in a series of song vignettes, and by musically-constructed cycles, such as Beethoven's and Schumann's, which cohere primarily through their musical structures. Upon close examination, topical cycles reveal closer and stronger connections than those found in collections and a sophistication that belies "primitive." Topical cycles feature techniques of coherence unlike but no less valid than those championed by Beethoven. To use a Romantic metaphor, these flowers cannot bloom in the dark of Beethoven's shadow.

Poets, Composers, Publishers, and Cycles

The text from one of Carl Maria von Weber's little-known songs reads,

> Meine Lieder, meine Sänge,
> Sind dem Augenblick geweiht,
> IhreTöne, ihre Klänge,
> Schwinden mit der flücht'gen Zeit.

> (My songs, my singing,
> Are dedicated to the moment;
> Their notes, their tones,
> Vanish with fleeting time.)

Most of Weber's songs, like those of the others contained in this volume, have vanished from modern concerts, overshadowed by weightier, more important works. A steady diet of weighty pieces, however, distorts who these people were and what their musical lives were like. To understand the early Romantics, one must cherish their lighter side as well. As another of Weber's songs advises,

> In dem Klang der Lieder
> Findet ihr mich wieder.

> (In the sound of songs
> You will find me again.)[12]

Beethoven and Schubert lend the impression that song cycles were a Viennese, or at least southerly genre, but in fact, the earliest song cycles appeared primarily in northern Germany, an uneasy amalgam of opera, lieder with the aesthetic ideals of the Berlin schools, a Romantic yearning for ancient cyclic forms, and an emerging nationalism. Cycles included in this edition were chosen without regard to their places of origin, yet all six were published in the north: Brunswick, Hamburg, two in Leipzig, and two in Berlin. Furthermore, all six composers were from the north, as were four of the five poets; only Castelli was Viennese. Berlin is especially prominent: Müchler, represented by two cycles, and von Gubitz, Hůrka, and Himmel were all in Berlin, and Weber wrote his cycle while in Berlin, inspired by its salons.

Until Beethoven composed *An die ferne Geliebte* and Schubert transformed lied into high art, song cycles were relatively insignificant works that were often omitted from composers' works lists, making it difficult to trace their history. They were composed within the context of more important genres such as the symphony, and especially that most influential of genres, opera. Three of the composers were associated closely with opera, Singspiel, and Liederspiel: Weber was an opera composer and director; Hůrka was an acclaimed tenor in Berlin; and Himmel replaced J. F. Reichardt as royal kapellmeister in Berlin, publicly argued music aesthetics with him, and composed his greatest work by imitating Reichardt's Liederspiele.

In the body of this edition, the cycles are arranged according to their underlying conceptual shapes; in this section, they are presented in their chronological order.

Müchler's Die Farben, *set by Hůrka and Himmel*

KARL FRIEDRICH MÜCHLER[13]

Born Stargard in Pommern, 2 September 1763; died Berlin, 12 January 1857. Civil servant, writer, and poet.

After completing his studies, Müchler began working as a civil servant, which he continued in a variety of capacities throughout his life. His career fluctuated with the times: he lost his income when Prussia lost the battle of Jena; he had to flee to avoid proscription into the occupying French army; and he oversaw the security police in Dresden, earning a life-long stipend for uncovering a counterfeiting operation.

Müchler published prolifically in a variety of genres. Brümmer cites Müchler's notable influence on *belles lettres* and his flair for puzzles and charades, anagrams and epigrams, for sociable conversation and gaity.[14] The numerous works of this type include *Meine Feierstunden* (1782), *Kriminalgeschichten* (1792), *Erotische Tändeleien* (1793), *Epigramme, Fabeln und Erzählungen* (1808), *Scherzhafte Erzählungen* (1818), *Taschenbuch für Kartenspieler* (1819), and *Polterabendscenen* (1830). Müchler also published dramatic works and novels, but was probably best known for his numerous almanacs and *Taschenbücher: Taschenbuch für Frauenzimmer* (six volumes, 1779–84); *Kleine Frauenzimmer-Bibliothek* (five volumes, 1782–86); *Berlinisches Taschenbuch* (1795); *Polterabende* (1798); *Vergißmeinnicht* (1809); *Taschenbuch der Liebe und des Frohsinns* (1811); and *Anekdoten-Almanach* (1808–13, 1815, 1817–45); and so on.

Müchler's first collection of poems, *Gedichte*, was published in 1782; more followed in 1786 (two volumes) and 1800 (two volumes, with copper engravings and music); it is this last set that contained the *Die Farben* cycle. Other collections of poetry include *Sechszehn Lieder* (1808), *Gedichte, niedergelegt . . .* (1813), and *Gedichte aus dem häuslichen Leben* (1827). Because of his fluid use of language and folk-like style, an aesthetic ideal for lieder, many of his poems were set to music by a wide variety of composers. Flowers were a popular theme: in addition to *Die Blumen und der Schmetterling*, Müchler also wrote *Die Blumensprache* (1820) and *Die Blumen* (1823).

Friedrich Franz (Franciscus Wenceslaus, František Václav) Hůrka[15]

Born Merklín near Přestice, Bohemia, 19 February 1762; died Berlin, 10 December 1805. Czech tenor and composer (almost entirely of songs), active in Germany; a Freemason.

Trained as a chorister in Prague, Hůrka joined Pasquale Bondini's theatrical troupe in 1783 and traveled to Germany, where he débuted at the Leipzig Fair in 1784. For the next twenty years, Hůrka made a living by singing concerts and in opera and by teaching, first as a royal Kammersänger in Schwedt beginning in 1788, then briefly in Dresden, and finally in Berlin from about 1789 on. His tenure in Berlin overlapped that of Himmel's between about 1800 and 1805, a time of intense activity for both. The two almost certainly knew one another: according to Gerber, Hůrka sang "with great artistry" the tenor solos in Himmel's opera *Semiramide* for a royal marriage and in Himmel's *Trauerkantate* for Friedrich Wilhelm II's funeral.

A prized and active singer, Hůrka received one thousand thaler annually from the court. He also participated in the Berlin Singakamedie from its founding in 1791 until 1802. Obituaries applauded Hůrka's understanding of music, the beauty of his voice, his vocal technique, and his dramatic expression. Gerber heard Hůrka in person and called him "one of the most glorious tenors of our time," but reported that Hůrka rarely if ever sang on Berlin's opera stage.[16] Gerber was presumably referring to the large Italian opera theater, because Hůrka is listed as singing in a number of operas, Singspiele, and Liederspiele. Eitner, on the other hand, claimed Hůrka sang only in concerts because his voice lost its power as he aged.

Regarding Hůrka's composing, Gerber described him as a "beloved composer of lieder,"[17] and some of his songs were sung as folksongs well into in the nineteenth century. In the preface to his first set of lieder, *Scherz und Ernst in 12 Liedern* (Dresden, 1787), Hůrka specified separate performers for the vocal and piano parts and was one of the first to speak out against singers accompanying themselves. In general, Hůrka composed in the aesthetic tradition of the second Berlin school of lied and is significant for some pre-Romantic traits. Although Hůrka was never particularly skilled or inventive as a composer, his works epitomize the quotidian style: he adhered to expectations in declamation and expression, and his choice of poets reflected contemporary fashion.

Hůrka gave his final public concert in Berlin on 21 April 1805 and died the following December.

Friedrich Heinrich Himmel

Born Treuenbrietzen, 20 November 1765; died Berlin, 8 June 1814. German composer. See below for his biography.

Himmel composed "Lob der violetten Farbe" sometime in his early thirties. Because individual songs are so difficult to track, attending circumstances or how his song ended up in a cycle of songs by Hůrka may never be known. "Lob der violetten Farbe" was not part of the original cycle (see below), and Himmel may not even have been thinking about cyclic forms when he composed it: all of his cycles, including *Die Blumen und der Schmetterling*, were composed after Reichardt invented the Liederspiel in Berlin in 1800.

Wilhelm Oehmigke

A publisher and printer in Berlin in the 1790s and 1800s. Little is known about him other than that he published mainly books, not music.

Nicolaus Simrock[18]

Born Mainz, 23 August 1751; died Bonn, 12 June 1832. German publisher.

Simrock, a horn player in Bonn's orchestra, began dealing in printed music and instruments in the 1780s and founded his publishing firm in 1793. He published works by Beethoven, who was a friend, Haydn, and Weber, and encouraged the reprinting of works by Bach and Handel. He published the second edition of *Die Farben* in 1802. His sons established branches in Paris in 1802 and Cologne in 1812; the firm passed to his son Peter Joseph Simrock in 1832. Nicolaus Simrock actively promoted German folk song, publishing works by Mendelssohn, Hiller, and Schumann, as well as Hůrka.

Johann Peter Spehr[19]

Born ca. 1770; died after 1859. German music publisher.

Spehr founded his Musik- und Kunsthandlung auf der Höhe in Brunswick in 1791, renaming it Musikalisches Magazin auf der Höhe in 1794. Spehr expanded rapidly through trading contacts; by 1816, he was able to offer a catalogue of over fifteen hundred works. Spehr published mainly popular music, including "Lob der schwarzen Farbe," as sheet music. In 1860, he sold the firm to Carl Weinholz, who in turn passed the firm to Julius Bauer, under whose name it continued until it was destroyed in 1944.

The Cycle

Main source. The Simrock edition:

Die Farben | Fünf Lieder | mit begleitung des Pianoforte | oder der Guittarre | von | F. F. Hurka. | Bey N. Simrock | in Bonn. | No.220. | Pr: Fl.

Plate no. 220. Date: probably 1802, as added by hand by the library in square brackets on the title page. Microfilm copy from the Staatsbibliothek zu Berlin—Preußischer Kulturbesitz, Musikabteilung mit Mendelssohn-Archiv, call no. O. 41229.

Additional source. The Oehmigke edition:

Müchler, Karl. *Gedichte*. 2 volumes. Berlin: Wilhelm Oehmigke, [1800].

No plate numbers. Date: 1800, as listed in Hirschberg, page 344. Photocopy from the Bayerische Staatsbibliothek, call no. P.o. germ. 2059 0/1.

Each volume is divided into "Books" of about fifty pages each, plus a final, shorter section containing a lyric cycle. At the end of the first volume, an otherwise blank page announces *Die Farben* and a woodcut of a rainbow over a mountain lake closes the cycle. The songs are printed on unnumbered inserts preceding or interrupting the verses of each poem.

Additional source. Spehr edition of "Lob der schwarzen Farbe":

Lob | der schwarzen Farbe | mit | Clavier Begleitung | von | F. F. Hurka. | 3 gg: | Braunschweig. | im Musikalischen Magazine auf der Höhe.

No plate number. Undated; the publisher's name change provides only the terminus post quem, 1794. Photocopy from Archiv der Gesellschaft der Musikfreunde, Vienna, call no. VI 12360 (Q 6153).

Surprisingly, the title page mentions no poet and the poem is written in a different style than the others. It is also the only one missing in Müchler's 1800 edition, so perhaps Müchler did not write it.

Comments. Of the six cycles presented in this edition, *Die Farben*, also occasionally called *Lob der Farben* or *Les Couleurs*, has the most complex history, in large part because it was remarkably popular, especially for such an early cycle: it was published in several cities and was listed in Gerber, Whistling's handbooks, Fétis, and Eitner.

The first edition, with five songs, was published by C. F. Himburg in Berlin in 1795 (see Eitner and *NG*;[20] listed as 1796 in Gerber). Exactly how many different editions appeared afterwards and with which songs is unclear (see table 6). *New Grove* lists an undated second edition "with addl song" and a third edition in 1796 "with addl song," either the same additional song for a total of six songs, or yet another additional song for a total of seven. The Staatsbibliothek zu Berlin has a card catalogue for a second edition, now lost, with six songs plus two added songs published without date, place, or publisher. Gerber lists a new edition with six songs in 1801, possibly the Oehmigke edition, and Eitner lists an undated edition with seven songs published in Berlin by Concha et Compl. By 1816, volume 1 of Whistling's handbooks lists four versions for sale—by Boehme in Hamburg, by Lischke, by Schott in Mainz (with piano or guitar accompaniment), and by Simrock in Bonn—as well as an arrangement for guitar by Bornhardt, published by Spehr in Braunschweig.

With so many editions, copies, and arrangements published, *Die Farben* should be readily available, but many were lost during the wars. Despite the numerous listings, the only copies available for this edition were (1) the 1802 Simrock edition containing five songs, apparently based on the first edition, and the primary source for this edition; (2) the six songs inserted into Oehmigke's 1800 edition of Müchler's *Gedichte*, used for comparison and as the primary source for "Lob der violetten Farbe"; and (3) the undated "Lob der schwarzen Farbe" from the Archiv der Gesellschaft der Musikfreunde, the only source for that song. The order of the songs in this edition compared to the contents of the three available editions and to the card catalogue description of the first edition (1795), from the Hessische Landes- und Hochschulbibliothek in Darmstadt, is as shown in table 7. To summarize, this edition presents the five songs of the Simrock edition (corresponding to those of the first edition) first, followed by the later addition of Himmel's song, and ending with "Lob der schwarzen Farbe," which may have been included in some later editions.

TABLE 6
Editions of *Die Farben*

1. Dated Editions Listed
   1795 (5 songs): Eitner; *NG* (listed as 1st ed.)
   1796 (5 songs): Gerber (listed as 1st ed.)
   1796 (7 songs): *NG* (listed as 3d ed.)
   1796 (9 songs): Fétis*
   1801 (6 songs): Gerber (listed as "Neue Auflage")

2. Undated Editions Listed
   n.d. (6 songs): *NG* (listed as 2d ed.)
   n.d. (6 + 2 songs): Berlin library
   n.d. (7 songs): Eitner

*Fétis's description of a 1796 Berlin edition having nine songs is probably an error, possibly an unclear "7" having been read as "9."

TABLE 7
Order of Songs in *Die Farben*

	1795	1800	1802	n.d.	This edition
"Lob der weissen Farbe" (C)	1	1	1	—	1
"Lob der rothen Farbe" (E♭)	2	2	2	—	2
"Lob der blauen Farbe" (A)	3	3	3	—	3
"Lob der violetten Farbe" (F)*	—	4	—	—	6
"Lob der gelben Farbe" (D)	4	5	4	—	4
"Lob der grünen Farbe" (F)	5	6	5	—	5
"Lob der schwarzen Farbe" (A♭)	—	—	—	1	7

*Composed by Himmel; the rest composed by Hůrka.

Müchler's Die Blumen und der Schmetterling, set by Himmel

Karl Friedrich Müchler

Born Stargard in Pommern, 2 September 1763; died Berlin, 12 January 1857. Civil servant, writer, and poet. See above for summary of biography.

Friedrich Heinrich Himmel[21]

Born Treuenbrietzen, 20 November 1765; died Berlin, 8 June 1814. German composer.

Under patronage of Friedrich Wilhelm II, Himmel studied with J. G. Naumann in Dresden in 1789–92, was appointed chamber composer, traveled in Italy for two years (where he composed two operas), and was appointed royal kapellmeister in 1795 to replace J. F. Reichardt, who had fallen into disfavor. In financial difficulty, and unable to interest the court in reviving

German opera, Himmel toured Russia and the Scandinavian countries, returning to Berlin by 1800.

According to Ludwig Rellstab, in the 1790s Himmel was "decidedly a representative of the modern age. Elegantly dressed, lightly powdered, somewhat portly but very agile, red-cheeked, his delicate white hands covered with splendid rings." But others described Himmel as alcoholic, gluttonous, coarse-mannered, and as one who took advantage of friends. Court intrigues being what they were, it is difficult today to separate fact from personal acrimony. Whatever the truth, Himmel retained the court's favor, first with Friedrich Wilhelm II and then with his successor Friedrich Wilhelm III.

Himmel's opera *Vasco da Gama*, performed in January 1801 shortly before Reichardt's *Rosmonda*, led to an acrimonious dispute over music aesthetics similar to that of Piccini and Gluck in Paris, with Himmel representing the neo-Neapolitan school and Reichardt defending Gluck's principles. Despite the court's bias against German opera, Himmel's best works were in German genres: Liederkreise, Liederspiele, Singspiele, and early German Romantic opera.

Himmel's *Frohsinn und Schwärmerey* of March 1801, an offshoot of Reichardt's new genre the Liederspiel, was an immediate success, overshadowed only in 1804 by his Singspiel *Fanchon das Leyermädchen*, which brought him wide reknown. *Fanchon* was performed repeatedly in Berlin until 1853 and songs from it were sung as folk songs throughout the nineteenth century. *Fanchon* was the only large work by Himmel to achieve lasting fame, and that fame owed more to its timeliness and historical context than to its compositional ingenuity.

Although few of Himmel's works are performed today, they were almost universally admired in their time, and they remain historically significant. In 1803, Himmel composed *Die Blumen und der Schmetterling*, a song cycle of the "sprung circle" variety that predates Beethoven's *An die ferne Geliebte* by thirteen years. In 1806, he composed *Die Sylphen: ein Zauberoper*, which although less successful than his other theater works, has been cited by H. J. Moser and E. Bücken as a forerunner of Weber's *Der Freischütz* and a "fully developed monument of Berlin early Romanticism."[22] And in 1814, he composed the Liederspiel *Alexis und Ida, ein Schäferroman*, op. 43, a forerunner of Schubert's *Die schöne Müllerin*.

In its diversity of style, Himmel's music reflects its era, one of great political, social, and artistic change; he exemplified contemporary aesthetics but did not challenge them. In 1814, E. T. A. Hoffmann wrote of Himmel's "genuinely charming music," yet by the mid-twentieth century, W. Pfannkuch of *Die Musik in Geschichte und Gegenwart* dismissed *Fanchon* as banal, "with all the characteristics of the 'popular hit.' " Not surprisingly, today we are more likely to study, say, Beethoven's *Leonore* than Himmel's *Fanchon*, although the latter had greater impact and is likely to reveal more about the era and its aesthetics.

Toward the end of his life, Himmel continued to travel widely in Europe; in fact, his final major work, the comic opera *Der Kobold*, premiered in Vienna in 1813. Although reports of his death occasionally arrived in Berlin ahead of him, Himmel was at home when he died of edema at age forty-eight.

Ambrosius Kühnel[23]

Born 1770; died 1813. Organist, publisher, and printer in Leipzig.

In 1801, Kühnel and Franz Anton Hoffmeister, a composer, kapellmeister, and publisher in Vienna, opened the Bureau de Musique in Leipzig, a publishing house connected to engraving and printing works and to a retail shop selling printed music and instruments. The Bureau de Musique, sometimes called the Musikalisches Bureau, published works by Haydn, Mozart, Bach, Beethoven, Reichardt, and Spohr, as well as books related to music, including Forkel's monograph. Kühnel published *Die Blumen und der Schmetterling* in 1803 as a *Prachtausgabe* with ten beautiful copper engravings.

Hoffmeister returned to Vienna in 1805, leaving Kühnel to carry on the business until his death in 1813. In 1814, the business was purchased by C. F. Peters, under whose name it continues today, which is why *Die Blumen und der Schmetterling* was later listed as a Peters edition (as in Whistling's handbooks).

Macarius (Franz de Paula) Falter[24]

Born Taiskirchen, 2 January 1762; died Munich, 24 September 1843. Piano teacher, then publisher in Munich.

Circa 1788, Falter began selling manuscript paper and printed music, moving into publishing in 1796, when he produced his first imprints. In 1813, his son Joseph (1782–1846) joined the firm. Although Falter und Sohn published works by masters such as Haydn and Pleyel, the firm concentrated on publishing local composers such as Stuntz, Cannabich, Winter, and Theobald Boehm. Falter was important for his early use of lithography.[25] There is no complete catalogue and numerous editions appeared without plate numbers.

On the title page of *Die Blumen und der Schmetterling*, the engraved line "München bey Falter und Sohn Residenz-Strasse No. 33" has been pasted over the earlier publisher, Rudolph Werckmeister, who founded his Bureau de Musique in Oranienburg in 1802, moved to Berlin in 1806, and sold the firm in 1809.[26]

In April of 1827, Falter und Sohn was sold to Sebastian Pacher. After Pacher's death in 1834, the firm passed first to his widow, Thekla Pacher (1805–79), then to a series of owners until 1888, when all rights were transferred to Joseph Aibl's publishing firm, also of Munich.

The Cycle[27]

Source. The Kühnel edition:

Die Blumen | und | der Schmetterling. | Zehn Lieder | von | Karl Müchler. | In Musik gesetzt | mit Begleitung des Pianoforte | und eines willkürlichen Violoncells | von | F. H. Himmel. | Mit zehn Kupfertafeln. | Bei A. Kühnel, | Bureau de Musique in Leipzig.

Plate number 220. Date: 1803, as listed in *NG*.[28] Microfilm copy from the Staatsbibliothek zu Berlin—Preußischer

Kulturbesitz, Musikabteilung mit Mendelssohn-Archiv, call no. Mus. Sig. 19,455 Rara.

Source. The Falter und Sohn edition:

Die Blumen | und | der Schmetterling | Zehn Lieder | von | Karl Müchler. | In Musik gesetzt | mit Begleitung des Pianoforte und eines willkürlichen Violoncells | von | Friedrich Heinrich Himmel, | Königliche Preussischem Kapellmeister. | München bey Falter und Sohn Residenz-Strasse No.33 | Preis 1 Rthlr. 8 Fr.

Plate no. 220. Date: 1803 edition, printed before 1809, when Werckmeister closed shop. Microfilm copy from the Bayerische Staatsbibliothek, call no. 4° Mus. pr. 18310.

Comments. Note that the plate numbers on both editions are 220. It is not a coincidence: the Falter und Sohn edition is identical to the Kühnel, right down to the incorrect plate number on page 3 (120 instead of 220); the Falter und Sohn is simply a *Titelauflage* lacking only the copper engravings. Thus, the four editions listed in various sources—by Peters, Falter und Sohn, Kühnel, and Werckmeister—are one and the same, the one from which this edition was prepared.

Die Blumen und der Schmetterling was reviewed in Leipzig's *Allgemeine musikalische Zeitung* in May of 1808, five years after it was first published (see discussion and quotation above, in "Coherence and Shape in Topical Song Cycles").

Scholz's Sechszehn Blumen, *set by Wineberger*

Joseph Scholz[29]

Born Hamburg, 1773; died Hamburg, 16 February 1811. Writer and poet. He also published under the pseudonym Claude Macario.

Scholz published several books of poetry, many of which were set to music by contemporary composers, including Berlin's Reichardt, but little is known about him today other than that he was the son of a pharmacist and that he lived in poverty. He is best remembered for *Hamburg und seine Umgebung* (1808), which was followed two years later by a second edition entitled *Hamburg oder vollständige Geschichte und Beschreibung dieser Stadt*.

Editions of poetry included *Lyrische Gedichte* in 1804 (a second edition entitled *Hamburgische Blumenlese* appeared in 1806), *Gedichte* also in 1804, and a separate volume of *Lyrische Gedichte* ca. 1807. Kosch lists *Sechszehn Blumen* as a separate publication, without a date. Kosch also mentions that Scholz wrote numerous poems and essays for periodicals; perhaps the poems first appeared in one of them.

Paul Anton Wineberger (Winneberger)[30]

Born Mergentheim, 7 October 1758; died Hamburg, 8 February 1822. German cellist, organist, and composer.

At age eight, Wineberger began singing alto for the Mergentheim court, moving on at age fourteen to organist for the Dominican church. While studying theology at the universities of Würzburg and Heidelberg in 1775–78, Wineberger supported himself by playing organ and teaching school. While in Mannheim, he studied composition under Holzbauer, violin under Fränzl, and music theory under Abbé Georg Joseph Vogler, the same teacher who piqued Weber's interest in the lied.

In 1782, Wineberger became a member of the Oettingen court orchestra at Wallerstein and, in 1785, principal cellist. In 1794, he moved to Hamburg, where he worked as a teacher and as a cellist at the French Opera for the rest of his career. Assessing Hamburg's musical life, a reviewer for Leipzig's *Allgemeine musikalische Zeitung* casually dismissed Wineberger with the following:

> This Mr. Wineberger is a very good orchestral and concert performer; he also possesses compositional knowledge; it appears he lacks only taste and suitable training.[31]

As a composer, Wineberger is best known for his instrumental music, especially his twenty-one *Harmoniemusik* pieces, but almost all of his music remains in manuscript. In addition to songs and piano works, Wineberger composed an opera, *Die Alpenhütte,* with text by August von Kotzebue (1814), three masses, and five symphonies. Scholz and Wineberger were both from Hamburg, so perhaps they were acquainted, but there is no direct evidence for that.

Johann August Böhme[32]

Born 1766; died 1847. Publisher and printer in Hamburg.

Böhme began his career in 1793 working as an art music and instrument dealer in a shop owned by Christoph Ehrenfried Günther. In 1794, they added a publishing firm to their retail store and issued their first list of new music available in 1796. Beginning with supplement no. 5 in 1799, Günther's name was dropped; Böhme had apparently acquired sole ownership. Böhme editions included works by Reichardt, Rellstab, and Zelter, as well as Schiller's ode "An die Freude." Böhme of Hamburg became one of the foremost European music publishers; *Sechszehn Blumen* was a minor early work.

In 1839, the firm passed to his son, Justus Eduard Böhme, and closed in 1886, when it was sold to August Cranz, although the retail store and an added concert agency remained under the Böhme name until 1907, when that was purchased by John Benjamin of the Anton J. Benjamin firm.

The Cycle

Source. The Böhme edition:

Sechszehn Blumen, ged: von Scholz. | in Musik gesetzt | von P. Wineberger | Hamburg bey J. A. Böhme

No plate number. Undated. Microfilm copy from the Staatsbibliothek zu Berlin—Preußischer Kulturbesitz, Musikabteilung mit Mendelssohn-Archiv, call no. O. 61891.

Comments. Dating *Sechszehn Blumen* is problematic. The terminus post quem is probably 1799, when J. A. Böhme separated from Günther and began publishing under his name alone, and the terminus ante quem 1816, when the cycle was listed in Whistling's volume 1: "Wineberger. Die Blumen von Scholz. Hamb. Boehme. 3 Mk."[33]

Gubitz's Die Temperamente, *set by Weber*

(Friedrich) Wilhelm Gubitz[34]

Born Leipzig, 27 February 1786; died Berlin, 5 June 1870. Wood carver, publicist, and poet.

Wilhelm Gubitz's father, Christoph, who worked as a typesetter, resettled his family in Berlin in 1790 in order to work for the printer J. Fr. Unger. Christoph, among others, carved the models for Unger's well-loved font, the *Unger'schen Typ*.

Wilhelm Gubitz learned the basics of wood carving from his father well enough that his carving attracted notice, and by 1800, Gubitz began receiving offers of positions with printers. Supported by his paternal grandmother, Gubitz chose instead to pursue theological studies, first from 1795 at the Gymnasium in Wittenberg and then from 1801 at the University of Jena. Throughout, Gubitz continued to receive commissions for woodcarving, even from outside Germany; in fact, Didot, the French printing/publishing firm, tried to convince the young man to move to Paris. In order to keep him in his Prussian homeland, officials promoted Gubitz, then just a nineteen-year-old theology student, to teacher and member of the Berlin Art Academy in 1805. In fact, Gubitz's lasting significance was primarily as an artist: he reawakened woodcarving in Germany, and his *Deutsche Volkskalender*, 1835–69, remain important works.

The difficult war years after 1806 induced Gubitz to try publishing, and between 1807 and 1809, he published a political and patriotic newspaper called *Das Vaterland*. When the wars were over in 1817, he began a long run of the attractive and influential periodical *Der Gesellschafter*. Gubitz also served as a long-time theater critic for Voss's *Musenalmanach* and wrote some moderately successful plays. At the end of his life, he wrote three volumes of memoirs titled *Erlebnisse* (1868 and 1873).

Gubitz's poetry, published in two volumes of *Gedichte* in 1860, are of uneven quality,[35] but their historical import remains difficult to evaluate. Carl Maria von Weber, for example, set more poems by Gubitz than by almost any other poet, but that probably reflects less Weber's aesthetic taste than his social life: as Degen points out, Weber usually set the poems of friends.[36]

Carl Maria (Friedrich Ernst) von Weber[37]

Born Eutin, 19? November 1786; died London, 5 June 1826. German composer, conductor, pianist, critic, and influential founder of Germany's Romantic movement.

Detailed biographies of Weber are readily available; the following summary focuses on events that pertain to his composition of lieder and the years surrounding 1816's *Die Temperamente* (J200–203).

Weber came from a musical family: his mother was a singer and actress, his father a composer of lieder, founder of the family's traveling theater company, and kapellmeister in Eutin. Not surprisingly, many of Weber's early works were German songs and operas.

As a young man studying with Abbé Vogler in Vienna, 1803–4, Weber developed a fascination with folksong, often singing in taverns and accompanying himself on guitar. His interest in folksong, encouraged by Vogler, intensified with Achim von Arnim's and Clemens Brentano's 1805 publication of *Des Knaben Wunderhorn*, a collection of folk poetry.

In his early professional life, Weber traveled extensively and held various positions. While working and studying again with Vogler in Darmstadt in 1810–11, Weber spent innumerable hours with fellow musicians, discussing music, criticizing each others' works, and singing and playing folk songs. According to Max Maria, Weber's son and biographer, describing an era before he was born,

> In Darmstadt, where Weber enjoyed Vogler's instruction along with Gänsbacher and Meyerbeer, the three "shook the dust from their pelts" whenever they left the company of the elders and went out in the evenings into the streets "collecting melodies"; i.e., drank wine, where[ver] [any]one sang or strummed zither or harp. In front of soldiers or young women, Carl Maria could toss a guitar around his throat, climb up on a table, and sing roguish songs, [so] that there was no end to the celebrating, until the tobacco smoke chased him out of the tavern. Thankfully, he received much stimulation in life and melody from folk song.[38]

Also during this time, Weber and his comrades—Gottfried Weber, Dusch, Meyerbeer, later Gänsbacher and others—formed a secret society called the "Harmonischer Verein," mainly to discuss and critique music, but also to promote each others' works. In composing as well as critiquing, Weber embraced the lied aesthetics of his time, with music following poetry's lead, especially in terms of declamation. As Weber noted in his diary of 24 September 1811,

> The creation of a new form must be engendered by the poem one composes. In my songs, my greatest struggle to render my poets truly and correctly declaimed has invariably guided me to some new configuration of the melody.[39]

And again, in a letter to Adolf Müllner, poet of the play *König Yngurd*, for which Weber composed music,

> In my opinion, the first and holiest duty of song, is to be, with the greatest possible loyalty, true in the declamation.[40]

After more travels, Weber arrived in Berlin in late February or early March 1812 for a stay of about five months. He found the intellectual atmosphere of Berlin stimulating, with the artistic camaraderie of his Darmstadt days. Through the salons, Zelter's *Liedertafel*, and the Singakademie, Weber met numerous talented and influential people, some of whom became lifelong friends, including F. W. Gubitz. As Max Maria described it,

> [T]he various social circles . . . gathered oftentimes, sometimes in the little drinking room of the castle, sometimes in the famous parlor of innkeeper Schwederer or at Höner's. Although mostly high spirits and exuberance reigned, still, many witty conversations were conducted as well, which more than once formed the point of departure for a song. In high spirits, then, these people—in very few cases poets by profession—ventured poetic endeavors that Weber, stimulated, often set at once to music. Thus, [his] choice of texts

becomes suddenly explicable. . . . But a reason for the quasi-improvisatory [feel] that occasionally clings to his style is also thereby furnished.[41]

Once again, it should be noted that Max Maria had not been born during this period, but biographers have long noted that Weber consciously chose the poetry of his acquaintances over that of the acclaimed masters.[42] In Berlin, lieder were less planned compositions than the product of social interaction, i.e., *Gelegenheitslieder*, never intended as great works of art.[43] If so, Gubitz's poems and Weber's settings reveal much about the quality of artistic endeavors and the role of improvisation in Berlin salons. Because many of these lieder were written and set so rapidly, composers unselfconsciously fulfilled contemporary aesthetic expectations ("die Modegeschmack"). Published, these works were perhaps more like sharing memoirs and activities than composing for posterity. Such cavalier, possibly naive, attitudes toward composing and publishing became inconceivable even twenty years later.

Seeking stability, Weber accepted a position with the opera in Prague, where he remained from 12 January 1813 to 5 June 1816. He had little time for composing while rebuilding Prague's opera, producing seventy-two French and German operas in some 430 performances, and he missed the camaraderie of the Berlin salons. In 1814, Weber began a stormy relationship with an acclaimed singer, Caroline Brandt, whom he eventually married in 1817. During the most serious of their separations, the summer, fall, and winter of 1815, Weber began composing his opus 46 cycle, with its telling subtitle: *Die Temperamente bei dem Verluste der Geliebten*.[44]

By fall of 1815, Weber had decided to resign his position at Prague, and he began to seek other positions as he fulfilled his contract, which ended in September of 1816. On 13 October, Weber returned to Berlin to await word on a promising new position. During the next three months, Weber became engaged to Caroline Brandt, with whom he had reconciled in spring, and was accepted as Dresden's kapellmeister, a position he assumed on 17 January 1817. Many of his best songs date from this period, including a two-song cycle (opus 47) and *Die Temperamente*.

Weber's songs seem conservative in retrospect, but contemporaries considered him one of the great composers of lied. Wilhelm Müller even dedicated his volume of poetry containing *Die schöne Müllerin* and *Winterreise* to Weber. Weber's lieder remain historically valuable precisely because they exemplified their era as Schubert's never did. Weber composed *Die Temperamente* in 1816, thirteen years after Himmel's *Die Blumen und der Schmetterling*, the same year Beethoven composed *An die ferne Geliebte*, and seven years before Schubert's first major cycle, *Die schöne Müllerin*. Weber composed within a tradition in the midst of transition, and largely because of that transition, Weber's songs, like most composed between 1790 and 1820, now languish in dusty archives.

Those who study Weber's songs often discover more than they expected. As early, and as long ago as 1871, when compiling his catalogue of Weber's works, Friedrich Jähns complained about the neglect of *Die Temperamente*:

> The work belongs among the those of W[eber]'s that have been—most unjustly—practically forgotten, although it contains four character pieces of the first rank. Each number surpasses the next with an impressive truth of expression; they are at once very grateful works for singer and accompanist, both presented as complete and full of expression. W[eber]'s full [range of] humor reveals itself here in all the nuances accessible mainly to him in his great mastery: now bubbling over, as in "Leichtmüthigen," now blustering, as in "Liebewüthigen," now dragging along in burlesque indolence, as in "Gleichmüthigen," this humor sparkles best, and only quite cleverly, through the musical expression of "Schwermüthigen's" bombastic fantasies.[45]

Adolph Martin Schlesinger[46]

Born Sulz, in Silesia, 4 October 1769; died Berlin, 11 October 1838. Publisher and printer in Berlin. A second Schlesinger publishing house, founded ca. 1821 by his eldest son Maurice, was based in Paris. The firm's signature varied: "Schlesinger," "Schlesinger'sche Buch- und Musickhandlung," or "Schlesinger'sche Buch- und Musikalienhandlung, Unter den Linden No. 34."

Schlesinger began as a book dealer in Berlin ca. 1790–95; he later added printed music and eventually expanded into music publishing, establishing his firm in April of 1810. From 1811, he did his own printing as well, usually of local Berlin composers such as Mendelssohn, Loewe, and Spontini. In 1814, he secured the rights to Weber's works and became his original publisher, including for *Der Freischütz*; he published *Die Temperamente* in 1817.

When Schlesinger died in 1838, his youngest son Heinrich, who had never married, managed the business until 1863, when he joined forces with Robert Emil Lienau, finally selling out to Lienau in 1864. For a time, Lienau maintained the Schlesinger name, adding his behind: "Schlesinger, Robert Lienau."[47]

Schlesinger became one of the most important of Prussian music publishers, issuing over two thousand publications by 1836. Important editions included works by Beethoven, Berlioz, Liszt, Cornelius, Mendelssohn, Spohr, Chopin (the posthumous works), and Bach (the *St. Matthew Passion*). The firm also published the *Berliner allgemeine musikalische Zeitung* under Adolph Bernhard Marx (1824–30) and *Echo* (1851–65), chiefly by Heinrich Schlesinger; both periodicals focused on promoting German music and revitalizing Berlin's musical life.

The Cycle

Source. The Schlesinger edition:

Die | Temperamente | bei dem Verluste der Geliebten. | Vier Gedichte von Gubitz, | in Musik gesetzt mit Begleitung des Pianoforte | von | Carl Maria von Weber. | Eigenthum des Verlegers | Berlin in der Schlesinger'schen Buch- und Musikhandlung. | Op. 46 No.234 Pr.1 rthl.

Plate number 234. Undated. Microfilm copy from the Bayerische Staatsbibliothek, call no. 4° Mus. pr. 11407.

Comments. According to Weber's diary, he began composing *Die Temperamente* in 1815 and completed it on 3 November 1816 in Berlin.[48] Jähns assigned the following numbers: J200, "Der Leichtmüthige"; J201, "Der Schwermüthige"; J202, "Der Liebewüthige"; J203, "Der Gleichmüthige." Schlesinger first announced the work in issue no. 15 of its *Voß'schen Zeitung: Musenalmanach* (Berlin, 1817).

Apparently, no autographs have survived;[49] this edition is based entirely on the first edition by Schlesinger.

Heinroth's Die Jahreszeiten, *set by Schneider*

T. L. A. HEINROTH

Entirely forgotten today, Heinroth was probably Schneider's friend or a member of the same circle; Schneider dedicated *Die Jahreszeiten* to him.

(JOHANN CHRISTIAN) FRIEDRICH SCHNEIDER[50]

Born Alt-Waltersdorf near Zittau, 3 January 1786; died Dessau, 23 November 1853. German composer, conductor, and teacher. Sometimes confused with his brothers, Johann (Gottlob) and (Johann) Gottlieb; with his son, Theodor; or with various members of other Schneider families.

When only four years old, Schneider began learning piano from his father, Johann Gottlob Schneider, a school master and organist in Alt- und Neu-Gersdorf. Inspired by a performance of Mozart's *Zauberflöte* in Dresden, Schneider decided to pursue a musical career and began studying diligently. By age eight, he was composing and entered the Zittau Gymnasium in 1798 to continue studying music. At one point, after despairing of ever performing in public, he considered giving up music, but at a performance of Haydn's *Die Schöpfung*, he met Mr. Lingke, a lawyer and proprietor in Görlitz, who became Schneider's patron, introducing Schneider into musical society and providing him opportunities to perform.

Schneider published his first three piano sonatas with Breitkopf und Härtel in 1803 and became director of Zittau's choral society in 1804 before entering the university in Leipzig in 1805. In the following years, Schneider changed positions frequently: singing teacher, organist, music director. Throughout this period, Schneider became known through performances of his own and others' works in the Leipzig concerts; his performance of Beethoven's Fifth Piano Concerto in Leipzig on 28 November 1811 is believed to have been the work's première.[51]

As of 2 April 1821, Schneider became Hofkapellmeister at Anhalt-Dessau, where he contributed much to improve musical life, founding a Singakademie, a schoolmasters' choral society, a *Liedertafel* in 1821, and a successful music school, ca. 1829–46, that was superceded by the Leipzig Conservatory. Between 1820 and 1851, he directed more than eighty German music and singing festivals, most of which included a performance of one of his oratorios. He belonged to numerous musical societies and received honorary doctorates from the universities of Halle and Leipzig in 1830.

Schneider composed prolifically, and in his day was considered a leading German composer; according to Fétis, his works were as remarkable for their quality and quantity as for their variety. Works included fifteen oratorios, six operas, fourteen masses, twenty-five cantatas, twenty-three symphonies, twenty overtures, seven piano concertos, ten string quartets, thirty-five piano sonatas, around 450 part songs, and around two hundred solo songs, as well as numerous smaller works. As opus 58, *Die Jahreszeiten* was one of his earlier works.

Schneider also wrote three treatises: an *Elementarbuch der Harmonie und Tonsetzkunst*, 1820, based on Gottfried Weber's principles (English translation, *Elements of Musical Harmony and Composition*, London, 1828); a *Vorschule der Musik*, 1827; and *Handbuch des Organisten*, 1829/30, in four parts. Fétis described Schneider's organ method as "one of the most important of its type."[52]

KARL CHRISTOPH TRAUGOTT TAUCHNITZ[53]

Born Grosspardau bei Grimma, 29 October 1761; died Leipzig, 14 January 1836. Printer, publisher, and book dealer in Leipzig. Not to be confused with his nephew and apprentice, (Christian) Bernhard Tauchnitz (b. 1816), who established a separate publishing firm in Leipzig in 1837 under the name Bernhard Tauchnitz, and who issued the so-called "Tauchnitz Editions."

Son of a school teacher who could not afford to finance a university education, Karl Tauchnitz turned to printing and publishing, a trade closely related to academic study.[54] Between 1777 and 1796, Tauchnitz apprenticed and then worked in print shops in Leipzig, Berlin, and Leipzig again. In 1797, thirty-six years old and armed with only one press, Tauchnitz opened his own print shop and married the daughter of fellow printer Christian Philipp Dürr. They had a son the following year, Karl Christian Philipp Tauchnitz (1789–1884), who realized his father's dreams by studying theology.

The Karl Tauchnitz firm grew quickly, adding a type foundry and retail store in 1800; the firm was selected as the city's book printer in 1806. In 1808, Tauchnitz began publishing his famous Greek and Latin classics—clean, accurate, and inexpensive editions that sold throughout Europe and reigned in German schools and universities for half a century.

One of twenty printers in Leipzig in 1804,[55] Tauchnitz distinguished himself through his tireless improvements in the quality and speed of printing. He experimented with lithography and stereotype, demonstrated the business advantages of combining publishing, printing, retailing, and type foundry under one roof, and employed faster, more efficient mechanical presses. Although stereotype had long been used in France and England, Tauchnitz was possibly the first, certainly one of the first, to introduce it in Germany. In 1819, he applied to the king for several years' exclusive rights to a stereotype foundry to protect his investment of having purchased the "secret" from the Englishman James Watt. The experiments paid off. Within only a few years, Tauchnitz issued over sixty volumes (around 20,000 plates) of Greek classics, four different editions of the Bible, and the first stereotype editions of music, piano scores of Mozart's *Don Giovanni* and Rossini's *Tancredi*, both previously published by Friedrich Schneider. It was during these early years of printing with stereotype that Tauchnitz published *Die Jahreszeiten*.

After Tauchnitz died in 1836, the firm passed to his son, who diversified into foreign language dictionaries and retired in 1865, selling the firm to Otto Holtze. The Tauchnitzes, father and son, operated at the forefront of printing and publishing in Leipzig for sixty-eight years and were recognized by the city through memorials, portraits, and displays in libraries and museums.

THE CYCLE

Source. The Tauchnitz edition:

Die | Jahreszeiten | Zwölf Lieder | gedichtet von T.L.A. Heinroth | componirt | und dem Dichter gewidmet | von | Friedrich Schneider | Herzl. Anhalt-Dessauischem Kapellmeister. | Mit Stereotypen gedruckt. 58. Werk. | Leipzig | bei Karl Tauchnitz.

Plate number 13. Undated. Microfilm copy from the Bayerische Staatsbibliothek, call no. 2° Mus. pr. 1020.

Comments. Dates for *Die Jahreszeiten* can only be approximated. Its title page suggests a terminus post quem by identifying Schneider as kapellmeister of Anhalt-Dessau, a position he assumed in 1821 but may have accepted earlier. Whistling's handbooks list *Die Jahreszeiten* for the first time in its second edition (1828), page 1095, providing the terminus ante quem: "Schneider—die Jahreszeiten, 12 Lieder von Heinroth. Ebend. [Leipzig, Tauchnitz] 16 Gr." The title page of *Die Jahreszeiten* notes that the music was printed with stereotype, a process Tauchnitz applied to music editions shortly after 1819; plate number 13, presumably the thirteenth stereotype music edition, suggests the cycle was printed earlier rather than later in the 1820s.

Castelli's Die Monate (An die Frauen), *set as* Die zwölf Monate *by Bornhardt*

IGNAZ VINCENZ FRANZ CASTELLI[56]

Born Vienna, 6 March 1781; died Vienna, 5 February 1862. Minor bureaucrat and secretary, collector, and poet. Pseudonyms included Bruder Fatalis, Kosmas, Rosenfeld, and C. A. Stille, among others.

Castelli began his career in 1801 at a bookshop in lower Austria, where he learned the French that had such impact on his life. For most of his life, Castelli worked as a bureaucrat, ending as Landschafts-Secretär. During the Napoleonic wars, Castelli vented his strongly patriotic, anti-French political views in widely circulated poems such as his *Kriegslied für die österreichische Armee*, which the Archduke Karl enjoyed so much that he had thousands of copies distributed. As a result, Castelli was forced to flee to Hungary during the French occupation.

During his career, Castelli assembled extensive and valuable collections of stage plays (over 12,000), tin boxes (over 1800), portraits of renowned actors and theater poets, and a gallery of paintings by contemporary Viennese artists. He also helped found the Viennese Humane Society (*Thierschutzverein*) and wrote a *Wörterbuch der Mundart in Oesterreich unter der Enns*, both in 1847.

Castelli attempted poetry in almost all genres, beginning in 1805 with his *Poetische Versuche* published under the pseudonym "Rosenfeld," and demonstrated a talent for folk-like lyric poetry written in dialect.[57] His *Gedichte in niederösterreichischer Mundart* (1828) founded a branch of poetry continued by Stelzhammer and J. G. Seidl. He also wrote numerous *Kriegslieder* and *Wehrmannslieder* but specialized in dramatic poetry for the theater.

In addition to writing his own plays, Castelli translated and adapted numerous plays (adding verses for music as needed) and operas from French, including Spontini's *Ferdinand Cortez* and Meyerbeer's *Die Hugenotten*. His best known work was the popular *Die Schweizerfamilie*, set to music by J. Weigl in 1811, which brought him the position of Hoftheaterdichter at the Kärntnertortheater, a position he relinquished in 1814. Between 1809 and 1848, Castelli also edited several periodicals and *Taschenbücher*, including *Huldigung den Frauen*, 1823–48.

A complete fifteen-volume edition of his works was published in Vienna in 1844–46 by Pichler, followed by six volumes of *Neue Folge seiner sämtlichen Werke* in 1858. *Die Monate (An die Frauen)* was reprinted in the 1844 edition, but without an explanation of where it first appeared. In 1861, the year before he died, Castelli wrote his *Memoiren meines Lebens: Gefundenes und Empfundenes*, four volumes that include his account of the "Ludlamshöhle," a society of Viennese writers that met between 1820 and 1826.

JOHANN HEINRICH KARL (CARL) BORNHARDT[58]

Born Braunschweig, 19 March 1774; died Braunschweig, 19 April 1840. German professor, pianist, guitarist, and composer. Bornhardt's name appeared in various guises: JHC, JGH, JFC, and FC as well as JHK.

Bornhardt apparently lived his entire life in Braunschweig. Although Fétis described him as one of the most prolific[59] composers of his time, and his works as achieving a "brillant succés" in Germany, little is known about him today. According to Gerber, Bornhardt composed primarily for Liebhaber, and Fétis noted that Bornhardt's reputation was based on his talent for writing lieder and Romanze. Bornhardt also composed several Singspiele, and at least one opera, *Der Eremit auf Formentera* in 1797; he was probably most well known for his guitar method, which was published widely and went through four editions.

Bornhardt devoted much of his time to transcribing popular works for piano, guitar, and voice, including Hůrka's *Die Farben*, a setting of (Karl) Theodor Körner's

Leyer und Schwert, and songs from the Singspiel *Rose die Müllerin,* Ludwig Berger's forerunner for Schubert's *Die schöne Müllerin.* Bornhardt and Castelli apparently never met, and Bornhardt's source for the poems is unknown.

GOTTFRIED MARTIN MEYER[60]

Died Brunswick, 1849. Publisher and printer.

Meyer founded his firm on 1 June 1828 as a combined music press and shop, which grew into a flourishing business. After Meyer died in 1849, his widow continued the business until 1851, when she married, and eventually deferred to, the French composer/pianist Henry Litolff, who renamed the firm Henry Litolff's Verlag.[61]

THE CYCLE

Source. The Meyer edition:

Die zwölf Monate. | An die Frauen. | Dichtungen von Castelli. | In Musik gesetzt mit | Begleitung des Pianoforte | von | J. H. C. Bornhardt. | Eigenthum des Verlegers. | Von Hildt in Beschm. ged. | No. 51 Pr: 18 gr. | Braunschweig bei G. M. Meyer jr.

Plate number 51. Undated. Microfilm copy from the Musiksammlung der Österreichischen Nationalbibliothek, call no. M.S. 19017.

Comments. Bornhardt published his setting of Castelli's *Die Monate* sometime between 1 June 1828, when G. M. Meyer founded his firm, and 1829, when the cycle was first listed in Whistling's handbooks, in the first supplement (1829) to his second edition, page 1234: "Bornhardt.—die 12 Monate (An die Frauen) von Castelli. Braunschweig, Meyer. 18 Gr."

Notes

1. Louise E. Peake pointed this out in "The Song Cycle: A Preliminary Inquiry in the Beginnings of the Romantic Song Cycle and the Nature of an Art Form" (Ph.D. diss., Columbia University, 1968), iii.

2. *The New Harvard Dictionary of Music,* s.v. "Song cycle," by Rufus Hallmark.

3. The definition previously considered to be the earliest, cited by Barbara Turchin in "Robert Schumann's Song Cycles in the Context of the Early Nineteenth-Century 'Liederkreis' " (Ph.D. diss., Columbia University, 1981), 4, was from Hermann Mendel's lexicon of 1876, *Musikalisches Conversations-Lexikon* (Berlin: L. Heimann), vol. 6, under "Liedercyklus." Arrey von Dommer's rather long explanation seems to have been the basis for Mendel's lightly reworded condensation. Dommer's complete definition reads:

> *Liederkreis, Liedercyclus.* Ein zusammenhängender Complex verschiedener lyrischer Gedichte. Jedes derselben ist in sich abgeschlossen, kann hinsichts des Versmaasses und Strophenbaues von den anderen auch äusserlich verschieden sein; alle aber stehen in innerer Beziehung zu einander, denn durch alle zieht sich ein- und derselbe Grundgedanke, die einzelnen Dichtungen geben immer nur verschiedene Wendungen desselben, stellen ihn in mannigfachen und oft auch contrastirenden Bildern und von verschiedenen Seiten dar, so dass das Grundgefühl in ziemlich umfassender Vollständigkeit ausgetragen wird. Die Musik anbelangend, pflegt zwar jedes einzelne Gedicht für sich durchcomponirt zu sein, doch im wesentlichen wird eine Hauptmelodie für alle Strophen (desselben Gedichts) beibehalten, und nur abgeändert und etwas anders gewendet, wo es passend oder erforderlich scheint. Ausserdem aber wechselt die Melodie und ganze Tongestaltung selbstverständlich mit jedem Gedichte, ebenso die Tonart, die einzelnen Sätze sind gewöhnlich durch Ritornelle und Ueberleitungen des begleitenden Instrumentes mit einander verbunden. Die Begleitung ist wesentlich entwickelt, in characteristischer Weise die Situation schildernd und malend, sowie ergänzend, was die Stimme hinsichts des Ausdruckes unerledigt lassen muss. Zur dramatisierenden Solocantate fehlt dem Liederkreise eigentlich nichts mehr als das Recitativ, und die arienartige Form der Gesänge anstatt der liedartigen; im übrigen wird man ihn der Cantate ziemlich nahestehend finden, oder als eine Mittelgattung zwischen durchcomponirtem Liede und Cantate ansehen.

Mendel writes:

> *Liedercyclus,* eine Reihe, dem Inhalt und Charakter nach zusammengehöriger lyrischer Dichtungen, z.B. W. Müller's "Die schöne Müllerin", componirt von Fr. Schubert, und Jeitteles' L. "An die ferne Geliebte", componirt von Beethoven, sowie "Liebeslust und Lied [*sic*]" von Rob. Schumann u.s.w.

4. Contemporary dictionaries show every indication of their authors trying to write for the present. To cite only a few examples, Koch's 1802 dictionary adds a new term as a result of an article published in 1800 (quoting the article at length); Mendel's 1876 lexicon speaks with pride of the German "Freiheitskrieg" of 1871; in 1922, after nine editions, Riemann suddenly adds a secondary meaning to a term, one year after the publication of a dissertation on it. Examples are numerous.

5. "Figürlich heißt *Kreis* jede Rückkehr zu dem Punkte, wo man ausgegangen war" and "*Cyklus* heißt, wörtlich übersetzt, der Kreis; daher auch jede gleichförmig wiederkehrende Reihe derselben Begebenheiten." *Allgemeine deutsche Real-Encyclopaedie* (Leipzig: F. A. Brockhaus, 1824), 5:454 and 2:878.

6. The second chapter of Peake's dissertation discusses in depth circles and their meanings in the seventeenth and eighteenth centuries.

7. Johann Friedrich Reichardt, ed., *Musikalisches Almanach* (Berlin: Johann Friedrich Unger, 1796), emphasis his. There are no page numbers; the reviews are in section 5, "Neue deutsche Lieder."

8. *Allgemeine deutsche Real-Encyclopaedie,* 2:878–79.

9. Columbia University Germanic Studies, ed. Robert Herndon Fife, new series, no. 17 (Morningside Heights, New York: King's Crown Press, 1946), 56–58.

10. "Man versteht hier unter *Cyklos* den Sagen- und Fabelkreis nicht blos der trojanischen Begebenheiten; die cyklische Poesie schlag sich um den ganzen Mythenstamm . . ." *Allgemeine deutsche Real-Encyclopaedie,* 4:385.

11. "Jetzt folgt ein längerer *Wechselgesang der Blumen,* wo, nach einem kurzen, dreystimmigen, muntern Tutti, mehrere nach einander auftreten, ihre Solos aus jenen Liedern zweckmässig und gut geordnet wiederbringen, und endlich sich zu jenem Tutti (mit einigen Abänderungen) nochmals verein-

igen. . . . Mit diesem Satze schlösse sich nun wol das Ganze am besten; auch ist er ganz so bearbeitet, als ob das geschehen sollte: aber es tritt noch, etwas isolirt, der *Schmetterling* auf, oder vielmehr der Dichter, der über den Schmetterling, als Bild des Sängers, manches Gute und wirklich im Tone inniger Rührung, aussagt. Der Komponist hat dies Lied im Ganzen lobenswürdig wiedergegeben. . . ."

The reviewer interprets the *Wechselgesang* "alle" as the three women whose solos do not return; obviously, the cycle will work both ways. Notice also the reviewer's phrase: "mehrere nach einander auftreten." This cycle lends itself to a presentation as a staged mini-drama. That the reviewer only mentions this in passing implies that the possibilities of staging were obvious and that staging a cycle was not unusual.

12. For these quotes, I am indebted to Kamillo Horn, who used them to introduce his edition of Weber's songs, *Ausgewählte Lieder und Gesänge für eine Singstimme mit Klavierbegleitung* (Vienna: Universal-Edition, Actiengesellschaft, 1902).

13. Compiled from Franz Brümmer, *ADB*, 22:438–39; *GGGDD*, 6:375, 11/1:536, 14:681, 14:1018.

14. Brümmer, *ADB*, 22:438: "M[üchler] hat auf dem Gebiete der schönen Litteratur eine erstaunliche Wirksamkeit entfaltet; er ist besonders der Mann der Räthsel und Charaden, der Anagramme und Epigramme, der geselligen Unterhaltung und des Frohsinns."

15. Compiled from Milan Poštolka and Undine Wagner, *NG2*, 11:883 (s.v. "Hůrka, Friedrich Franz"); Fétis, 4:390–91; Gerber, 2: cols. 748–50; Eitner, 5:235–36; Riemann, 1:794.

16. Gerber, 2: col. 748: "einer der herrlichsten Tenoristen unseres Zeitalters"; cols. 749–50: "Und dieser vortreffliche Sänger hat während der vorigen Regierung, meines Wissens, das große Berliner Opernheater nur wenig oder gar nicht betreten. Glücklicher Weise für das Berliner mus. Publikum stand er mehrere Jahre mit an der Spitze des mit Recht so berühmten großen Konzerts in der Stadt Paris, wo auch ich obige Scenen hörte."

17. Ibid., col. 750: "beliebter Liederkomponist."

18. Compiled from Rudolf Elvers, *NG2*, 23:414–15 (s.v. "Simrock").

19. Compiled from Alec Hyatt King, *NG2*, 24:169 (s.v. "Spehr, Johann Peter").

20. Milan Poštolka, *NG*, 8:819 (s.v. "Hůrka, Friedrich Franz").

21. Compiled from Gerhard Allroggen, *NG*, 8:571–73 (s.v. "Himmel, Friedrich Heinrich"); Fétis, 4:335–36; Eitner, 5:152–57; Gerber, 2: cols. 679–86; Riemann, 1:760–61.

22. Allroggen, *NG*, 8:572.

23. Compiled from Donald W. Krummel, *NG2*, 20:367 (s.v. "Printing and publishing of music. II. Publishing. 3. The age of engraving, 1700–1860"); Hans-Martin Plesske and Frances Barulich, *NG2*, 19:489–91 (s.v. "Peters"); Alexander Weinmann, *NG2*, 11:598–600 (s.v. "Hoffmeister, Franz Anton"); also Otto Erich Deutsch, *Musikverlagsnummern: Eine Auswahl von 40 datierten Listen 1710–1900*. 2d ed. (Berlin: Verlag Merseburger, 1961), 13–14.

24. Compiled from Hans Schmid, *NG-MPP*, 235 (s.v. "Falter & Sohn").

25. Donald William Krummel, *NG-MPP*, 106; Alec Hyatt King mentions that Falter issued music using lithography as early as 1797, *NG-MPP*, 423 (s.v. "Senefelder, Alois").

26. Dieter Spatschek of the Bayerische Staatsbibliothek in a letter to the editor, 21 May 1999, in which he attached the library description: "Die Blumen und der Schmetterling . . . Berlin, bei Rudolph Werckmeister. ([überklebt von:] München bey Falter und Sohn Residenz-Strasse N.o [sic] 33.). . . ." Spatschek concurred, "Vermutlich ist Ihre Annahme richtig, daß Falter Exemplare nach dem Ende des Verlages Werckmeister 1809 aufgekauft und vertrieben hat." History of Werckmeister compiled from Rudolf Elvers, "Datierte Verlagsnummern Berliner Musikverleger," in *Festschrift Otto Erich Deutsch zum 80. Geburtstag am 5. September 1963*, ed. Walter Gerstenberg, Jan LaRue, and Wolfgang Rehm (Kassel: Bärenreiter Verlag, 1963), 291–95; Hans-Martin Plesske, "Bibliographie des Schrifttums zur Geschichte deutscher und österreichischer Musikverlage," *Beiträge zur Geschichte des Buchwesens* 3 (1968): 135–222; Liesbeth Weinhold and Alexander Weinmann, *Kataloge von Musikverlegern und Musikalienhändlern im deutschsprachigen Raum 1700–1850: Verzeichnis mit Fundortnachweisen und einem historischen Überblick*, Catalogus Musicus, vol. 15 (Kassel: Bärenreiter, 1995), 102.

27. Compiled from Eitner, 5:155; Gerber, 2: col. 686; Whistling, vol. 1 (1816), 562.

28. See Allroggen, *NG*, 8:572.

29. Compiled from Kosch-2, 3:2574; Kosch-3, 16:150; Karl Goedeke, *Grundrisz zur Geschichte der deutschen Dichtung aus den Quellen von Karl Goedeke*, 2d ed., revised, ed. Edmund Goetze (Dresden: L. Ehlermann, 1906), s.v. "Scholz, Joseph Heinrich," which appears in vol. 7 ("Zeit des Weltkrieges: 1790–1815"), ch. 6 ("Romantik: Norddeutschland"), 395–96.

30. Compiled from Sterling E. Murray, *NG2*, 27:435–36 (s.v. "Wineberger, Paul Anton"); Fétis, 8:478; Eitner, 10:272; Gerber, 3: col. 587; Riemann, 2:2035.

31. *Allgemeine musikalische Zeitung* (Leipzig), vol. 2 (5 March 1800), col. 413, letter of February 1800: "Dieser Herr Wineberger ist ein sehr guter Orchester- und Konzertspieler, auch besitzt er Kompositionskenntnisse, nur scheint es ihm an Geschmack und gehöriger Ausbildung zu fehlen."

32. Compiled from Eitner, 2:87; Hugo Riemann, *Riemann Musik Lexikon*, 12th ed., ed. Wilibald Gurlitt (Mainz: B. Schott's Söhne, 1959), 1:185; Krummel, *NG-MPP*, 105–10; Theodor Wohnhaas, *NG2*, 3:271 (s.v. "Benjamin, Anton J."); Rita Benton, *NG*, 15:6–10 (s.v. "Pleyel"); Gerber, supplement 2: cols. 446–47; Weinhold and Weinmann, *Kataloge von Musikverlegern*, 45–46.

33. More accurate dating may be found in Günther's and Böhme's lists of published works, possibly available at the Gesellschaft der Musikfreunde, Vienna. Lists began in 1796; Günther's name was dropped with supplement no. 5 in 1799; the lists ceased with supplement no. 22 in 1814.

34. Compiled from Dohme, *ADB*, 10:86; Max Degen, *Die Lieder von Carl Maria von Weber* (Basel: Inaugural-Dissertation, Universität Basel, 1923), 12–19, 38, 49, 64–65; *GGGDD*, 3:638f. (list of poetry), 9:435, 14:205; Leopold Hirschberg, *Der Taschengoedeke Bibliographie deutscher Erstausgaben*, 2d ed. (Munich: Deutscher Taschenbuch Verlag, 1990), 182.

35. Degen, *Die Lieder von Carl Maria von Weber*, 16.

36. Ibid., 13.

37. Compiled from John Warrack, *NG* 20:241–64 (s.v. "Weber. Carl Maria [Friedrich Ernst] von Weber"); John Warrack, *Carl Maria von Weber* (Cambridge: Cambridge University Press, 1976); Friedrich Wilhelm Jähns, *Carl Maria von Weber in seinen Werken: Chronologisch-thematisches Verzeichniss seiner sämmtlichen Compositionen* (Berlin: Schlesinger'schen Buch- und Musikhandlung [Rob. Lienau], 1871; reprint, Berlin-Lichterfelde: Robert Lienau, 1967), 215; Degen, *Die Lieder von Carl Maria von Weber*; Horn, introduction to Weber, *Ausgewählte Lieder und Gesänge*.

38. Quoted in Degen, *Die Lieder von Carl Maria von Weber*, 14, from Max Maria von Weber, *Carl Maria von Weber: ein Lebensbild* (Leipzig: E. Keil, 1864–66), 99ff.: "In Darmstadt, wo Weber zusammen mit Gänsbacher und Meyerbeer den Unterricht Voglers genoß, 'schüttelten sich die drei den Staub aus dem Pelz', wenn sie aus der Gesellschaft der Alten abends auf die Straße hinauskamen und 'Melodien sammeln' gingen, d.h. da Wein tranken, wo man sang oder Zither oder Harfe schwirrte. Vor Soldaten oder Mädchen konnte da Karl Maria die Gitarre um den Hals werfen, auf einen Tisch steigen und Schelmenlieder singen, daß des Jubels kein Ende war, bis ihn der Tabaksdampf aus der Kneipe jagte. Zum Dank empfing er vom Volksgesange manche Anregung in Leben und Melodie." "Staub aus dem Pelz schütteln" was one of Weber's sayings; the "Alten" are Vogler and his friend Hofkammerrat Hoffmann; and "Melodien sammeln" was a humorous reference to Vogler's interest in folk melodies, which Weber adopted.

39. Quoted in Degen, *Die Lieder von Carl Maria von Weber*, 19; Weber recorded a remark made to Friedrich Wieck (Clara

Schumann's father): "Die Schopfung einer neuen Form muß durch die Dichtung, die man komponiert, erzeugt werden. Bei meinen Gesängen hat mich immer nur das größte Streben, meinen Dichter wahr und korrekt deklamiert wiederzugeben, zu manchen neuen Melodiegestalten geführt."

40. Degen, *Die Lieder von Carl Maria von Weber*, 19, quoting Carl Maria von Weber, *Sämtliche Schriften von Carl Maria von Weber*, ed. Georg Kaiser (Berlin: Schuster and Loeffler, 1908), 372: "Nach meiner Ansicht ist es die erste und heiligste Pflicht des Gesanges, mit der möglichsten Treue wahr in der Deklamation zu sein."

41. Degen, *Die Lieder von Carl Maria von Weber*, 13–14, paraphrased from the biography, no page number specified: "Die verschiedenen gesellschaftlichen Kreise . . . vereinigten sich des öftern, teils in den Trinkstübchen des Schlosses, teils in der berühmten Wirtsstube des Gastwirts Schwederer oder bei Höner. Wenn auch Übermut und Ausgelassenheit meistens vorherrschen, so wurde doch auch manches geistvolle Gespräch geführt, das mehr als einmal den Ausgangspunkt zu einem Liede bildete. In gehobener Stimmung wagten dann diese Leute, die in den wenigsten Fällen Dichter von Beruf waren, poetische Versuche, die Weber, der sie angeregt, oft sogleich in Musik setzte. Dadurch wird einmal die Textwahl erklärlich. . . . Aber auch für das Improvisationsartige, das seinem Stil bisweilen anhaftet, ist damit ein Grund gegeben."

42. See Michael C. Tusa in his article on Weber, *NG2*, 27:151; Degen, *Die Lieder von Carl Maria von Weber*, 13–14, and in his summary, 19: "Das Verhältnis Webers zu seinen Texten ist, wie wir gesehen haben, ein besonderes und nicht etwa mit dem Schuberts zu vergleichen, dessen Lieder mehr Konzertlieder sind, während Webers Lieder im Konzertsaal nie Erfolg haben werden. Seine Lieder werden einzig und allein richtig genossen und letzten Endes auch richtig beurteilt werden können, wenn man sich stets ihrer Entstehung bewußt bleibt und möglichst bestrebt ist, sie in den Kreisen erklingen zu lassen, für die sie bestimmt sind."

43. Degen, *Die Lieder von Carl Maria von Weber*, 13–14, 19. While Weber's lieder obviously cannot be heard in the same way as Schubert's, Degen probably overstates the case. Most important here, however, is Degen's justified admonition to evaluate salon lieder in terms of their context rather than in comparison to lieder from other contexts.

44. There is no proof that Weber's break with Caroline Brandt was related in any way to composing opus 46, but the coincidence invites speculation. Tusa stated (see *NG2*, 27:151), "In certain cases Weber, an accomplished interpreter of his own songs, set texts pertinent to the circumstances in his own life . . . and it is tempting to relate the incipient song cycle op. 46 (J200–203), on four poems by F. W. Gubitz about rejection, to the nadir of Weber's relationship with Caroline Brandt in autumn 1815, about which time he began to think about these poems."

45. Jähns, *Carl Maria von Weber in seinen Werken*, 215 (emphasis omitted): "Das Werk gehört in die Reihe derjenigen W.'s, die mit hohem Unrechte von der musikalischen Welt fast vergessen sind, obwohl es 4 Characterstücke ersten Ranges enthält. Eine Nummer überbietet die andere an schlagender Wahrheit des Ausdrucks; sie sind zugleich höchst dankbare Aufgaben für Sänger und Begleiter, beide als fertig und ausdrucksvoll vorausgesetzt. W's ganzer Humor entwickelt sich hier in allen ihm vorzugsweise in hoher Meisterschaft zugänglichen Nüancen; bald sprudelnd, wie beim Leichtmüthigen, bald polternd, wie beim Liebewüthigen, bald in burlesker Trägheit sich hinschleppend, wie beim Gleichmüthigen, durchschimmert dieser Humor am feinsten und nur wie ganz heimlich den musikalischen Ausdruck der hochgetriebenen Schwärmerei des Schwermüthigen."

46. Compiled from Rudolf Elvers, *NG-MPP*, 410 (s.v. "Schlesinger"), and in *NG2*, 22:520. Riemann gives A. M. Schlesinger's dates as 1769–1833 and mentions that he dealt in music and maps as well as books while working as a dealer in Berlin in the 1790s.

47. Rudolf Elvers, *NG-MPP*, 321–22 (s.v. "Lienau").

48. Jähns, *Carl Maria von Weber in seinen Werken*, 215.

49. Jähns, *Carl Maria von Weber in seinen Werken*, 215, listed the cycle's autograph as "unbekannt," and Eveline Bartlitz, ed., in *Carl Maria von Weber: Autographenverzeichnis*, Handschrifteninventare, vol. 9 (Berlin: Deutsche Staatsbibliothek, 1986), mentioned neither the cycle nor any of the four songs.

50. Compiled from Franz Gehring, *NG*, 16:684–85 (s.v. "Schneider"); Gerber, 3: cols. 100–103; Riemann, 2:1637; Fétis, 7:490–93.

51. Reviewed in *Allgemeine musikalische Zeitung*, vol. 14 (1812), col. 8.

52. Fétis, 7:493: "Cet ouvrage est un des plus importants en son genre."

53. Compiled from Friedrich Kapp and Johann Godfriedrich, *Geschichte des deutschen Buchhandels*, published by the Historischen Kommission des Börsenvereins der Deutschen Buchhändler, 5 vols. (Leipzig: Börsenvereins der Deutschen Buchhändler, 1886–1913; Unveränderter fotomechanischer Nachdruck des Originalausgabe, Leipzig: Zentralantiquariat der Deutschen Demokratischen Republik, 1970), 3:47–48, 3:242–46, 4:17–21, 4:55–57, 4:139–42, 4:197–200, 4:461–62; G. Wustmann, *ADB*, 37:441–43; Joachim Kirchner, ed., *Lexikon des Buchwesens*, 2 vols. (Stuttgart: Hiersemann Verlag, 1952), 2:761; Reinhard Wittmann, *Geschichte des deutschen Buchhandels: Ein Überblick* (Munich: Verlag C. H. Beck, 1991), 163–64, 204, 353.

54. G. Wustmann, *ADB*, 37:441, "Da ihm sein Vater den Wunsch, zu studiren, nicht erfüllen konnte, so wollte er wenigstens ein 'den wissenschaftlichen Studien verwandtes' Gewerbe ergreifen, trat 1777 als Lehrling in die Sommer'sche Buchdruckerei in Leipzig ein und zeichnete sich dort bald durch Fleiss und Geschmack aus." Wustmann did not give a citation for the quoted phrase, which he may have borrowed from the sources he used in compiling the biography: *Nekrolog der Deutschen*, vol. 14 (1836): 52–59; *Verwaltungsbericht der Stadt Leipzig* (1884); *Acten des Leipziger Rathsarchivs*; and "etc." Kapp and Godfriedrich, writing at the end of the nineteenth century, attested to publishers' high level of education, whether acquired through schooling or through self-education (see *Geschichte des deutschen Buchhandels*, esp. 3:522–24), and emphasized publishers' important role in Germany's political history, in the education of the population, and in the development and exportation of German literature (see esp. vol. 4, chapters 1–3).

55. Kapp and Godfriedrich, *Geschichte des deutschen Buchhandels*, 3:478.

56. Compiled from K. Weiß, *ADB*, 4:63–64, based on Castelli's memoires and C. von Wurzbach's biography of Castelli; Kosch-2, 2:302 and 11:376; *GGGDD*, 6:583, 9:51, 11/2:42; and Gero von Wilpert and Adolf Gühring, *Erstausgaben deutscher Dichtung: Eine Bibliographie zur deutschen Literatur 1600–1990*, 2d ed., revised (Stuttgart: Alfred Kröner Verlag, 1992), 234–37.

57. Weiß, *ADB*, 4:63: "volksthümliche Behandlung der lyrischen Dichtung."

58. Compiled from Eitner, 2:136–38; Gerber, 2: cols. 478–80; Riemann, 1:207; and Fétis, 2:29–30.

59. Fétis, 2:29–30: "laborieux," which could mean either hard-working or laborious.

60. Compiled from Fritz Stein, *NG2*, 14:892–93 (s.v. "Litolff").

61. Fritz Stein, *NG-MPP*, 322–23 (s.v. "Litolff").

Texts and Translations

Texts from three of the cycles (*Die Jahreszeiten, Sechszehn Blumen,* and *Die Blumen und der Schmetterling*) have been excerpted from the music sources, there being no available editions for comparison. Texts for the other three (*Die Monate, Die Farben,* and *Die Temperamente*) are from editions of poetry as cited below. All were published later than the cycles; readers cannot, therefore, attribute discrepancies to composers' choices, but they can compare the two versions. Notes for these latter cycles are detailed, in order to document the poetry as it appeared in the music.

The following poems are printed exactly as in the sources cited, except that unnumbered verses have been numbered, abbreviations such as "u." and "weñ" have been spelled out, underlaid first verses have been capitalized and formatted to match subsequent verses, and hyphenated spellings have been converted into their unhyphenated form ("Flok-ken," for example, is printed as "Flocken"). Accompanying prose translations are by the editor and are intended only to convey the sense of the poetry.

The Poems

Ignaz Vincenz Franz Castelli: Die Monate (An die Frauen)

Text source: *J. F. Castelli's sämmtliche Werke,* Vollständige Ausgabe letzter Hand, in strenger Auswahl (Vienna: Ant. Pichler's sel. Witwe, 1844), 3:157–61.

[1.] Jänner
Den ersten Monat hieße füglich
   Man wohl den Lügenmonat auch;
Denn Schmeichelei'n und Wünsche plappern,
   Die man nicht fühlt, ist da der Brauch;
Doch wenn wir Männer Euch versichern,
   Daß wir Euch stets mit Wonne schau'n,
Und ohne Euch nicht leben könnten,
   So ist das wahr, Ihr holden Frau'n!

January
One could also aptly call
   the first month "Lying Month,"
for it is customary to blabber flatteries and
   congratulations that one doesn't feel;
yet when we men assure you that we always
   look upon you with joy,
and could not live without you,
   that is true, you charming Ladies!

Comments on music setting. Title is "Januar." M. 32, "können" (compare l. 7, "könnten"), or "and *can*not live without you." M. 33, "es" (compare l. 8, "das"), or "*it* is true."

[2.] Februar
Gott Komus fasset jetzt das Zepter,
   Durch Tanz, Musik und Mummerei'n
Macht er die Welt auf einmal närrisch,
   Wenn's aus ist, stellt sich Langweil' ein,
Nur mag dabei sich jeder hüten,
   Daß er kein Liebesfünkchen fang',
Wer Euch zu stark in's Auge gucket,
   Bleibt närrisch auch sein Lebelang.

February
The god Komos now wields his scepter
   in dance, music, and mummery;
he makes the whole world foolish at once;
   when it's all over, boredom sets in.
Yet, may each take care to
   inflame no sparks of love:
whoever gazes too intently into your eyes
   will remain foolish his whole life long, as well.

Comments on music setting. M. 9, "führet" (compare l. 1, "fasset"), or "now *leads* [with] his scepter." M. 24, "Frau'n" (compare l. 7, "Euch"), or "into *women's* eyes."

[3.] März
Noch wehen rauh und kalt die Lüfte,
    Doch blickt im einfach blauen Kleid
Bescheiden aus dem Schnee das Veilchen,
    Uns kündend eine schön're Zeit;
So kündet auch das blaue Auge
    Der guten und bescheid'nen Frau,
Dem Manne Freude, Trost und Frieden,
    Wenn um ihn stürmt das Leben rauh.

March
The winds blow still harsh and cold,
    yet the violet, in its simple blue dress,
peeps modestly out of the snow,
    heralding a lovelier time.
So, too, the blue eyes of a good and
    modest woman herald joy,
solace, and peace to man
    when harsh life storms about him.

Comments on music setting. Title is "Maerz." M. 9, "kalte" (compare l. 1, "kalt die"), or "*cold* winds still blow." M. 15, "da" (compare l. 2, "Doch"), or "*there*, the violet." M. 19, "und kündet" (compare l. 4, "uns kündend"), or "*and* heralds." M. 29, "im Leiden" (compare l. 7, "und Frieden"), or "solace in *sorrow*."

[4.] April
Das ist der Mann, der alle Tage
    Ein anderes Gesicht uns macht,
Wir haben mit ihm uns're Plage,
    Weil er ohn' Ursach weint und lacht,
Ach, diesem launenhaften Herren,
    Ihr Frauen gleicht ihm viel zu sehr,
Wir bitten Euch, seid doch beständ'ger,
    Und quält durch Launen uns nicht mehr.

April
That is the man who daily shows us
    a different face;
we are tormented by him, because he
    cries and laughs without reason.
Ah, you women are far too similar
    to this capricious gentleman;
we beg you, be more constant and vex us
    no longer with caprices.

Comments on music setting. M. 20, "diesen" (compare l. 5, "diesem"), or "*these* capricious gentle*men*." M. 23, "gar" (compare l. 6, "viel"), or "*entirely* too similar." Mm. 27–28, "beständig" (compare l. 7, "beständ'ger"), or "*be constant*."

[5.] Mai
Du Herrlichster von deinen Brüdern,
    Belebst durch deinen Hauch die Flur,
Und Alles prangt in frischer Jugend,
    Und Alles athmet Liebe nur;
Seht Frauen, wie Euch jedes Blümlein
    Und jede Mück' ein Beispiel gibt,
Daß Ihr zur Liebe nur geschaffen,
    Drum öffnet Euer Herz und liebt.

May
You, most glorious of all your brothers,
    animate the meadow with your breath,
and everything sparkles in the freshness of
    youth, and everything breathes only love;
see, Ladies, how each little blossom and
    every gnat sets an example for you:
you are created for love alone, so open
    your heart[s] and love.

[6.] Junius
Ihr holden Frauen! dieser Monat
    Ist vorzugsweise Euch geweiht,
Ich möcht' ihn Euern Vater nennen,
    Denn er erzeugt die Rosenzeit;
Ihr seid die Rosen dieses Lebens
    Und die Natur, sich stets getreu,
Gab Euch wie allen andern Rosen
    Auch leider viele Dornen bei.

June
You charming Ladies! This month is
    dedicated primarily to you;
I would like to call it your father, for
    it begets the bloom of youth;
you are the roses of this life, and
    nature, ever true to itself,
unfortunately also gave you,
    as all other roses, many thorns.

Comment on music setting. M. 5, "Ihr mögt" (compare l. 3, "Ich möcht'"), or "you [plural] might call him."

Comment on text. L. 4, "Rosenzeit," lit., "time of roses," or figuratively, "youth," maintaining an allegory between women and roses.

[7.] Julius
Der heiße Strahl der Mutter Sonne
    Durchdringet selbst die tiefste Schlucht,
Das Werk der Liebe ist vollendet,
    Die schöne Blüthe weicht der Frucht;
Drum seid Ihr ja des Lebens Sonnen,
    Das macht das Weib zur Königinn:

July
The hot rays of Mother Sun penetrate
    even the deepest ravines;
the work of love is ended, the lovely
    blossoms yield to fruit;
thusly are you indeed life's sun,
    which makes a woman into a queen,

Daß sie für süße Frucht der Liebe
    Die Blüthe opfert willig hin.

for she is willing to sacrifice the
    blossom for the sweet fruit of love.

Comments on music setting. Mm. 5–6, "Morgensonne" (compare l. 1, "Mutter Sonne"), or "of the morning sun." M. 16, "Sonne" [*sic*] (compare l. 5, "Sonnen").

[8.] August

Das Jahr steht nun auf seiner Spitze,
    Es scholl bis jetzt ihm Lob und Preis,
Nun aber wird der frohe Knabe
    Zum ernsten Mann, zum finstern Greis;
Der höchste Punkt führt immer abwärts,
    Ihr Frauen nehmt ihn wohl in Acht,
Und sammelt Euch für Euern Winter,
    Was Schönes Euch der Lenz gebracht.

August

The year stands now at its peak;
    until now, praise and glory resonated unto it,
but now the happy boy becomes the
    serious man, the gloomy old man;
the highest point leads ever downward—
    Ladies, pay close heed,
and gather for your winter whatever
    of beauty spring brought you.

[9.] September

Durch Wald und Flur, im Thal', auf Bergen
    Erschallt des Hüfthorns froher Ton,
Das arme Rehlein will entwischen,
    Da trifft's das Blei des Jägers schon:
Ihr lieben Frauen, arme Rehlein!
    Der bösen Jägerschar entflieht,
Die Jagd auf Eure Tugend machet,
    Und zielt,—und trifft—und dann entflieht.

September

Through woods and meadows, in valleys, on mountains,
    the joyful tone of the hunting horn resounds;
the poor little deer tries to escape,
    but the hunter's lead scores already:
Dear Ladies, poor deer!
    flee the wicked band of hunters,
who hunt down your virtue,
    and aim—and score—and then flee.

Comments on text. L. 2, a "Hüfthorn" is, literally, a "hip horn" or a horn that is carried on the hip and is used for signalling during hunts. L. 5, the pun between "dear ladies" and "poor deer" is unintentional and does not occur in German. L. 6, "böse" does not translate easily—it can mean "bad, evil, angry, ill-tempered, sore, malicious, or virulent," none of which applies exactly; in this context, "die böse Jägerschar" means a group of boisterous, ill-mannered hunters intent on a deed that is somewhere between mischievous and malicious. Ll. 4 and 8, "treffen" means more exactly "to hit, strike, or meet"; I have chosen "score" to reflect the sexual connotations so important to the allegory.

[10.] Oktober

Die Rebe schwillt, Gott Bachus feiert
    Sein Fest in dieser Jahreszeit,
Ihr lieben Frauen betet, betet,
    Damit der Rebensaft gedeiht,
Bedenket, daß ein altes Sprichwort
    Mit vollem Rechte demonstrirt:
Daß ohne Ceres, ohne Bachus,
    Gewöhnlich auch Frau Venus friert.

October

The grape swells, the god Bacchus
    celebrates his festival in this season;
Dear Ladies, pray, pray, so that the
    grape juice may flourish;
consider, that an old proverb
    demonstrates, with perfect reason,
that without Ceres, without Bacchus,
    Lady Venus generally freezes as well.

Comment on music setting. Title is "October."

Comment on text. L. 5, the proverb is possibly "Venus leidet Noth ohne Wein und Brot" (Venus suffers without wine and bread), which was current at the end of the eighteenth century.

[11.] November

Die rauhen kalten Winde wehen,
    Und ihren Schmuck verliert die Flur,
Nicht trotzen können Frau'n den Stürmen,
    Und eine Frau ist die Natur;
Doch seht ihr wohl, sie weiß zu hüllen
    Sich in der Unschuld weißes Kleid,
Und unter ihm wirkt sie im Stillen;—
    Folgt ihr bei stürmisch rauher Zeit.

November

The cold harsh winds blow,
    and the meadow loses its adornment;
women cannot defy the storms,
    and nature is a woman;
yet note well—she knows to envelop
    herself in the white dress of innocence,
and she works in silence underneath it;—
    follow her [example] in harsh, stormy times.

[12.] DECEMBER

Erreicht hat nun das Jahr sein Ende,
   Nur Jener kann ganz ungetrübt
Zurücke schauen, der sich saget:
   Gelebet hab' ich und geliebt,
Drum bitten wir, daß Ihr, o Frauen!
   Uns ja durch Sprödigkeit nicht quält,
Sonst seid Ihr Schuld, wenn von uns Einer
   Das ihm bestimmte Ziel verfehlt.

DECEMBER

The year has now reached its end;
   only he who says to himself,
"I have lived and loved"
   can look back without misgivings;
thus we beg you, O Ladies!
   do not vex us with prudery, or you
will be to blame if one of us misses
   his destined target.

Comment on text. L. 6, "Sprödigkeit" has several connotations, all of which seem to apply here: "hardness, friability, obstinacy, coldness, reserve, coyness, shyness."

T. L. A. Heinroth: Die Jahreszeiten

Text excerpted from the music source.

I. WINTER

1. WINTERS ANKUNFT

1. Welch Tosen da draussen!
Welch Wehen, welch Sausen
   in stöbriger Nacht!
Die Flocken, sie jagen
ans Fenster geschlagen!
Ins Land zieht der Winter
   mit stürmischer Macht!

2. Doch lustig! im Zimmer
da fürchten wir nimmer
   den Winter-Ocean!
Uns halten die Flammen
vertraulich beisammen:
Rückt Alle, rückt näher
   zum Feuer heran!

3. Die Gläser gehoben!
Wir ehren, wir loben
   den köstlichen Wein!
den kräft'gen, den alten!
Des Winters Gewalten
bezwingt er und führt uns
   den Frühling herein!

I. WINTER

1. WINTER'S ADVENT

Such raging outside!
Such blustering, such howling
   in turbulent night!
The snowflakes race by,
beaten against the window!
Winter sweeps into the country
   with stormy might!

Yet [be] merry! Indoors,
we never fear the
   winter-ocean!
The flames keep us
companionably together:
come all, come closer
   to the fire!

Glasses raised!
We honor, we praise
   the delectable wine!
The robust, the aged [wine]!
It subdues winter's fury
and leads us to
   the springtime within!

Comment on text. V. 1, l. 3, "stöbriger," lit., "stewing."

2. WINTERRUHE

1. Die Sonne weicht nach kurzem Lauf
   vom eisigen Gefild!
am Winterhimmel steigt herauf
   manch funkelnd Sterngebild.

2. Es fleucht der Vogel in sein Nest
   der Mensch zu Hüttchens Ruh:
auch Mutter Erde deckt sich fest
   mit weisser Hülle zu.

3. Es ruht und schläft so Hain als Flur
   im sichern Winterhaus:
die weite Welt doch ruht sie nur
   zu neuem Leben aus!

3. WINTERNACHTLEBEN

1. Fachet zum Feuer die glimmende Kohle!
Schneuzet die dunkelnden Kerzen noch hell!

2. WINTER REPOSE

The sun retires, after [its] brief circuit,
   from the icy field!
In winter heavens rise
   many a twinkling constellation.

The bird flees to its nest,
   man to the quiet of his little hut:
even Mother Earth blankets herself
   tightly with a white cover.

Glade, as meadow, rests and sleeps
   in a secure winter house:
but the wide world is only resting up
   for new life!

3. WINTER NIGHT'S LIFE

Fan the glimmering embers into fire!
Trim the dimming candles bright again!

Spät noch zur Nacht eine dampfende Bowle!
Hurtig herbei sie, du wack'rer Gesell!
Kurz bringt der Winter und trübe den Tag:
Lebe zur Nacht jezt, wer leben noch mag!

2. Munter herbei nun zum traulichen Kreise!
Eilt nicht so hastig, ihr Gäste, nach Haus!
Singt noch ein Liedchen in fröhlicher Weise!
Sorgenlos leert mir die Bowle noch aus!
Augen und Herzen macht hell sie und frisch.
Frisch auf! und spottet des Schlafers am Tisch!

3. Winter und Nacht sie vereinen die Herzen!
Sommer und Tag sie zerstreuen den Bund!
Winter und Nacht sie entzünden mit Scherzen
Leben am Leben im fröhlichen Rund,
Leben am Leben beim traulichen Heerd.
Winternacht, sey uns willkommen und werth!

II. Frühling

1. Frühlingshimmel

　1. Es schauet vom Himmel
kein winterlich Grau,
kein Wolkengewimmel,
nur lächelndes Blau!

　2. Es wehen die Lüfte
balsamisch und rein,
als saugten sie Düfte
der Blumen schon ein.

　3. Es strahlet die Sonne
nur Leben und Lust.
Schon athmet in Wonne
den Frühling die Brust.

2. Frühlingserde

1. Willkommen, trautes Baches Rieseln,
zu dem des Hügels Quellen ziehn
und scherzend über bunten Kieseln
der Winterfessel rasch entfliehn.

2. Willkommen, junges Grün am Bache,
willkommen, junges Grün am Rain:
ihr Veilchen unterm Hirtendache,
ihr Glöckchen dort im Buchenhain!

3. Willkommen, all du Knospenfülle
so reich am Strauch, so reich am Baum!
O, junges Frühlings zarte Hülle,
du birgst, doch du verbirgst ihn kaum!

3. Frühlingsleben

　1. Unter blauem Himmelsbogen,
hoch und herrlich ausgespannt,
kommt mit segensreicher Hand
auf der Blumendüfte Wogen
hold der Frühling eingezogen
in sein Reich, das Blüthenland.

　2. Jedes Knöspchen hat erschlossen
seiner Blüthe zarten Schoos!
neues Leben ringt sich los

[Keep] a steaming [punch]bowl late into the night!
Quickly gather 'round it, you stouthearted fellows!
Winter brings a short and dreary day:
live now at night, you who still wish to live!

Now gather 'round gaily in [our] cordial circle!
Don't hurry away so hastily to your homes, guests!
Sing yet another merry little song!
Carefree, [I] empty out my [punch]bowl!
It brightens and refreshes eyes and hearts.
Lively, now! And flout he who sleeps at the table!

Winter and night unite [our] hearts!
Summer and day disperse our fellowship!
Winter and night kindle with jests
life to life in the merry circle,
life to life 'round the cordial hearth.
Winternight, may you be welcomed and cherished by us!

II. Spring

1. Spring's Skies

　No wintery grey,
no mass of clouds
looks down from the skies,
only smiling blue!

　The winds blow
balmy and clear,
as though they have already imbibed
the fragrance of flowers.

　The sun radiates only
life and delight.
Already, [one's] breast joyfully
inhales spring.

2. Spring's Earth

Welcome, rippling of the beloved brook,
welling up from the hills' springs
and playfully, over many-colored pebbles,
fleeing the shackles of winter.

Welcome, fresh verdure beside the brook,
welcome, fresh verdure along the banks,
your violets under the shepherd's roof,
your bluebells there among the beech groves!

Welcome, you abundance of buds,
so plentiful on the bush[es], so plentiful on the tree[s]!
Oh, fresh spring's delicate shell,
you contain [spring], but hardly conceal it!

3. Spring's Life

　Under the blue arch of heaven,
high and gloriously outstretched,
with blessed hand upon the waves
of flowers' fragrance,
spring comes, pleasantly drawn
into its realm, the land of blossoms.

　Each little bud has disclosed
the bosom of its blossom!
New life struggles free

in den Luft- und Erd-Genossen.
Bund des Friedens ist geschlossen:
Liebe heisst des Tages Loos.

   3. Liebe weht durch junge Schatten,
Liebe tönt die Nachtigall,
Liebe der Schalmeye Schall,
Liebe spielt auf grünen Matten,
wo sich Taub' und Täubin gatten;
Lieb' ist Frühlings Wiederhall.

with companions of air and earth.
The league of peace is ended:
love commands the day's fortune.

   Love blows through young spirits;
love, the nightingale sings;
love, the sound of the shawm;
love plays on green meadows
where doves mate;
love is spring's reverberation.

III. Sommer

1. Im Walde

   1. Es treibt uns die Glut in den Hain jetzt hinaus;
wir wählen und suchen
im Schatten der Buchen
ein kühlendes Plätzchen, ein luftiges Haus.

   2. Hier wehen die Lüftchen, hier rieselt der Bach:
hier ist es gefunden!
Vor glühenden Stunden
beschirmt uns des Haines breitblättriges Dach.

   3. Hier lagert bekränzt euch am moosigen Hang!

Hier soll uns erfrischen
auf rasigen Tischen
die Beere des Waldes bei Scherz und Gesang!

III. Summer

1. In the Woods

   Now the heat drives us out into the glade;
we search and select
a cooling spot, an airy house,
in the shade of the beech trees.

   Here the breezes waft, here the brook trickles:
here it is!
During sweltering hours,
the glade's broadleafed roof shelters us.

   Here encamp, crowned with garlands, on the mossy slope!
Here berries from the woods,
on grassy tables,
shall refresh us, along with jesting and song!

Comment on text.   V. 2, l. 2, lit., "here it is found!"

2. Auf dem Flusse

   1. Die Sonne sinkt,
der Abend winkt
mit sanftem Purpurschein.
Bekränzt, geschmückt,
vertraut, beglückt,
nimmt uns der Nachen ein.

   2. Vom Strom bespült,
vom Strom gekühlt,
so schiffen wir dahin.
Der Tag erbleicht,
das Ufer weicht
und uns ist wohl zu Sinn.

   3. Wir schiffen fort
von Ort zu Ort,
vor Berg und Thal vorbei.
Das Feste weilt,
das Schiffchen eilt
und wir sind froh und frei.

2. On the River

   The sun sets,
evening beckons
with a soft crimson glow.
Bedecked, adorned,
intimate, blessed,
our skiff charms us.

   Propelled by the current,
cooled by the current,
so we sail along.
Day fades,
the riverbank recedes,
and all is pleasant.

   We sail forth
from place to place,
past mountain[s] and valley[s].
The fête lingers on,
the skiff hurries along,
and we are happy and free.

Comment on text.   V. 2, l. 6, lit., "and is pleasing to our senses."

3. In der Laube

   1. Lieblich weht die duft'ge Kühle
durch die Sommernacht;
und der heissen Mittagsschwüle
wird nicht mehr gedacht.

   2. In der trauten Laube Runde,
vom Jasmin umwebt,

3. In the Arbor

   Fragrant coolness wafts delightfully
through the summer night
and the hot, sultry midday
comes to mind no longer.

   Under the arch of the cosy arbor
intertwined by jasmine,

sitzen wir in später Stunde
Wein- und Lied-belebt.

   3. So, von Blätternacht umdunkelt,
würzen wir das Mahl.
Lauschend durch die Bäume funkelt
sanft des Mondes Strahl.

   Comment on text.   V. 1, l. 4, lit., "is no longer thought of."

IV. Herbst

1. Garten

   1. Die holden Rosen sind erbleicht,
die Lilie hat ihr Haupt geneigt,
verschwunden ist der Frühlingsglanz,
verwelkt ist Flora's schönster Kranz.

   2. Nur bunte Blumen ohne Duft,
sie blühn auf ihrer Schwestern Gruft.
Ihr Astern blau, ihr Astern roth:
ihr kündet uns des Schönsten Tod!

   3. O Frühlingskraft, o Jugendkraft,
Die warmes Leben rings erschafft
das süss mit Duft die Welt durchzieht:
Dich scheucht der Herbst, dein Hauch entflieht!

   Comments on text.   V. 3, l. 2, "warmes Leben," lit., "warm life." V. 3, l. 4, "Hauch," lit., "breath."

2. Weinberg

   1. Lustig den Hügel hinan!
Durch die gewundenen Gänge
zeigen mit Traubengepränge
Rebengeländer die Bahn.

   2. Frisch, um die Wette den Lauf
über veralterte Stufen!
Muntere Winzer sie rufen
freundlich die Wand'rer hinauf!

   3. Trauben in schwellender Pracht,
köstlicher Lese das Beste,
schmecken wir fröhliche Gäste
hier, wo der Himmel uns lacht.

   4. Sende, du Sonne, den Strahl,
sende das heitere Leben,
uns in der Traube gegeben,
auch für das Leben zumal!

   Comments on text.   V. 2, l. 1, "um die Wette den Lauf," lit., "in rivalry the course." V. 3, l. 4, lit., "here, where heaven laughs at us."

3. Herbstöde

   1. Durch Herbsteslüfte,
durch Nebeldüfte
geht Wand'rers Tritt.
Die kahlen Raine,
die öden Haine
durcheilt sein Schritt.

   2. Kein Leben aussen;
die Winde sausen
durch dürres Laub.

IV. Autumn

1. Garden

   The lovely roses have faded,
the lily has bowed its head,
the luster of spring has vanished,
Flora's fair wreath has wilted.

   Only bright, unscented flowers
that bloom upon their sisters' grave[s].
Asters blue, asters red,
you announce the death of the most beautiful [flowers]!

   O vigor of spring, O vigor of youth,
that creates vitality all around,
that permeates the world, sweet with fragrance:
autumn frightens you away; your bloom flees!

2. Vineyard

   Up the hill, merrily!
The trellises overladen with grapes
show the way
through winding paths.

   Briskly vie [along] the course
over antiquated steps!
Cheerful vintners amicably
call up to the hikers!

   We, happy guests, savor here,
where the heavens smile upon us,
grapes swelling in splendor,
the best of an exquisite vintage.

   Above all—send, O sun, [your] rays,
send the cheerful life
granted us [while] among the grapes,
for [the rest of] life as well!

3. Autumn Barrenness

   Through autumnal air,
through misty vapors
falls the wanderer's tread.
The barren banks,
the desolate meadows
hasten his step.

   No life outside;
the winds whistle
through withered foliage.

Die Blätter fallen	Leaves fall
aus Wipfel-Hallen,	from treetop arcades,
des Winters Raub.	the plunder of winter.
3. An Heerdes Flammen	Around the hearth's flames,
drängt jetzt zusammen	life's zest
sich Lebenslust.	now concentrates.
Hinab zum Thale!	Down into the valley!
zum frohen Mahle!	To merry repast!
an Freundes Brust!	To the breast of a friend!

Karl Friedrich Müchler: Die Farben

Text source: Karl Müchler, *Gedichte* (Berlin: Oehmigke, [1800]), 1:176–92. Müchler's book contains neither the eighth verse of "Lob der gelben Farbe," excerpted here from the 1802 Simrock edition, nor the entire "Lob der schwarzen Farbe," excerpted here from the undated Spehr edition (see "Poets, Composers, Publishers, and Cycles"). Those verses may have been written by someone else.

[1.] Lob der weissen Farbe

In Praise of White

1. Zartes Weiss, die Feier meiner Lieder
   will ich dir aus voller Seele weih'n,
   mögte sie so fleckenlos und rein,
wie des königlichen Schwans Gefieder,
   wie der Schnee auf hohen Alpen sein.

Delicate white, the celebration of my songs
   I dedicate to you from the fullness of my soul;
   may [my soul] be as unblemished and pure
as the plumage of the royal swan,
   as the snow upon the high alps.

2. Wohl dem Manne, der in seinem Herzen,
   heil'ge Unschuld, deine Farbe trägt,
   wenn Verfolgung ihn in Ketten schlägt,
kann er noch mit diesen Ketten scherzen,
   weil ein Gott mit rechter Waage wägt.

Happy the man, who carries holy innocence,
   your color, in his heart;
   when persecution throws him in irons,
he can still laugh at his chains,
   because God weighs with a just scale.

3. Wohl ihm, harret sein am Traualtare
   die Geliebte, wie der Friede mild,
   in ein weisses Brautgewand gehüllt,
einen Liljenkranz im blonden Haare,
   ihrer engelreinen Seele Bild.

Happy he, who is awaited at the altar
   by his beloved, gentle as peace,
   enveloped in a white bridal gown,
a crown of lilies in her blond hair,
   the image of her angel-pure soul.

4. Dass des Vaters Tugenden nicht sterben,
   werden Kinder seiner Ehe Glück;
   wie der Mond den hohen Sonnenblick,
eines ungetrübten Abends Erben,
   strahlen sie des Greises Licht zurück.

So that the virtues of the father do not die out,
   children become the fortune of his marriage;
   as the moon, inheritance of a clear evening,
[becomes the fortune] of the noble glance of the sun;
   they reflect the light of their elder.

5. Er erbebt nicht an des Grabes Rande,
   denn er fühlet seines Herzens Werth;
   und der Tod, der seinen Köcher leert,
wird ein Genius im Lichtgewande,
   der die Fackel lächelnd niederkehrt.

He does not tremble at the edge of his grave,
   for he senses his heart's merit;
   and death, which empties its quiver,
becomes a guardian angel robed in light,
   who smilingly dims the torch.

   Comment on text. V. 4, l. 3, besides its literal translation, "Sonnenblick" more commonly means "cheerful glance"; both meanings apply here.

[2.] Lob der rothen Farbe

In Praise of Red

1. Dir gebühren meine Huldigungen,
darum sei dir auch dies Lied gesungen,
   Bild der Liebe, wunderschönes Roth;
welche Farbe kann sich dir vergleichen,
deinem Schimmer muss die schönste weichen,
   gegen dich sind alle, alle todt.

My homage belongs to you;
thus this song, as well, is sung to you,
   magnificent red, symbol of love.
What color can compare to you?
[Next] to your luster, the most beautiful must yield;
   compared to you, all, all are lifeless.

2. Wann in Nacht das Heer der Sterne schwindet,
wann Aurorens Blick den Tag verkündet,
   Phöbus sich aus blauer Fluth erhebt,

When at night the host of stars fades,
when Aurora's glance proclaims the day,
   Phoebe rises from the blue flood,

färbt sein Antlitz den getrübten Aether	colors his countenance, the cloudy ether
triumphirend roth und immer röther,	a vanquishing red and ever redder,
bis er flammend über Wolken schwebt.	until he soars, flaming, over the clouds.

3. Purpur ward der Schmuck der zarten Rose,
von Cytheren in Adonis Schosse,
   einst mit ihrem Götterblut benetzt,
und der Stolz von allen Blumenbeeten
mahlt uns nun der ersten Lieb' Erröthen,
   hat uns Amors Pfeil die Brust verletzt.

Crimson became the adornment of the delicate rose,
of Cytherea in Adonis' lap;
   once [we are] anointed with her divine blood,
and the pride of all flowerbeds
paints us [with] the blush of first love,
   [when] Cupid's arrow has pierced our breasts.

4. Purpurrosen schmücken Hymens Lauben,
pupurn glänzen Libers Nektartrauben,
   Purpur färbt des Mädchens zarten Mund,
und die sanfte Röthe ihrer Wangen
macht dem holden Jüngling das Verlangen
   ihres liebekranken Herzens kund.

Crimson roses adorn Hymen's bower,
crimson glisten Liber's grapes of nectar,
   crimson colors the girl's tender mouth,
and the soft red of her cheeks
informs the charming youth of the yearnings
   of her love-sick heart.

5. Selig, wem Liäens Traube glänzet,
Amors Hand die Stirn mit Rosen kränzet,
   Hymens Fackel rothe Flammen strahlt,
wem nicht Sorgen seine Freuden tödten,
wem des Mädchens banges Schaamerröthen
   noch das Bild der zarten Unschuld mahlt.

Blessed, for whom Liäen's grapes glisten,
[for whom] Cupid's hand crowns the brow with roses,
   [for whom] Hymen's torch shines red flames,
for whom sorrows do not kill his joys,
for whom a girl's anxious blush of shame
   still portrays the image of tender innocence.

6. Selig, wann er dann zu ew'gem Bunde
von des trauten Mädchens Rosenmunde
   früh den Kuss der Treu' und Liebe küsst;
sagt ihm das Erröthen ihrer Wangen,
und ihr Blick voll zärtlichem Verlangen,
   dass sie treu, und dass er glücklich ist.

Blessed [is he], when he then, to everlasting union,
precipitously kisses the kiss of love and loyalty
   from the dear girl's rosy mouth;
[when] the blushing of her cheeks,
and her glance full of tender longing
   tells him that she is faithful, and that he is fortunate.

Comment on text. V. 6, l. 6, here, "treu" means both "faithful" and "sincere" or "honest"; "glücklich" means both "fortunate" and "happy."

[3.] Lob der blauen Farbe

In Praise of Blue

1. Von allen Farben auf der Welt
mir doch am meisten blau gefällt,
blau ist des Himmels lichter Bogen,
hat ihn kein Nachtgewölk umzogen.

Of all the colors in the world,
I like blue best;
blue is the bright vault of heaven,
when night clouds have not obscured it.

2. Blau ist des holden Veilchens Kleid,
wann es sich voll Beschcidenheit
in dunkelgrüne Blätter hüllet,
und doch die Luft mit Balsam füllet.

Blue is the charming violet's dress
when it modestly wraps itself
in dark green leaves,
and yet fills the air with perfume.

3. Blau ist das Blümchen, welches spricht:
"Ich bitte dich, vergiss mein nicht!"
das sich die Freundschaft ausersehen,
für Liebe, Liebe zu erflehen.

Blue is the little flower that says,
"I beg you, forget me not!"
which, for love's sake, friendship
chooses to plead for love.

4. Aus blauen Augen strahlet rein
der Huld und Liebe milder Schein,
drum haben immer auch vor allen
nur blaue Augen mir gefallen.

The tender shine of grace and love
radiates clearly from blue eyes;
thus, only blue eyes have always
pleased me best of all.

5. Blau ist schon seit der Fabelzeit
die Farbe der Beständigkeit,
das Roth der Liebe zu erheben,
und schöne Dauer ihm zu geben.

Since the age of mythology,
blue has been the color of constancy,
to highlight the red of love,
and to give it splendid permanence.

6. Drum soll die blaue Farb' allein
stets meine Lieblingsfarbe sein;
drum will ich nur in blau mich kleiden
und mich an blauen Auge weiden.

Thus, the color blue alone
shall always be my favorite color;
thus, I want to dress only in blue
and to feast my eyes on blue eyes.

7. Und führt mich Hymen einst zur Trau,
sei meine Braut geschmückt in Blau,
wünsch' ich, aus himmelblauen Augen
der Treue schönsten Lohn zu saugen.

And should Hymen ever lead me to marriage,
may my bride be adorned in blue;
I hope to drink the most beautiful reward of fidelity
from sky-blue eyes.

[4.] Lob der gelben Farbe

In Praise of Yellow

1. Der gelben Farbe bin ich hold;
drum sei ihr auch dies Lied gezollt,
viel schönes kenn' ich in der Welt
das doppelt Reiz durch gelb erhält.

I am partial to the color yellow;
thus, may this song, too, be bestowed upon it;
I know much that is beautiful in the world,
[much] that obtains doubled charm through yellow.

2. Gelb ist das Gold, und wie bekannt
ersetzt es Tugend und Verstand,
erkaufst du dir für blankes Gold
Vergnügen, Ruhm, selbst Minnesold.

Yellow is gold, and as is known,
it replaces virtue and judgment,
[if] you buy yourself
pleasure, fame, even love's reward for shiny gold.

3. Doch darum sing' ich freilich nicht
der gelben Farb' ein Lobgedicht,
wer trifft des Goldes Talisman
wohl je bei einem Dichter an.

Yet, I do not, of course,
sing a eulogy to the color yellow because of that;
who ever comes across
gold's talisman around a poet?

4. Doch gelb ist auch der Sonne Licht
wenn sie hervor aus Wolken bricht,
wenn sie im Lenz der Wiese Kleid
mit bunten Blümchen überstreut.

Yet yellow is also the light of the sun
when it breaks through the clouds,
when, in spring, it strews the meadow's gown
with bright little blossoms.

5. Gelb, wie die goldne Ananas,
gelb wie im vollen Deckelglas
der Wein, den Nierenstein gebahr,
ist meines Liebchens blondes Haar.

Yellow as the golden pineapple,
yellow as wine in a full goblet
that begets the kidney stone
is my beloved's blond hair.

6. Und Heil dem vaterländ'schen Rhein,
er giebt uns reichlich edlen Wein,
gelb, wie der Morgensonne Strahl
glänzt er im schäumenden Pokal.

And hail to the fatherland's Rhine;
it gives us an abundance of noble wine,
yellow as the radiance of the morning sun;
it glistens in the foaming goblet.

7. Heil diesem Wein!—er schenkt uns Muth
er wärmt des Greises kaltes Blut,
und flammt den Jüngling und den Mann
zu kronenwerthen Thaten an.

Hail to this wine!—it lends us courage,
it warms an old man's cold blood,
and inflames youth and man
to deeds worthy of a crown.

8. Auch kenn' ich noch in braunem Haar
Ein zartes gelbes Rosenpaar,
O, solltet [I]hr's nur einmal seh[']n,
Ihr riefet alle: Gelb ist schön!

I also acknowledge in brown hair
A pair of pale yellow roses;
Oh, should you see that but once,
You would all cry, "Yellow is lovely!"

Comments on text. V. 2, l. 3, "erkaufen" also means "to bribe, to corrupt." V. 5, l. 3, this is a double entrendre: wine begets kidney stones, but it also begets "Niersteiner," a famous white Mosel wine that has a pale golden color. Verse 8 was not included in Müchler's 1800 version of this cycle and may not have been written by him. Note the change in style: the verse sounds as though the author was apologizing for praising blondes because he had a beloved who was a brunette.

[5.] Lob der grünen Farbe

In Praise of Green

1. Singt roth und blau
und gelb und grau,
schwarz, feuerfarb und weiss;
Singt carmosin,
ich singe grün,
denn ihm gebührt der Preis!

Sing [of] red and blue
and yellow and grey,
[of] black, the color of fire and white;
Sing [of] crimson,
[but] I sing [of] green,
for it deserves the prize!

2. Seht die Natur!
die Blumenflur
schmückt sich im Lenz mit Grün,

Look at nature!
In spring, the flower field
adorns itself with green,

wenn hin zum Tanz
  bei'm Mondenglanz
die Hirten fröhlich ziehn.
	when the shepherds traipse
	  off to the dance
	by the light of the moon.

3. Im grünen Wald,
    dem Aufenthalt
der Unschuld, singt allein
    die Nachtigall
    dem Wiederhall
melodisch silberrein.
	In the green forest,
	    the dwelling place
	of innocence, the nightingale
	    sings alone
	    to its echo,
	melodiously clear as a bell.

4. Des Mädchens Haar
    am Brautaltar
schmückt grünes Mirtenreiss;
    ein grünes Blatt
    lohnt Heldenthat,
lohnt Dichtergeist und Fleiss.
	A green sprig of myrtle
	    bedecks the girl's hair
	at [her] wedding altar;
	    a green leaf
	    rewards the heroic deed,
	rewards the poet's wit and diligence.

5. Der Göttin, die
    des Lebens Müh'
durch schönen Traum versüsst,
    ist grün geweiht,
    grün ist das Kleid,
das flatternd sie umfliesst.
	To the goddess who
	    sweetens life's labor[s]
	with lovely dreams,
	    green is sacred;
	    green is the garment
	that encircles her, fluttering [in the wind].

6. O Göttinn, sei
    mir immer treu,
bis an des Grabes Rand;
    ich folge gern,
    glänzt nur von fern
mir tröstend dein Gewand.
	O goddess, may you be
	    ever true to me,
	unto the brink of [my] grave;
	    I will gladly follow,
	    if only your garment
	will glitter consolingly at me from afar.

Comment on music setting of the Oehmigke edition. In mm. 8–10, the text in verse 1 is "Singt roth und blau, singt gelb und grau" (Sing [of] red and blue, sing [of] yellow and grey); interestingly enough, the poetry with "und" faces the song with its "singt."

Comment on text. V. 3, l. 6, "silberrein," lit., "silver-pure."

[6.] Lob der violetten Farbe	In Praise of Violet

1. Farbe, die Cytherens Götterhand
einst erschuf aus Blau und Morgenröthe,
und damit des Veilchens Schmuck erhöhte,
    als es farbelos im Grase stand.
	Color that Cytherea's divine hand
	once created out of blue and the red of morning,
	and with which [she] enhanced the violet's finery,
	    as it stood colorless in the grass.

2. Dir, nur dir ertön' ein Feierlied,
wie ich keiner Farb' es noch gesungen,
Bild der Treue, die mein Herz durchdrungen,
    Bild der Liebe, die mein Herz durchglüht.
	To you, only to you, do I sing lauds,
	as I have not yet sung to any other,
	symbol of the loyalty that has permeated my heart,
	    symbol of the love that inflames my heart.

3. Als ich, Jenny, dich zuerst erblickt,
war dein Haar, das sanft die Stirn umflossen,
mit Violen, die sich kaum entschlossen,
    schön, als wär's ein Diadem, geschmückt.
	Jenny, when I first caught sight of you,
	your hair, which softly encircled your brow,
	was beautifully decked with violets,
	    which suddenly seemed to be a diadem.

4. Heilig soll mir diese Farbe sein,
löscht sich auch im raschen Strom der Zeiten
Amors Fackel,—all' die Seeligkeiten
    der Erinnerungen bleiben mein!
	Hallowed shall this color be for me,
	even if Cupid's flare should extinguish itself
	in the swift current of the times,—
	    all the joys of memories remain mine!

5. Ewig, ewig schlägt mein Herz wie heut,
glühn für mich auch nicht mehr Amors Kerzen,
jedes Veilchen spricht zu meinem Herzen:
    ohne Freundschaft keine Seeligkeit!
	Forever and ever, my heart will beat as [it does] today,
	and although Cupid's candles no longer shine for me,
	each little violet speaks to my heart:
	    no happiness without friendship!

Comment on text. V. 3, ll. 3–4, lit., "beautifully, had just then resolved [to appear] as though it were a diadem."

[7.] Lob der schwarzen Farbe

1. Schwarz der Nacht, von dir umgeben,
zittert nur der Bösewicht;
wer mag schaudern, wer mag beben
wem sein Herz kein Urtheil spricht!
Schwarz der Nacht, von dir umgeben
sinkt in Ruh zum neuen Leben,
Mensch und Thier und Feld und Wald
in des sanften Schlafs Gewalt.

2. Wenn am seegnenden Altare
Ehrfurchtsvoll die Andacht kniet;
Wenn an des Geliebten Bahre
Iedes Auge niedersieht;
Wenn du weinst wo Freunde starben,
Dann verlöschen andre Farben
Dann bleibt heil'gem Schmerz geweih't
Schwarz der Wehmuth Feierkleid.

3. Nicht im leuchtenden Gewande
Bist du stille Trau'r gehüllt,
Schwarz verweilest du am Strande
Deiner Trennung, denkst das Bild,
Denkst das Haben, denkst das Missen,
Malest es in Schattenrissen,
Denkst was war, was wird gescheh'n,
Ahndest frohes Wiedersehn.

4. Nacht, durch deine Einsamkeiten
Schimmert eines Weisen Pfad,
Und aus deinen Heimlichkeiten
Spriesset manche grosse That!
Schwarz, aus deinen Finsternissen
Möge Menschenglück entspriessen:
Dann wird Liebe und Vertrau'n
Sich bei Völkern Hütte bau'n.

In Praise of Black

Black of night, surrounded by you,
only the villain trembles;
he, for whom his heart renders no judgment,
[indeed] may shudder, may quake!
Black of night, surrounded by you,
man and beast and field and forest
sinks [sic] peacefully into a new life
in the power of gentle sleep.

Whenever devotion kneels reverentially
at the consecrating altar,
whenever any eye looks down
on the bier of a loved one,
whenever you weep where friends have died,
then other colors fade away,
then black, the ceremonial garb of sorrow
remains dedicated to sacred grief.

Not in radiant garment[s]
are you, silent mourning, wrapped;
black, you linger on the shore
of your parting, [and] reflect [on] the image,
reflect [on] having, reflect [on] missing,
paint it in silhouettes,
reflect [on] what was, what will be,
[and] foreshadow a happy reunion.

Night, through your solitudes
the path of a sage gleams,
and from your privacy,
many a great deed sprouts!
Black, from your darknesses
may the happiness of man sprout [anew]:
for shelter among the people will
rest upon love and trust.

Comments on text. Notice the change in style of this poem. The title page on this song (see "Poets, Composers, Publishers, and Cycles") does not mention a poet, which was unusual for the time; the song is simply " by Hůrka," so perhaps the poetry is as well. The last two lines of verse 4, "Dann wird Liebe und Vertrau'n / Sich bei Völkern Hütte bau'n," are awkward even in German.

Joseph Scholz: Sechszehn Blumen
Text excerpted from the music source.

[1.] Das Stiefmütterchen

1. Es blühet auf Hügel und Auen
Ein Blümlein, gar lieblich zu schauen,
　Mit niedlichen Farben geschmückt.
Oft hab' ich in schwärm'rischen Stunden
Das Blümlein am Wege gefunden,
　Oft hat mich sein Anblick entzückt.

2. Nicht stolz auf die schimmernde Hülle,
Erkeimt in bescheidener Stille,
　Das Blümlein das jedem gefällt.
Fünf Blätter nur zieren die Kleine,
Drei Farben im schönen Vereine,
　Hat Flora für sie sich erwählt.

3. Die gelbe den Argwohn bedeutet,
Der immer die Liebe begleitet,

The Pansy

On hills and in meadows there blooms
a little flower, quite lovely to see,
　adorned with pretty colors.
Often, in rapturous hours, I have
found the little flower along the path;
　often, the sight of it has delighted me.

Not proud of its glistening sheath,
the flower that everyone likes
　sprouts in modest repose.
Only five petals embellish the little one;
Flora chose for it
　three colors in fair alliance.

The yellow signifies distrust,
which always accompanies love,

Wenn Treue das Herz nicht bewacht;	whenever loyalty does not guard the heart;
D'rum ward von der Göttin aufs neue	For that reason, the goddess allied anew
Der Unschuld, ätherische Bläue	the ethereal azure of innocence [to yellow]
Gesellet zu schützender Macht.	as a protective force.
4. Oft pflückt' ich die lieblichen Blüthen	I often plucked the lovely blossoms
Und deutete dann ihre Mythen	and then explained its tale
Der Holden, die lieb ich gewann.	to my darling, whom I gladly won.
Es sprachen die lehrenden Farben,	The instructive colors,
Die unser Vertrauen erwarben,	which earned our trust,
Dann freundlich und tröstend uns an.	then appealed to us amiably and comfortingly.
5. Weswegen den drolligten Namen	The reason for the droll name
Die zierlichen Blümchen bekamen,	the charming little flower acquired:
Dies Räthsel, traun, lös't' ich noch nicht.	that [is a] puzzle, indeed, [that] I have not yet solved.
Doch sollt' ich's in Zukunft erfahren	But should I discover it in the future,
Dann will ich es gern offenbahren,	then I will gladly disclose it;
Jtzt [sic] end' ich mein kleines Gedicht.	[for] now, I conclude my little poem.

Comment on text. V. 5, l. 1, "the droll name," "Stiefmütterchen," means "little stepmother."

[2.] Die Sonnenblume   The Sunflower

1. Blume, die von Phöbus Glanz umflogen,	[This] flower, strewn from Phoebe's splendor,
Über viele Blumen ragt hervor,	surpasses many flowers,
Die zur Sonne, zu des Aethers Bogen	lifts its head majestically
Majestätisch hebt ihr Haupt empor:	towards the sun, towards Aether's arch:
Jener Schönheit Fülle singt mein Lied,	my song sings of the fullness of that beauty,
Die in deinem Kelche strahlend blüht.	which radiantly blooms in your cup.
2. Wie im Dunkel niedrer Regionen,	[Just] as the proud mind of the brave
Nie des Kühnen stolzer Sinn verweilt,	never lingers in the dark of nether regions,
Wie er hin zu lichterfülltern Zonen	[just] as it hurries towards more luminous regions,
Sehnend auf des Geistes Schwingen eilt:	yearning for the spirit's sway,
So, o Sonnen-Blume, strebt dein Blick	thus, oh sun-flower, your gaze gravitates
Auf dein hohes Ideal zurück.	back towards your [own] high ideal.
3. Schmetterling und Biene summen lüstern	Butterfly and bee buzz greedily
Um den Kelch, aus welchem Nektar quillt;	around your cup, from which nectar springs;
Sie umgaukeln dich mit leisem Flüstern,	they flutter around you with faint whispering;
Süsser Wonne-Rausch hat sie erfüllt.—	a sweet intoxication of joy has filled them.—
Du bist dem Inseckt auf stiller Flur,	To the insect on the quiet meadow,
Sonnen-Strahl belebender Natur!	you are the sunshine of invigorating nature!
4. Haucht um dich, du segenschwangre Blume,	No pleasant scent exudes delicate fragrance around you,
Auch kein Wohl-Geruch den zarten Duft,	you flower fecund with blessings;
Schimmern doch in Floras Heiligthume	yet indeed, few in Flora's realm
Wen'ge schöner durch die Sommer-Luft.	shimmer more beautifully through the summer air.
Wie am blauen Himmel Eos lacht,	As Eos laughs in the blue heaven[s],
Winkt, o Blume, deine stolze Pracht!	display, oh flower, your proud splendor!
5. Mag auch deiner Schönheit Reiz entschweben,	Although the charm of your beauty may vanish
Wenn des Herbstes Stürme feindlich drohn,	when autumn storms threaten inimically,
Du erwachst im Lenz zum neuen Leben,	you awake in spring to new life;
Alles kehret wieder, was entflohn!—	all that fled returns again!—
Und der Sonne mächtige Gewalt	And the mighty power of the sun
Ruft zurück die liebliche Gestalt.	summons [your] lovely form.

Comments on text. The bushy sunflower of Europe, unlike the giant sunflower common in the United States, remains facing the sky while blooming and seeding. V. 2, ll. 5–6, in other words, the sunflower, having come down from Phoebus, faces back toward him. V. 3, l. 4, "erfüllen" can also mean "to impregnate," a meaning not incompatible with the imagery here.

[3.] Das Vergissmeinnicht

1. In feuchten Schatten-Gründen,
Entfernt vom Sonnen-Licht,
Lässt sich ein Blümchen finden,
Es heisst: Vergissmeinnicht.

2. Unschuldig, sanft, bescheiden,
Blüht still es und versteckt,
Und scheint den Blick zu meiden
Der freudig es entdeckt.

3. Den zarten Kelch umziehet
Kein süsser Balsamduft
Und seine Farbe glühet
Nicht schimmernd durch die Luft.

4. Es schmückt des Aethers-Bläue
Das Blümchen, ach, so mild!
Ein Sinnbild ew'ger Treue
Hat sich in ihm enthüllt.

5. Die kleine holde Blume,
Die ohne Prunk gefällt,
Hat sich zum Heiligthume
Empfindung ausgewählt.

6. Der Freundschaft und der Liebe
Ist sie allein geweiht,
Dass die Erin'rung bliebe
Der schön-verlebten Zeit.

7. Es reicht, ist sie gefunden,
Dann die geliebte Hand
In bangen Trennungs-Stunden
Sie uns als Minne-Pfand.

8. Mit warmer Liebe sorgen
Wir für das Blümchen nun
Und lassen es verborgen
An unserm Herzen ruhn.

9. Dort mahnt es an die Stunde
Des Abschieds, zärtlich spricht,
Wie aus geliebtem Munde,
Es sanft: Vergissmeinnicht!

The Forget-me-not

In the damp, shadowy ground,
removed from sunlight,
a little flower can be found;
its name is Forget-me-not.

Innocent, tender, modest,
it blooms quietly and hidden,
and seems to shun the glance
that joyfully discovers it.

No sweeter perfume
surrounds the delicate cup
and its hue glows
unwaveringly through the air.

The little flower, oh, so tender!
is bedecked in ethereal blue.
In it, a symbol of eternal loyalty
unveils itself.

The small, lovely flower,
which pleases without ostentation,
nominated itself
to the shrine of sentiment.

It alone is sacred
to friendship and to love,
[so] that remembrance [may] remain
of time well spent.

When found, it comes to
a beloved hand
in anxious hours of separation
as a pledge of love for us.

With warm love we now
attend to the little flower
and let it lie hidden
upon our heart[s].

There it reminds [us] of the hour
of parting; it speaks tenderly, softly,
as from a beloved mouth:
forget-me-not!

Comment on text. V. 7, l. 4, technically, "Minne" is the courtly love of the Middle Ages, but it is often used in poetry to refer to more mundane love, platonic and romantic.

[4.] Die Nelke

1. Gepflanzet durch des Gärtners Hand,
Und treu von ihm bewacht
Mit kluger Sorgfalt und Verstand,
Erblüht der Nelke Pracht.

2. Wie Iris Bogen, glänzen bald
Die Farben hell und rein,
Bald hüllt die liebliche Gestalt
Ein traurig Dunkel ein.

3. So würzig, wie aus ihr, ergiesst
Sich keiner Blume Duft
Und weit umher, wo sie entspriess't,
Füllt Wohlgeruch die Luft.

The Carnation

Planted by a gardener's hand,
and faithfully watched over by him
with clever care and understanding,
the carnation's splendor blooms.

Like Iris's bow, the colors soon
shine bright and clear;
soon its lovely form enfolds
a melancholy darkness.

The fragrance of no flower
flows forth as spicily as from it;
and wherever it sprouts,
[it] fills the air far and wide with scent.

4. Ist oft mit wenig Blättern nur
Der Nelke Kelch umlaubt.
Gesellt die Kunst sich der Natur,
Und schöner prangt ihr Haupt.

The carnation's cup is often
foliated with only a few leaves.
[So it is when] art accompanies nature,
and its head shines more beautifully.

5. Die Kunst gebeut, und üppig schwillt
Und ründet sie sich dann;
Vollendet zeigt sich nun ihr Bild,
Das höhern Reiz gewann.

Art is humbled: [the carnation's head] swells luxuriantly
and then rounds itself out;
then its figure emerges complete,
the greater charm won.

6. Des Menschen Geist der Nelke gleicht,
Gelähmt bleibt seine Kraft,
Wenn ihm nicht die Erziehung zeigt
Denn [sic] Pfad zur Wissenschaft.

The carnation is like the human spirit:
its vigor remains crippled
if its training does not show it
the path to knowledge.

7. Doch, wenn er sich durch sie erhebt
Und Psyches Flügel schwingt,
Er muthig nach dem Lichte strebt
Und Weisheit sich erringt.

For when he elevates himself through [training],
and wields Psyche's wings,
he strives valiantly towards the light
and achieves wisdom.

8. Das Schöne, das verborgen wohnt,
Lockt Fleiss und Kunst hervor,
Wie beide der Erfolg belohnt,
Dies zeigt der Nelken Flor.

Beauty that lies hidden
entices diligence and skill,
as success rewards both;
this, the carnation's florescence demonstrates.

Comments on text. V. 4, the analogy here is weak; the idea is that when art is combined with nature, it rises above nature and shines more beautifully because of that association. V. 5, l. 1, the phrase "üppig schwellen" contains connotations of putting on airs, of being uppity. V. 7, l. 2, "Psyche" here refers to mental processes and activities as opposed to physical.

[5.] Die Nachtviole

The Dame's Violet

1. Es sinkt Asträa von den Bergen nieder,
    Ihr brauner Schlei'r umhüllet Thal und Flur;
Der Hain verstummt, es schweigen seine Lieder,
    Entschlummern will die lebende Natur.

Astraea sinks down from the mountains,
    her brown veil envelops valley and meadow;
the glade quiets down, its songs fall silent;
    living nature wishes to sleep.

2. Schon glänzet an des Himmels hohem Bogen,
    Im dunklen Blau, der Sterne leuchtend Meer,
Auf sanftbewegten silberhellen Wogen,
    Schwebt Luna majestätisch still einher.

The glimmering sea of stars already shines
    in the dark blue of the sky's high vault;
Luna floats along majestically quiet
    upon softly undulating, silver-bright waves.

3. Ietzt schwimmen durch die lauen Abend-Lüfte,
    Getragen auf der Weste leichtem Flug,
Der Nacht-Viole süsse Balsam-Düfte,
    Und streuen um uns süssen Wohl-Geruch.

The sweet balsam fragrances of the dame's violet
    now float through the mild evening breezes and,
carried on the slender wing of [its] waistcoat,
    strew sweet aroma around us.

4. Wenn Flora wandelt in der Töchter Kreise,
    Verweilt auf dieser Blume gern ihr Blick,
Denn dankbar schweben ihre Düfte leise
    Und liebevoll von ihr auf sie zurück.

When Flora ambles in the circle of her daughters,
    her glance lingers gladly upon this flower,
for, thankfully, her fragrances float delicately
    and lovingly from her and back again.

5. Ihr gilt mein Lob, die in bescheidner Hülle,
    Vom goldnen Farben-Schimmer ungeschmückt,
Im leisen Wehn der lauen Abend-Stille
    Mit eignem Reiz uns wunderbar entzückt!

My praise is meant for her, who in modest raiment,
    unadorned by gold-colored luster,
in the quiet waving of mild evening stillness,
    enchants us wonderfully with her own charm!

6. Ist auch ihr Wohl-Geruch dem Sinn entschwunden,
    Wenn Phöbus früh an Thetis Brust erwacht,
Doch kehrt zurück er in den Abend-Stunden
    Und wehet würzig durch die Sommer-Nacht.

Although her scent has vanished from the senses,
    when Phoebus awakes early upon Thetis's breast,
yet it returns in the evening hours
    and drifts fragrantly through the summer night.

7. Die zarte Nacht-Viole sey vor allen
    Die liebste mir, auf Floras Blumen-Flur!

The delicate dame's violet may be my favorite
    among all of Flora's flower-field!

Bescheiden, anspruchlos muss sie gefallen,	She must please modestly, without pretension,
Denn schmucklos ist am schönsten die Natur!	for nature is most beautiful unadorned!

Comments on text. The title, "Die Nachtviole," lit., "night violet." V. 4, the articles are ambiguous: "sie" refers to both Flora and the flower. V. 6, l. 2, "Thetis Brust," i.e., a sunrise.

[6.] Die Lilie / The Lily

1. Dir sing' ich, holde Lilie,
    Die kühn empor sich hebt,
Um deren Kelch der Blüthen-Schnee
    Ein zart Gespinste webt;
Die durch des Sommer-Abends laue Lüfte,
    So würzig haucht die süssen Balsam-Düfte!

I sing to you, dear lily,
    who lifts yourself up boldly,
around whose snow-white cup
    a delicate tissue floats;
who, through the mild breezes of a summer evening,
    exhales sweet balsam scents so fragrantly!

2. Wie wenn des Mondes sanftes Licht
    Die Blumen-Flur umzieht,
So strahlt des Mädchens Angesicht,
    Wo deine Farbe blüht.
Sie weichet nie, küsst auch die schönen Wangen
    Des holden Scham-Erröthens leises Bangen.

As when the soft light of the moon
    transforms the flower field,
so the maiden's countenance beams
    where your color blooms.
She never yields, even when the faint worry of
    a charming blush of shame kisses her lovely cheeks.

3. Die Blume königlicher Pracht,
    O, Lilie, bist Du!
Geweiht zum Symbol der Macht,
    Umschwebt dich stolze Ruh.
Du warst es, welche Könige bekränzte,
    Als einst der Bourboniden Thron noch glänzte!

The flower of royal magnificence,
    you, O lily, are!
Consecrated to the symbol of power,
    proud repose surrounds you.
It was you who crowned kings,
    when once the Bourbon throne still sparkled!

4. Im grauen Alterthume wies
    Die Dichtung auf dich hin,
Wenn sie der Tugend Würde pries
    Und unschuldsvollen Sinn.
Es wählte die Natur ein irdisch Zeichen,
    Das Himmlische der Tugend zu vergleichen.

In remote antiquity,
    poetry alluded to you
when it glorified the value of virtue
    and a chaste mind.
Nature chose an earthly symbol
    to compare the heavenly to virtue.

5. Von heil'ger Unschuld treu bewacht,
    Und makellos und rein,
Beschützet durch der Tugend Macht,
    Soll unser Seele seyn!
Dann gattet liebend sich der Herzens-Güte
    Die Lilie mit ihrer Schönheits-Blüthe.

Loyally guarded by sacred innocence,
    and immaculate and pure,
may our souls be
    defended by virtue's might!
For then the lily, with its blossom of beauty,
    fondly pairs itself with kindheartedness.

Comment on text. V. 1, l. 3, "Kelch der Blüthen-Schnee," lit., "cup of blossom-snow."

[7.] Die Kamille / The Chamomile

1. Ich kenn' ein Blümlein klein und zart,
Es ist von ganz besondrer Art,
    //: Kein gleiches wird gefunden. ://
Kamillenblümlein ist's genannt
Und wird geliebt im ganzen Land,
    //: Von Kranken und Gesunden. ://

I know a little flower, small and fine;
it is of a quite unusual sort;
    none similar is found.
It is called the little chamomile flower,
and is loved throughout the land,
    by the sick and by the well.

2. Den Magen-Schmerz, das Podagra,
Das Fieber und die Kolika
    //: Vertreiben die Kamillen. ://
Drum, Kranke, trinkt Kamillen-Thee!
Traun, dann velässt [sic] euch jedes Weh
    //: Und trollt sich fort im Stillen. ://

Stomach ache, podagra,
fever and colic,
    the chamomile dispels.
Therefore, invalids, drink chamomile tea!
Indeed, then every ache will desert you
    and toddle off in silence.

3. Den Frauen und den Mädchen ist
Dies Blümelein zu jeder Frist,
    //: Vor allen zu empfehlen, ://
Wenn Nerven-Krampf und Hysterie,

For every reprieve, this little flower
is to be recommended above all
    to women and to girls,
when nervous fits and hysteria,

Und Herz-Gespann und Kopf-Weh sie
   //: Mit Höllen-Martern quälen. ://
	and palpitations of the heart and headache
	   plague them with infernal torment.

4. Zu Olims grauen Zeiten gab
Den Kranken sie schon Aeskulap,
   //: Der Ahnherr der Dockteren ://
Und, glaubt es meinem Dichter-Schwur,
Es gieng bei der Kamillen-Kur
   //: Kein Kranker ihm verlohren! ://
	In the distant days of yore,
	Asclepius, the forefather of doctors,
	   already gave it to the sick,
	and, trust me,
	no invalid ever went astray
	   with the chamomile cure!

5. Was Doctor Brown auch immer spricht,
Gott Aeskulap kurirte nicht
   //: Mit Portwein und mit Schinken. ://
Dafür gebot der alte Herr,
Sah in Gefahr die Kranken er,
   //: Kamillen-Thee zu trinken. ://
	And as Doctor Brown always says,
	the god Asclepias did not cure
	   with port wine and with ham.
	For that, the old man prescribed
	drink[ing] chamomile tea
	   when he saw the sick in danger.

6. Drum stimmet alle mit mir ein
Und lobt das holde Blümelein,
   //: Das wohlthut in der Stille. ://
Vor ihm fliegt Meister Klapperbein,
Des könnt ihr alle Zeugen seyn,
   //: Es lebe die Kamille! ://
	Therefore, everyone join with me
	and praise the lovely little flower
	   that succors in silence.
	Death flies before it;
	you all could be witness to that:
	   long live the chamomile!

Comments on text. V. 2, l. 1, podagra is more commonly known as gout. V. 4, l. 4, lit., "and, believe it by my poet's oath." V. 6, l. 4, "Meister Klapperbein," lit., "Mister Rattle-bones," i.e., a skeleton.

[8.] DIE ROSE	THE ROSE
1. Wenn prangend sich der Rose Kelch entfaltet, Winkt noch des Lenzes heitre Blüthenzeit, Von Floras Hand ward sie so schöngestaltet Und liebevoll den Liebenden geweiht.	When the rose's cup gloriously unfolds, spring's merry flowering still beckons; [the rose] was fashioned so beautifully by Flora's hand and lovingly dedicated to lovers.
2. Die Rose glühet auf der Iungfrau Wangen, Wenn des Geliebten Mund um Liebe fleht Und schüchtern sie, mit nie empfundnem Bangen, Was sie gefühlt, erröthend ihm gesteht.	The rose glows upon the maiden's cheeks, when [her] beloved's mouth beseeches love and she shyly, without perceiving the anxiety that she feels, blushingly yields to him.
3. Sie blühet in dem seidnen Locken-Haare, Vereinigt mit der Myrthe dunklem Grün, Führt sie als Braut der Iüngling zum Altare, Wo Hymens Opfer-Flammen hell erglühn.	It blooms in silken curls of hair; the youth escorts her, along with the dark green of the myrtle, as a bride to the altar, where Hymen's flames of worship glow brightly.
4. Mit Rosen kränzt die Hoffnung unser Leben, Die leere Zukunft glänzt in ihrem Licht Wenn schöne Möglichkeiten uns umschweben, Die ihre Hand in unser Schicksal flicht.	Hope crowns our life with roses; the vacant future sparkles in its light when lovely possibilities surround us, [possibilities] that its hand weaves into our fate.
5. Sie strahlt am Morgen, wenn Auroras Schleier Umhüllt des Aetherslichte Purpur-Gluth, Und wenn Hyperion in stiller Feier, Am Abend sinkt in Thetis kühle Fluth.	She is radiant in the morning, when Aurora's cloak envelops the crimson glow of ethereal light, and in the evening, when Hyperion, in quiet celebration, sinks into Thetis's cool flood.
6. Wir pflanzen Rosen auf den Grabes-Hügel, Der unsrer Lieben Hülle hier umschliesst; Es wehen der Erinnrung Rosen-Flügel Um uns, wo unsrer Wehmuth Thräne fliesst.	We plant roses on the burial mound that encloses therein the bodies of our beloved; rose petals of remembrance flutter around us, where the tears of our grief flow.
7. Sind ihre zarten Blätter einst gefallen, Hat sich ihr Haupt zur Erde matt geneigt, Wird nimmer doch der Rose Lob verhallen, Die selbst im Welken keiner andern weicht!	Once her delicate petals have fallen, her head has feebly bowed to earth, yet praise of the rose, who even in wilting yields to no other, will never fade away!

Comments on text. Throughout this poem, where "sie" refers to both rose and maiden, I have used female pronouns. V. 1, l. 2, "Blüthenzeit," lit., "blossom-time," i.e., its apex. V. 3, l. 2, the myrtle is used in bridal wreaths and is a symbol of marriage. V. 6, l. 4, "fliesst" should read "fließen," but has been truncated to fit the rhyme.

[9.] Das Gänseblümchen

1. Dir, kleine Blume, weih' ich ein Gedicht,
   Die still verblüht,
Und die so oft des Menschen Angesicht
   Stolz übersieht.

2. Kaum schmilzt des rauhen Winters Schnee-Gewand
   Der Sonnenschein,
So trittst du schon, geführt von Floras Hand
   Ins Leben ein.

3. Wenn kaum ein andres Grün in der Natur
   Das Aug' entzückt,
Bist du es, holdes Blümchen, das die Flur
   Bescheiden schmückt.

4. Du zauberst uns des Frühlings Lächeln her,
   Wenn überall
Verödet trauern, blüthenlos und leer
   Noch Berg und Thal.

5. Iezt ist die Zeit, wo Iung und Alt dich liebt
   Und gern dich pflückt;
Doch bist du, wenn es schön're Blumen giebt,
   Nicht mehr beglückt.

6. Dann sieht der Mensch dich mit Verachtung an,
   Des Spottes Ziel
Wirst du, die einst im Lenze Iedermann
   So wohl gefiel.

7. So welkst du Arme, still und freudenlos,
   Vom Hohn geneckt,
Bis wieder liebend aus der Erde Schooss
   Der Lenz dich weckt.

The Little Daisy

I dedicate a poem to you, little flower,
   who quietly fades,
and who so often overlooks the pride
   [in] man's face.

The sunshine has hardly melted harsh winter's
   vestment of snow,
when you, led by Flora's hand,
   already begin life.

When hardly anything green in nature
   delights the eye,
it is you, dear little flower, who modestly
   adorns the meadow.

You conjure up for us spring's smile,
   when all around,
mountain and valley still mourn, desolate,
   flowerless, and empty.

Now is the time when young and old love you
   and like to pick you;
But when there are lovelier flowers [around], you
   are no longer favored.

Then man looks on you with disdain; you become
   the butt of jokes,
[you], who once in springtime
   pleased everyone so well.

So you wither, poor one, silent and friendless,
   chafed by scorn,
until spring lovingly awakens you once again
   from the earth's bosom.

[10.] Die Kornblume

1. Wer kennt sie nicht, die Blume, die umflossen
   Von goldnen Halmen, lieblich blüht?
In deren Kelch, hat er sich auf geschlossen,
   Ein dunkles Blau so schön erglüht?

2. Dort auf der Flur, wo Ceres Saaten glänzen,
   Habt ihr als Knaben sie gepflückt,
Und öfters euch mit selbst geflochtnen Kränzen
   Die jugendliche Stirn geschmückt.

3. Wenn sie verblüht, neigt sich der Aehre Segen,
   Zur Aerndte reif, der Sichel hin
Und fröhlich jauchzt der schönen Zeit entgegen
   Der Schnitter und die Schnitterin.

4. Bald schimmert dann im bunten Aehren-Kranze,
   Ihr brennend Blau durchs falbe Stroh,
Mit ihr bekränzt, eilt hin zum Reihen-Tanze
   Die muntre Schaar, beglückt und froh.

5. Wie himmlisch glänzt ihr Blau in Mädchen-Augen,
   So hell und rein beim blonden Haar!

The Cornflower

Who doesn't know the flower that blooms,
   charmingly encircled by golden stalks?
in whose cup, if opened up,
   a deep blue glows so beautifully?

There upon the meadow, where Ceres' crops glisten,
   as children you picked it,
and oftentimes adorned your youthful brows
   with wreaths you wove yourselves.

When it [begins to] fade, the bountiful seedhead,
   ripe for harvest, bows down for the sickle,
and [each] harvester, man and woman,
   rejoices gaily in anticipation of a lovely time.

Soon its fiery blue shines through flaxen straw
   in bright wreaths of grain;
wreathed with it, the merry crowd hurries off
   to the round dance, blessed and happy.

How heavenly its blue shines in maidens' eyes,
   so bright and clear next to blonde hair!

Es stellt der Blick, aus dem wir Wonne saugen,
    Des Herzens Blüthen-Unschuld dar!
	[Its] appearance represents the heart's blossom-like purity,
	    from which we imbibe joy.

6. Mag immer der Cyane Kelch verwelken,
    Erbleichen ihrer Farben Licht!
Wir lieben sie, wie Lilien und Nelken,
    Wie Rosen und Vergissmeinnicht!
	Although the cup of the cornflower may wither,
	    the light of its color may fade,
	we love it, [as much] as lilies and carnations,
	    as roses and forget-me-nots!

Comments on text. V. 5, l. 2 ends with a question mark; an exclamation mark has been used in the edition. V. 5, l. 4, "Herzens Blüthen-Unschuld," lit., "heart's blossom-purity." V. 6, l. 1, "Cyane," now spelled "Zyane," is another name for the cornflower; its Greek root refers to the dark blue color.

[11.] Die Wasser-Lilie   The Waterlily

1. Aus den Fluthen keimt ein Blumen-Leben, Üppig, wie aus Tellus Schooss, hervor, Und aus blauen Wasser-Spiegeln heben Goldne Blüthen stolz ihr Haupt empor. Auf der Wogen feuchtem Pfad, Schwimmt ihr wunderbares Blatt.	Out of the floods, a blossom's life sprouts forth richly, as from Tellus's womb, and from blue water-mirrors, golden blossoms proudly raise their heads. Its amazing leaf floats upon the damp path of the waves.
2. Dort, wo oft die zartgeformten Glieder Die Najad' im Gauckel-Tanz bewegt, Wo des königlichen Schwans Gefieder Alpen-Schnee durch Aether-Bläue trägt; Dort im schilfumkränzten See Wohnt die Wasser-Lilie!	There, where the Naiad often stirs delicate limbs into a chimerical dance, where the plumage of royal swans carries alpine snow through Aether's blue, there, in [a] lake encircled by reeds, the waterlily lives!
3. Wenn des Sommer-Abends Pupur[sic]-Gluthen Rosig glänzen auf dem Wellen-Schaum Und die Spiegel-Fläche dunkler Fluthen Wiederzeigt des Himmels weiten Raum: Rudern wir auf leichtem Kahn Durch die schöne Blumen-Bahn.	When the crimson glow of summer evening sparkles rosily on the waves' foam, and the glassy surface of dark floods reflects the broad expanse of heaven; we row through the lovely lane of flowers in a small skiff.
4. Schweigend werfen Garn und Angel-Schnüre Neben Wasser-Lilien wir hin, Dass Betrug die sichern Fische führe In die Netze, die wir um sie ziehn. Oft, wenn unsre List gelang, Lohnt uns dann ein reicher Fang.	Falling silent, we toss lure and fishing line near the water lilies, so that deception will lead the trusting fish into nets we draw around them. If our cunning has succeeded, then a rich catch often rewards us.
5. So, gebohren auf den blauen Wogen, Von der Welle zartem Schaum geküsst, Blüht die Blume, her- und hingezogen Von der Fluth, die murmelnd sie umfliesst, Bis des rauhen Winters Hand Auf sie wirft ein Eis-Gewand.	So, borne upon the blue ripples, kissed by the delicate foam of the waves, the flower blooms, pulled to and fro by the flood, which flows murmuring around it, until winter's harsh hand tosses a raiment of ice over it.

[12.] Die Hyacinthe   The Hyacinths

1. In des Winters trüben Stunden
    Sehn am lodernden Kamin,
Wir gesellig uns verbunden,
    Still die Hyacinthe blühn.
	In the dreary hours of winter,
	    beside the blazing fireplace,
	companionably engaged, we see
	    the hyacinth quietly bloom.

2. Aus der Zwiebel strebt ihr Leben
    Schnell und wunderbar hervor,
Unterm Drohn des Nord-Sturms heben
    Ihre Blüthen sich empor.
	Its life struggles forth, quickly
	    and wondrously, out of [its] bulb;
	under threat of a northern storm,
	    its blossoms raise themselves up.

3. Ueppig ihre Kelche schwellen,
    Die des Gärtners Kunst gefüllt,
Zarter Ambra-Düfte Wellen,
    Schweben um sie leis' und mild.
	Its cups swell luxuriously,
	    filled by the gardener's skill,
	waves of delicate amber-fragrance
	    hover around it, faint and mild.

4. Proteus wechselnde Gestalten
   Gleiten über sie dahin,
Doch die Form hat sich erhalten
   Und der Wechsel wird Gewinn.

      Proteus' changing aspects
         pass over it,
      yet it has retained its form,
         and the change becomes profit.

5. Bald umziehen Rosen-Gluthen,
   Bald des Himmels Blau ihr Haupt,
Bald hat Flora gar der Fluthen
   Weissen Schaum für sie geraubt.

      Now [it has] the glow of roses,
         now its head the blue of heaven;
      now Flora has even robbed
         the white foam of the waters for it.

6. Bald umstrahlt im goldnen Scheine
   Brennend gelb ihr volles Blatt,
Bis im lieblichsten Vereine,
   Ieden Farben-Schmuck sie hat.

      Now its entire petal radiates
         fiery yellow in golden sheen,
      until, in the most lovely alliance,
         it is adorned by every color.

7. Sorgsam pflegen wir das Leben,
   Das aus ihren Blumen lacht,
Denn die Hyacinthen geben
   Frühlings-Reiz der Winter-Nacht!

      We carefully cultivate the life
         that laughs out from its flowers,
      for hyacinths give
         the charm of spring to winter's night.

Comments on text. V. 5, ll. 1–3, "Bald," lit., "soon." V. 6, l. 4, lit., "every color-ornament it has."

[13.] DIE MOHN-BLUME

1. Kennt ihr die Zeit, die süsse Ruh' uns reichet,
Wo jeder Schmerz vor holden Träumen weichet,
Wo Trauer flieht, die Hoffnung lieblich lacht,
Und rosenfarb erscheint der Zukunft Nacht?
Ihr kennt sie, des Schlummers goldne Zeit,
Wo seinen Kranz von Mohn uns Morpheus beut!

2. Kennt ihr sie wohl, die Blume, die, geweihet
Von Götter-Hand, uns diesen Trost verleihet,
Den Einzigen, dem wir nicht widerstehn
Und ach, um den wir alle sehnend flehn?
Ihr kennt sie! Seht, liebend liess Natur
Für uns erblühn den Mohn auf stiller Flur!

3. Ihr kennt ihn doch? wenn Krankheit oder Kummer
Verscheuchten einst von euch den sanften Schlummer,
Wenn euren Sinn kein goldner Traum umschlich
Und jeder Trost aus eurer Nähe wich:
Was gab euch Ruh? Dann warf von seinem Thron
Gott Phantasus auf euch den Schlummer-Mohn!

4. Kennt ihr das Glück, das oft ein Traum gewährte,
Der das Gemüth mit zarter Hoffnung nährte,
Der schmeichelnd kos'te, wenn des Schicksals Hand
Uns Dornen in das Blüthen-Leben wand?
Ihr kennt es wohl! Euch gab es öfters schon
Die Blume, die den Schlaf erzeugt, der Mohn!

THE POPPY FLOWER

   Do you know when sweet repose comes to us,
when every pain retreats before lovely dreams,
when sorrow flees, hope laughs charmingly,
and approaching night seems rose-colored?
You know it, the golden time of slumber,
when Morpheus grants us his wreath of poppies!

   Do you know it well, the flower that,
sanctified by the hand of gods, grants us this solace,
the only one we cannot resist
and ah, for which we all longingly implore?
You know it! See, nature lovingly let
the poppy bloom for us upon the quiet meadow!

   Surely you know it? When sickness or cares
betimes chased gentle slumbers away from you,
when no golden dream roved your mind
and every comfort retreated from your presence,
what gave you peace? Then, from his throne,
the god Phantasos tossed you the poppy of slumber.

   Do you know the happiness that a dream often imparted,
that nourished the soul with tender hope,
that fawningly caressed, whenever fate's hand
wound thorns into the prime of life?
You know it well! The flower that begets sleep
has already given it to you often—the poppy!

Comments on text. In this poem, the opening lines of each verse recall Goethe's "Kennst du das Land?" V. 4, l. 4, "Blüthen-Leben," lit., "blossom-life."

[14.] DAS VEILCHEN

1. Holdes Blümchen,
Sey willkommen
   Auf der öden Flur!
Du erwachst schon,
Wenn noch leise
   Schlummert die Natur.

2. Wenn noch feindlich
Hain und Hügel

THE VIOLET

Lovely little flower,
welcome
   to the deserted meadow!
You awaken already
when nature still
   slumbers softly.

When winter night still
inimically blankets

Decket Winternacht;
Und von Floras
Zarten Kindern
    Wenig sind erwacht.

3. Eh' noch Phöbus
Feuerblicke
    Auf die Erde sehn,
Eh' noch laue
Frühlings-Lüfte
    Um die Wangen wehn.

4. Schöne Hoffnung
Näher Freuden,
    Die der Lenz gewährt,
Hat, o Veilchen,
Dein Erscheinen
    Liebend uns beschert!

5. Mädchen-Lächeln,
Jünglings-Wonnen
    Hast du mitgebracht,
Ahnend sehn wir
Nun des Maies
    Volle Blüthen-Pracht!

6. Veilchen-Kränze
Reicht die Jungfrau
    Dem Geliebten hin,
Blumen-Sprache
Wählt die Treue,
    Lieb' verräth den Sinn!

7. Schwärmerische
Augenblicke
    Reiner Seligkeit!
O erheitert
Oft hienieden
    Unsre Lebens-Zeit[.]

8. Ewig blühe,
Liebes Veilchen
    Nie vergess ich dein!
Treuer Liebe,
Schöner Hoffnung
    Sollst geweiht du seyn!

glade and hill,
and few of Flora's
delicate children,
    are awake.

Even before Phoebe's
fiery glances
    are seen upon the earth,
Even before mild
breezes of spring
    waft about [our] cheeks.

Your appearance,
O violet, has lovingly
    bestowed upon us
the lovely hope,
nearer to joy,
    that spring imparts.

You have brought with you
maidens' smiles,
    youths' delights;
now we look forward to
the full flowering
    splendor of May.

The maiden gives
violet wreaths
    to [her] beloved;
faithful, she chooses
the language of flowers—
    love betrays the mind!

Rapturous
moments
    of pure bliss,
oh, enliven
often here below
    our lifetime!

Bloom forever
beloved violet—
    I will never forget you!
May you be dedicated
to true love,
    to fair hope!

Comments on text. V. 6, l. 5, "die Treue," lit., "the faithful one" (female). V. 6, l. 6, "Sinn" means not only "mind" but also "meaning"—both connotations are relevant here: the language of flowers is more reliable than spoken language.

[15.] Die Tulpe

1. Die Schönheit bleibt auch ohne Seele schön—
Wir weilen gern bei lieblichen Gestalten,
der glühnde Blick will ewig nicht erkalten,
die zarte Form bewundernd anzusehn.

2. Doch das Gefühl muss jeden Reiz erhöhn!
Bis in des Herzens tiefverborg'ne Falten
dringt seine Macht mit zaubrischen Gewalten,
und lässt dort sanft den Götter-Odem wehn.

3. Schön bist du, Tulpe! Deiner Reize Schimmer
erhellt mit stolzer Pracht den Blumen-Hayn.
Doch können wir dir nur Bewund'rung weihn.

The Tulip

Beauty remains beautiful even without a soul—
we tarry gladly before lovely figures;
[an] ardent gaze will never grow cold
contemplating [a] delicate form with admiration.

Yet feeling must enhance every charm!
Until its might penetrates with magical powers
into the heart's deeply hidden recesses
and there lets the breath of gods gently blow.

You are beautiful, tulip! The luster of your charm
illuminates the flower field with proud splendor.
Yet we can devote only admiration to you.

4. Drum glaubt es, Mädchen! Blosse Schönheit nimmer,	Therefore, believe this, maiden! Mere beauty will never
wird euch der Liebe dauernd Glück verleihn,	grant you the abiding happiness of love;
Denn wisst, der Mann liebt Schönheit nie allein.	understand then, that man never loves beauty alone.

Comment on text. V. 1, l. 1 ends with no period and a dash in the top voice and a period and dash in the lower voice; the version without the period has been given preference in the edition.

[16.] Der Lavendel — The Lavender

1. Ein Liedchen dir zu singen	A little song to sing to you,
Lavendel-Blümelein,	little lavender flower,
Muss traun, soll es gelingen,	must certainly be short and edifying,
Kurz und erbaulich seyn.	if it is to succeed.
Dich streut die Göttinn Mode	The goddess of fashion strews you
Verschwendrisch durch die Luft,	lavishly through the air;
Im Leben und im Tode,	in life and in death,
Flieht nie dein Balsamduft.	your balsam fragrance never goes away.
2. Lavendel-Düfte wehen	Lavender fragrances float
In Logen und Parterr,	in loges and on the parterre,
Wo wir Beaumonde sehen	where we see the beau monde
Um Herrn und Damen her.	round about ladies and gentlemen.
Beim Ball, bei Maskeraden,	At the ball, at masquerades,
Im raschen Walzer-Flug,	in the dashing flight of the waltz,
Ia selbst auf Promenaden	yes, even in promenades,
Küsst uns dein Wohl-Geruch.	your fragrance kisses us.
3. So manches holde Weibchen	So many lovely little ladies,
Durch dich süss parfümirt,	sweetly perfumed by you,
Ward wie ein Lirres Täubchen	are tracked down in the dark,
Im finstern aufgespürt.	like a little Lirres dove.
Dein Spiritus beseelet	Your essence animates
So manchen dummen Tropf,	so many dumb peabrains;
Du giebst den Geist, der fehlet,	you give to the empty headed
Dem leeren Titus-Kopf!	the spirit that is missing!
4. Beaten und Hetären	Beatrices and hetaerae,
Schön, hässlich, warm und kalt,	beautiful, ugly, warm, [or] frigid,
Sie halten dich in Ehren,	they honor you;
Dich liebet Jung und Alt!	young and old love you!
Dich musst' ich hier besingen,	Here, I must laud you,
Du holdes Blümelein!	you lovely little flower!
Mag auch mein Lied verklingen,	Although my song may fade away,
Du wirst unsterblich seyn!	you will be immortal!

Comments on text. V. 3, l. 5, "Spiritus" here refers to both "spirit" and the alcoholic essence of perfume. V. 3, l. 7, "Geist," lit., "spirit," refers to intellect; i.e., lavender perfume gives the empty-headed the illusion of intellect.

Karl Friedlich Müchler: Die Blumen und der Schmetterling

Text excerpted from the music source.

[1.] Zueignung an Deutschlands Töchter — Dedication to Germany's Daughters

1. Euch ihr Guten, Euch ihr Schönen,	To you who are good, who are pretty,
Die ihr zart wie Blüthen seid,	who are tender as blossoms,
Euch sei unter sanften Tönen	to you may this wreath of flowers
Dieser Blumenkranz geweiht.	set amongst delicate notes be dedicated.
Aus dem Mutterschoos der Erde	From the womb of the earth
Sprossten sie an Anmuth reich:	they sprang, rich in grace:
Deutsche Mädchen, jedes werde	German girls, may each [of you] become
Diesen holden Blumen gleich.	like these charming flowers.

2. Wie das Veilchen, blüht bescheiden,
   Wie das Maienblümelein
Frost erduldet, traget Leiden,
   Hüllend Euch in Demuth ein.
In der Lilien weissem Kleide,
   Wie der Rose Knospe schön
Mögt Ihr einst im Festgeschmeide
   An dem Brautaltare stehn.

3. Auf der Pfirsichwange male
   Die Gesundheit Rosenlicht,
Aus dem offnen Auge strahle
   Sanftmuth wie Vergissmeinnicht.
Fest wie Ephen rankt, umgürte
   Sittsamkeit die keusche Brust;
Dann nur blühet Hymens Mirte
   Euch zu dauerhafter Lust.

Like the violet, like the lily-of-the-valley,
   [may each of you] bloom demurely,
endure frost, bear sorrows,
   enveloping yourselves in humility.
In the lily's white dress,
   lovely as the rosebud,
may you some day stand in ceremonial jewels
   at the wedding altar.

On [your] downy cheek,
   may health paint a rosy glow;
from [your] candid eye[s],
   may gentility radiate like the forget-me-not.
As firmly as ivy twines, may modesty
   gird your chaste breast;
only then will Hymen's myrtle bloom
   for you in everlasting joy.

Comment on text. V. 3, l. 1, "Pfirsichwange," lit., "peach-cheek."

[2.] Das Schneeglöckchen

1. Wenn noch Eis die Fluren drückt,
Sich noch keine Schwalbe zeiget,
Noch kein Halm der Erd' entsteiget,
   Und kein Knöspchen freundlich nickt,
   Hebst du schon dein Haupt empor,
Zeigst du rein wie Winterflocken
Deine zarten weissen Glocken,
   Blühst du schon im hell'sten Flor.

2. Holde Lenzverkünderin,
Du des Frühlings Erstgeborne,
Von der Unschuld Auserkohrne,
   Bildlich zeigend ihren Sinn.
   Sanft erduldest du den Sturm,
Und der Schnee muss in Gefahren
Ist er gleich dein Feind, dich wahren,
   Dich zerstört kein böser Wurm.

3. Liebliche, dies ist dein Bild,
Mädchenunschuld, fromm, bescheiden
Blühet schöner unter Leiden,
   Das Gemüth macht Kummer mild.
   Sieh! so strahlen unterm Schnee
Heller dieses Blümchens Blätter
Fröhlich blüht's in Sturm und Wetter
   Und spriesst muthig in die Höh'.

4. Bleibe diesem Blümchen gleich,
Such' in trüben rauhen Zeiten
Fried' und Freude zu verbreiten,
   Schaff' um dich ein Himmelreich.
   Es steht ganz in deiner Macht,
Wenn du im Verborg'nen blühest,
Und das Gift der Anmuth fliehest,
   Schnöden Stolz und eitle Pracht.

The Snowdrop

When ice yet weighs down the meadows,
no swallows yet appear,
no blade [of grass] yet emerges from the earth,
   and no little buds nod amiably,
   you already lift up your head,
you reveal your delicate white bells,
pure as snowflakes,
   you already bloom in brightest florescence.

Charming harbinger of spring,
you, spring's firstborn,
innocence's chosen,
   symbolically displaying its meaning.
   Placidly, you endure the storm,
and the snow, although also your foe,
must protect you in danger;
   no noxious worm disturbs you.

Lovely one, this is your metaphor:
female innocence, piously, modestly,
blooms more beautifully amidst sorrow;
   a good nature mitigates troubles.
   Look! the petals of this little flower
thus shine brighter amidst snow;
it blooms cheerfully in wind and weather
   and sprouts courageously towards the sky.

Remain like this little flower:
in dreary, harsh times, seek
to spread peace and joy;
   create a heavenly realm around yourself.
   It is entirely within your power,
if you bloom in seclusion,
and flee the poison of charm,
   vile pride, and vain display.

Comments on text. V. 2, the verse's meaning is twofold: in early spring, the vermin that eat and destroy plants are not yet active; and the evil "worms" of society both cannot and do not dare destroy such purity. V. 4, l. 7, "Anmut" here refers to the negative charms of society (flirtation, for example) rather than the positive (grace, pleasantness, etc.) cited above (see "Zueignung an Deutschlands Töchter," v. 1, l. 6).

[3.] Das Veilchen / The Violet

1. Von dunklem Laub umschlossen
   Blüht heimlich auf der Au,
Wo wild nur Gräser sprossen
   Ein Blümchen dunkelblau.
	Enveloped by dark leaves,
	   a dark blue little flower
	blooms secretly on the meadow
	   where only grasses sprout wildly.

2. Es prangt nicht stolz im Garten
   Und keines Künstlers Hand
Müht sich es treu zu warten
   Mit Vorsicht und Verstand.
	It does not flaunt itself proudly in the garden
	   and no master gardener's hand
	takes the trouble to wait for it faithfully
	   with care and understanding.

3. Es schimmert nie in Kränzen,
   Die leere Prunksucht flicht,
Es strebt auch nie zu glänzen
   Durch bunter Blätter Licht.
	It never gleams in wreaths,
	   which empty ostentation weaves;
	it also never strives to [out]shine
	   the luminescence of more colorful petals.

4. Nur einsam und bescheiden,
   Sich keines Werths bewusst,
Schmückt es der Hirten Weiden,
   Der Schäfferinnen Brust.
	But solitary and humble,
	   unaware of its worth,
	it adorns the shepherds' meadows,
	   the shepherdesses' breast.

5. Des Leichtsinns Tritte schweben
   Vorüber, wo es steht,
Und kürzen roh sein Leben
   Weil es nicht keck sich bläht.
	Frivolity's footsteps float past
	   overhead where it stands,
	and roughly shorten its life
	   because it does not boast brazenly.

6. Doch durch die Frühlingslüfte
   Wenn es versteckt auch blüht,
Verstreut es Balsamdüfte,
   Wo es kein Auge sieht.
	Yet, although it blooms concealed,
	   where no eye can see it,
	it dispenses a balsamic fragrance
	   through the spring breezes.

7. O, es ist zu beneiden
   In seinem Kindersinn,
Der Einfalt reine Freuden
   Gewähren nur Gewinn.
	Oh, it is to be envied
	   in its childlikeness;
	the pure joys of naïveté
	   yield only dividends.

8. Von allen Blumen wählen
   Zu einem Lieblingsstrauss
Sich fromme Mädchenseelen
   Das holde Veilchen aus.
	Out of all the flowers,
	   girls' innocent souls select
	the lovely violet
	   as a favorite nosegay.

9. Es ruht an ihren Herzen,
   Sinkt dort in süsse Ruh,
Und schliesset ohne Schmerzen
   Den Kelch auf ewig zu.
	It rests upon their hearts,
	   languishes there in sweet repose,
	and painlessly closes
	   its calyx forever.

Comments on text. V. 2, l. 2, "Künstlers Hand," lit., "artist's hand." V. 4, l. 2, lit., "aware of no worth." V. 5, l. 4, lit., "because it does not boldly puff itself up."

[4.] Die Myrthe / The Myrtle

1. Dir Myrthenreiss,
Gebührt der Preis
   Vor jeglicher Blume und Pflanze.
Denn dich ersah
Einst Cypria
   Der Unschuld zum lohnenden Kranze.
	To you, myrtle branch,
	the prize belongs,
	   above any other flower or plant.
	For Cyprus once
	desired you
	   for a wreath rewarding innocence.

2. Dich Zarte schuf,
Auf Amors Ruf,
   Einst Flora für Hymens Entzücken,
Der Jungfrau Haar
Am Brautaltar
   Mit schimmernden Knospen zu schmücken.
	Flora once created you,
	delicate one, at Cupid's request,
	   for Hymen's delight,
	to adorn the virgin's hair
	with shining buds
	   at [her] wedding altar.

3. Stets bleibst du grün,
Und dauernd blühn
    Die Blüthen der bräutlichen Krone;
Was Liebe flicht
Verwelket nicht,
    Dich schützet allmächtig Dione.

4. Ihr Töchter Teuts!
Den höchsten Reiz
    Verleiht Euch die Krone von Myrthen,
Wenn froh und frei
Euch Lieb' und Treu
    Die Stirne der Unschuld umgürten.

You remain ever green,
and the blossoms of the bridal crown
    bloom perennially;
what love entwines
does not wither;
    almighty Dione protects you.

Sister Teutons!
the myrtle crown
    bestows upon you incomparable charm,
when, happy and free,
love and loyalty
    gird your innocent brows.

Comment on text. V. 4, l. 3, "Krone von Myrthen" could be translated as "laurel wreath"; myrtle and laurel are closely related.

[5.] Die Narzisse

1. Horch, was tönt vom Felsenhange
    Traurig dort am Wasserfall,
Gleich dem klagenden Gesange
    Der verlassnen Nachtigall.

2. Echo seufzet, die Verschmähte,
    Ach, die für Narziss entbrannt,
Schwärmerisch um Liebe flehte,
    Doch nie Gegenliebe fand.

3. Er bleibt kalt wie Meeresfluthen,
    Höhnend ihren zarten Sinn,
Und verzehrt von ew'gen Gluthen
    Welkt die Liebende dahin.

4. Doch die mitleidsvollen Götter,
    Fühlend ihres Busens Pein,
Wandeln, als gerechte Retter,
    Die Verschmachtende in Stein.

5. Und sie werden Echo's Rächer,
    Der Olymp hält strengen Rath:
Schrecklich büsse der Verbrecher
    Seine rohe Frevelthat.

6. Einst im klaren Bach erblicket
    Er sein Bild mit hoher Lust,
Und der Gott der Liebe drücket
    Gift'ge Pfeil' in seine Brust.

7. Ihn ergreift ein thörigt Schmachten,
    Wahnsinn dunkelt sein Gemüth,
Und ihn züchtigt das Verachten,
    Dass er für sich selber glüht.

8. So, der Eitelkeit zum Raube,
    Schliesst sich ungeliebt sein Lauf,
Und es spriesst aus seinem Staube
    Eine Blume warnend auf.

The Narcissus

Listen [to] what resounds sadly from the cliff,
    there by the waterfall,
like the plaintive song
    of the forsaken nightingale.

Echo sighs, the rejected girl,
    ah, who burned [with love] for Narcissus,
[who] begged rapturously for love,
    but never found requited love.

He remains cold as ocean currents,
    scorning her tender feelings,
and, consumed by everlasting ardor,
    the loving girl fades away.

But the compassionate gods,
    feeling the pain in her heart,
as just deliverers transform
    the languishing girl into stone.

And they become Echo's avengers;
    Olympus holds strict counsel:
may the offender suffer terribly
    for his cruel misdeed.

One day, in the clear stream, he glimpses
    his reflection with great delight,
and the god of love shoots
    a poisonous arrow into his heart.

A foolish yearning seizes him,
    madness darkens his soul,
and his disdain that he is enamored
    of himself punishes him.

Thus, falling prey to his vanity,
    [he] ends his days unloved,
and from his dust,
    a flower sprouts in warning.

Comments on text. V. 5, l. 2, technically, Olympus is a mountain; Müchler refers either to the Olympian gods as a unit or to one unspecified god as the supreme Olympian god. V. 6, l. 3, "drücket," lit., "to press, to impress, to stamp." V. 8, l. 2, lit., "his course ends itself unloved."

[6.] Das Vergissmeinnicht

1. Freundlich glänzt an stiller Quelle,
　　Wie des Mondes Silber-Licht,
Eine Blume zart und helle,
　　O, verkenn' dies Blümchen nicht!

2. Schimmernd, wie des Äthers Bläue
　　Wenn ihn kein Gewölk umflicht,
Ist es ein Symbol der Treue,
　　Das zum Herzen tröstend spricht.

3. Mild, wie Deiner Augen Sterne,
　　Wie verklärter Unschuld Licht,
Ruft es warnend aus der Ferne:
　　O, vergiss, vergiss mein nicht!

4. Wann der Trennung Zähren fliessen,
　　Folgsam dem Gebot der Pflicht,
Soll es deinem Pfad entspriessen,
　　Bittend: ach! vergiss mein nicht!

5. Doch, geliebte Seele, höre,
　　Was aus jedem Blättchen spricht:
Ach, sein Thau ist eine Zähre,
　　Und sie seufzt: vergiss mein nicht!

The Forget-Me-Not

In a quiet spot, a flower,
　　delicate and bright, shines amiably
like the silver light of the moon;
　　oh, do not fail to recognize this little flower!

Shimmering, like Aether's azure
　　when no clouds enlace it,
it is a symbol of faithfulness,
　　which speaks consolingly to hearts.

Mild, like the stars of your eyes,
　　like the light of lucent innocence,
it cries warningly from afar:
　　oh, forget, forget me not!

When the tears of parting flow,
　　obedient to the call of duty,
it shall floreate your path,
　　entreating: ah, forget me not!

Yet hear, dear soul,
　　what utters from every leaflet:
ah, its dew[drop] is a tear,
　　and [the tear] sighs: forget me not!

[7.] Die Palme

1. Es mag der Held den Lorbeer preisen,
Der um des blut'gen Schwerdtes Eisen
　　Nach langem Kampf als Lohn sich schlingt;
Ich preise nur Irenens Palme,
Die uns die seegenreichen Halme,
　　Des friedlich frommen Landmanns bringt.

2. Des Lorbeers dunkle Blätter spriessen
Nur dort, wo Kummerthränen fliessen,
　　Wo schuldlos Blut die Fluren düngt;
Die Palme wächst auf stiller Haide,
Wo zu der Einfalt reiner Freude
　　Die Friedensgöttin lächelnd winkt.

3. Der Zwietracht Furien, wo die wüthen
Verdorren schnell des Lebensblüthen,
　　Erstirbt des Herzens Zartgefühl;
Nur wo sich Fried' und Freude gatten,
Nur in der edlen Palme Schatten
　　Lacht, süsse Liebe, dein Asyl.

The Palm

The hero may praise the laurel,
which coils 'round the iron of his bloody sword
　　as a reward after long battle;
I praise only Irene's palm,
which brings us the prosperous grains
　　of the peaceful, pious farmer.

The laurel's dark leaves sprout
only there, where tears of sorrow flow,
　　where blameless blood fertilizes the fields;
the palm grows on quiet heaths,
where the goddess of peace smilingly
　　nods to the pure joy of naïveté.

Where they, the Furies of discord rage,
life's blossoms wither rapidly,
　　the heart's sensitivity fades away;
only where peace and joy unite,
only in the shadow of the noble palm,
　　does your sanctuary, sweet love, thrive.

Comments on text. V. 1, l. 5, "Halme," lit., "stalks." V. 3, l. 6, "Lacht," lit., "laugh," as in, "only in the sanctuary of the noble palm's shadow does love laugh for joy."

[8.] Die Rose

1. Bild der jungfräulichen Tugend,
　　Die in hoher Schaam erglüht,
Bild der Schönheit, Bild der Jugend,
　　Dir, o Ros'! ertön' ein Lied.

2. Flora schloss, um dich zu schützen
　　Deine Knosp' in Dornen ein,
Um der Frevler Hand zu ritzen,
　　Die mit frechem Raub dir dräun.

3. Deine Purpurblüthen glänzen
　　In der Charitinnen Haar,
Und mit deinen vollen Kränzen
　　Schmücket Hymen den Altar.

The Rose

Symbol of maidenly virtue,
　　which glows amid peerless modesty,
symbol of beauty, symbol of youth,
　　to you, O rose!, [I] sing a song.

To protect you, Flora enclosed
　　your bud in thorns,
to scratch the hand of the offender
　　who threatens you with brazen plunder.

Your crimson blossoms gleam
　　in Charities' hair,
and Hymen decks [her] altar
　　with your abundant wreathes.

4\. Zarte Liebesgötter kosen
   Um der Knospen süssen Mund,
Und auf einem Thron von Rosen
   Herrscht Cyther' in Amathunt.

5\. Sanfter Weste Schmeichellüfte,
   Wenn die Knospen dir entblühn,
Rauben dir die Balsamdüfte,
   Die durch deine Lauben ziehn.

6\. Aller Haine Sänger preisen
   Dich, du Blumenkönigin,
Du umschlingst den Kelch des Weisen,
   Und die Brust der Schäferin.

7\. Ämsig Honig suchend, gaukelt
   Hin die Bien' an deine Brust,
Und auf deinen Blättern schaukelt
   Sich der Schmetterling mit Lust.

8\. Dich bewundernd, weilt die Quelle,
   Wo dein Liebreiz sich enthüllt,
Und in jeder leichten Welle
   Spiegelt sich dein schönes Bild.

9\. Aber ach, nach kurzen Stunden
   Ist der zarten Blätter Pracht,
Ist der Zauber hingeschwunden,
   Der aus jedem Knöspchen lacht.

10\. Zephyr eilt mit raschen Flügeln
   Den verwelkten Blättern nach,
Keine Purpurblüthen spiegeln
   Sich im klaren Silberbach.

11\. Vogel, Schmetterling und Biene
   Flattern, suchend dich, umher,
Doch verwandelt ist die Bühne,
   Du, o Rose, bist nicht mehr!

Tenderhearted gods of love caress
   the bud's sweet mouth,
and Cytherea reigns in Amathus
   upon a throne of roses.

Caressing breezes of gentle westerlies,
   when the buds fade away,
they rob you of the balsamic fragrances
   that waft through your bowers.

Singers of all coteries praise
   you, queen of flowers;
you entwine the wise man's goblet
   and the bosom of the shepherdess.

Busily searching for honey,
   the bee flits in to your breast,
and on your petals,
   the butterfly sways with joy.

Admiring you, the fountain lingers
   where your charm is exposed,
and in each gentle ripple,
   your lovely image is reflected.

But ah, after a few short hours,
   the splendor of your delicate petals,
the enchantment that laughs from
   every little bud, has vanished.

Zephyrus hastens with nimble wings
   after faded petals;
no crimson blossoms are reflected
   in the clear, silver stream.

Bird, butterfly, and bee
   flutter around, looking for you,
but the stage has transformed;
   you, O rose, are no more!

Comments on text. V. 4, ll. 1–2, lit., "Delicate gods of love caress around the sweet mouth of the buds." V. 4, l. 4, Amathunt, a city on the southern coast of Cyprus, Cytherea's home, was of Phoenecian origins, dating back to 1000 B.C., and was located near modern Limassol; it was the center of a joint cult for Adonis and Aphrodite (Cytherea) and was the origin of one of Aphrodite's pseudonyms, Amathusia. V. 6, l. 1, "Aller Haine Sänger" probably refers to the Göttingen "Hainbund" of 1770–74, a small but well-known coterie of poets.

[9.] Wechselgesang der Blumen

Alle
1\. Wir Kinder des Lenzen,
wir keimen und spriessen
im Garten und Hain,
auf grünenden Wiesen
zu duftenden Kränzen
uns lieblich zu reihn.

2\. Wir krönen die Musen mit Blüthen,
und fröhnen Cytherens Altar.
Wir zieren der Schönen
sanft wallenden Busen,
leicht flatterndes Haar.

Das Veilchen
3\. Ich liebe nur Trifften,
mich nährt nur der Morgen

Alternating Song of Flowers

All
Children of spring,
we germinate and sprout
in garden and grove,
on greening meadows,
to arrange ourselves into
lovely, fragrant wreaths.

We crown the Muses with blossoms,
and attend Cytherea's altar.
We grace the softly flowing hair
and the gently undulating bosoms
of beauties.

The Violet
I love only pastures;
only the morning nourishes me

mit labendem Thau
ich blühe verborgen,
doch würz' ich mit Düften
die lachende Au!

Das Vergissmeinnicht
4. An ländlicher Hütte
umgürt ich die Quelle
und brüste mich nicht,
an heimlicher Stelle
entkeim' ich und bitte,
ach! vergiss mein nicht.

Die Myrthe
5. Wir kränzen die Haare
der schmachtenden Bräute
der Keuschheit Symbol
der Jünglinge Beute
an Hymens Altare,
ihr schönstes Idol.

Die Rose
6. Zur Fürstin der Beete
ernannte mich Flora
als Amor mich nahm,
mich malet Aurora
mit lieblicher Röthe,
ein Sinnbild der Schaam.

Alle
7. Wir alle, wir grünen
in Iris Geschmeide,
in kunstloser Zier,
der Schönheit zu dienen,
der Unschuld zur Freude
wir huldigen ihr.

with refreshing dew;
I bloom concealed,
but I season the laughing meadow
with fragrance!

The Forget-Me-Not
By a rustic cabin,
I encircle the spring
and do not boast;
in a secluded spot,
I sprout and entreat,
forget me not!

The Myrtle
We wreathe the hair
of yearning brides,
the symbol of chastity,
the plunder of youths
[laid at] Hymen's altar,
her most beautiful idol.

The Rose
When Amor captured me,
Flora named me
the princess of [flower]beds;
Aurora painted me
with lovely red,
a symbol of modesty.

All
We all, we sprout
into Iris's jewels,
into unaffected adornment
to serve beauty;
we joyfully pay homage
to innocence.

Comments on text. V. 6, l. 6, "Schaam," lit., "shame," red representing blushing. V. 7, l. 5, "Unschuld" implies both innocence and purity.

[10.] DER SCHMETTERLING

1. Von Knosp' auf Knospe schwebend,
Vom Duft der Blüthen lebend,
   Sich badend in des Äthers Blau,
Bestrahlt vom Sonnenspiegel,
Hebt er die goldnen Flügel,
   Und flattert fort von Au zu Au.

2. Den schönen Lenz verkündend,
Der Liebe Wonn' empfindend,
   Auf Myrth' und auf Orangenbaum,
Und unter flücht'gen Küssen,
Auf Veilchen und Narzissen,
   Umgaukelt ihn des Lebenstraum.

3. Doch wenn die Blätter fallen,
Des Herbstes Nebel wallen,
   Beschliesst sich auch sein kurzer Lauf,
Sein Grab ein Kelch der Rose;
Froh steigt die fessellose,
   Verklärte Psyche himmelauf.

4. Dies ist des Sängers Leben;
Viel' holde Träum' umschweben,

THE BUTTERFLY

Hovering from bud to bud,
living off the fragrance of blossoms,
   bathing in Aether's blue,
illuminated by the heliotrope,
he raises his golden wings,
   and flutters off, from meadow to meadow.

Heralding the lovely spring,
sensitive to the joy of love,
   on myrtle and on orange tree[s],
and among hurried kisses,
on violets and narcissi,
   life's dream hovers around him.

But when the leaves fall,
[when] autumn mists rise,
   his brief life also comes to an end,
his grave, the cup of a rose;
the unfettered, transfigured
   Psyche rises joyfully heavenward.

This is the singer's life:
many lovely dreams hover around

Den reinen, frommen Kindersinn.	the pure, innocent minds of children.
Weit von der Heimath Hügeln,	Far from the hills of home,
Trägt ihn sein Geist auf Flügeln,	his spirit carries him on wings
Ins Reich der Phantasieen hin.	into the realm of fantasy.

5. Die Nachtigall, die Blume / Führt ihn zum Heiligthume, / Das nur dem Reinen sich erschliesst, / Enträthselt wird ihm vieles / In Taumel des Gefühles, / Wenn süsser Wehmuth Thräne fliesst.

The nightingale, the flower, / lead him to the sanctuary / that admits only the pure of heart; / much will be explained to him / in an ecstasy of emotion, / when a tear of sweet melancholy flows.

6. Der Erde Druck entbunden, / Blickt in geweihten Stunden, / Sein Seherauge himmelwärts, / Gleichfühlenden verkündet / Sein Lied, was er empfindet, / Und flieht die Jugend, bricht sein Herz!

The weight of the earth released, / his prophetic eye looks / heavenward in sacred hours, / his song proclaims what he perceives / to those who feel as he does, / and should youth flee, his heart would break!

Comments on text. V. 1, l. 3 and v. 5, l. 5 both end with periods; commas have been used in the edition. V. 1, l. 4, the "Sonnenspiegel" (heliotrope) is a variety of flower that faces the sun, turning as the sun moves across the sky. Its English name derives from that characteristic: "helio" referring to the sun, "trope" to turning. The German name, literally "sun mirror," provides the imagery here: the flower reflects the sun's light onto the butterfly. V. 5, l. 2, "Führt," lit., "leads" [*sic*].

Friedrich Wilhelm Gubitz: Die Temperamente der Liebe

Text source: Friedrich Wilhelm Gubitz, *Gedichte* (Berlin: Vereins-Buchhandlung, 1860), 1:214–21. (Bayerische Staatsbibliothek FN.11634.)

I. Der Schwermüthige

1. Sel'ge Zeiten sah ich prangen / Und den Erdball glaubt' ich mein / Als mich Liddy's Blick befangen, / Unschuldklar wie Heil'genschein.

2. Als der Lippen Siegel sprangen, / Herrschte Gott nicht mehr allein, / Denn der Liebe Klänge schwangen / Siegend mich zum Himmel ein.

3. Ach, die Wonnen all zerklangen, / Ewig kann nicht Frühling seyn! / Traum und Treue sind vergangen, / Ausgelöscht der Heil'genschein.

4. Fern von ihr muss ich verbangen, / Von der Welt, ist nichts mehr mein: / Glühend fasset Allverlangen / Nur der Hoffnung Leichenstein.

5. Doch zum Todesengel drangen / Meines Herzens Oed' und Pein, / Liebend bald von Erd' umfangen / Wird der Himmel wieder mein!

I. The Melancholic [Lover]

I saw happy times flourish, / and I thought the earth was mine / when Liddy's glance caught me, / clear as innocence, like an aureole.

When the seal of our lips sprang [open], / God no longer reigned alone, / for the reverberations of love / swung me, triumphantly, up to heaven.

Ah, all [our] joys are discordant, / Spring cannot last forever! / Dream and fidelity are past, / the aureole extinguished!

Far from her, I must die of anguish, / nothing more of this world is mine: / all [my] longing fixes ardently / only on hope's tombstone.

Yet the despair and agony of my heart / have impressed the angel of death, / soon lovingly embraced by earth, / heaven will again be mine!

Comment on music setting. M. 7, "Lyddis" (compare v. 1, l. 3, "Liddy's"), or "when *Lyddis's* glance."

II. Der Leichtmüthige

1. Lust entfloh und hin ist hin! / Blanda will mich nicht mehr lieben, / Ich wär' ihr, so wahr ich bin! / Noch vier Wochen treu geblieben,

II. The Sanguineous [Lover]

Passion has fled and what's gone is gone! / Blanda doesn't want to love me any more, / I would have been (honestly!) / faithful yet another month,

Kam ihr Hochzeit nicht zu Sinn.	if marriage hadn't occurred to her.
Dafür hat mich Gott bewahrt!	God saved me from that!
Lebe wohl, mein Kind, ich wandre	Farewell, my child, I'm already
Schon zu neuer Liebefahrt:	roving to a new affair:
Morgen Die, und heut die Andre,	one girl tomorrow, and another today,
Das ist mir die rechte Art.	that's the right style for me.
2. Scheiden wird mir nimmer schwer,	Parting never burdens me,
Weinen kann ich nicht, noch fluchen—	I can neither cry, nor curse—
Doch da kommt ein Mädchen her,	wait, there comes a girl,
Frisches Glück will schnell ich suchen,	I must quickly seek my luck anew,
Ohne Lieb' ist's All mir leer!	without love, [life] is empty for me!
"Sprödes Kind, wirf ab dein Joch,	"Timid child, throw off your yoke,
Lass' von Himmelskost mich nippen.	let me sip from heaven's nectar.
Eh' wir bleichen, lebe noch!	Before we fade away, live on!
Mädchen, reiche mir die Lippen,	Maiden, offer me [your] lips,
Denn geküsst wirst du ja doch!["]	for you will surely be kissed!"
3. Sieh, man darf sich im Genuss	See, in pleasure one may exact revenge
Für der Sehnsucht Träume rächen;	for dreams of longing;
Lass' der Seelen Genius	let your spirit's soul speak
Aus dem Schlag der Herzen sprechen:	through the beating of [your] heart:
Doppelsprache ist der Kuss!	a kiss is twice [as good as] talk!
Ah, du magst mich nicht? Nun gut!	Ah, you do not like me? Well then!
Kann ich's auch nicht gern ertragen.	I can't much endure it either.
Halt' ich doch mir fest den Muth;	But I'll hold fast to my courage;
Morgen will ich wieder fragen,	I'll ask again tomorrow;
Hast vielleicht dann wärmer Blut.	perhaps then you'll have warmer blood.
4. Lieben muß man, schönes Kind!	One must love, pretty child!
Soll dereinst ich selig werden,—	Should I someday die—
Was schon hier recht gut beginnt!	I'll ask the Lord of the Earth right away
Frag' ich gleich den Herrn der Erden,	[about] what has begun so well here:
Ob die Engel weiblich sind?	whether the angels are female?
Wenn er etwa "Nein!" nun spricht,	If he should, by chance, say, "No!"
Sag' ich keck und voll Vertrauen:	I'll say, impudently and full of confidence,
["]Herr, dein Reich gefällt mir nicht,	"Lord, I do not like your realm,
Denn ein Himmel ohne Frauen	for a heaven without women
Ist die Sonne ohne Licht!"	is [like] the sun without light."
5. Hebt die Treue hoch empor,	If you exalt fidelity,
Quälend Glück kann ich euch schenken!	I will give you agonizing happiness.
Schwatzt nur mir Moral nicht vor,	Only, don't prattle morality at me,
Bei der Liebe will ich denken,	I [only] want to think about love,
Wenn ich den Verstand verlor.	when I have lost my wits.
Alle Wesen huld'gen ihr,	All beings pay homage to [love],
Liebe ist das Herz vom Leben,	love is the heart of life,
Nur durch Liebe sind wir hier:	we are here only through love:
Liebe will ich wieder geben,	love I will reciprocate.
Mädchen alle, kommt zu mir!	Maidens all, come to me!

Comments on music setting. Mm. 1–2 (v. 2), "Scheiden macht mein Herz nicht schwer" (compare v. 2, l. 1), or "Parting doesn't burden my heart." Mm. 9–10 (v. 1), "acht Tage" (compare v. 1, l. 4, "vier Wochen," lit., "four weeks"), or "eight days" (i.e., a week). Mm. 9–11 (v. 2), "schnell muss ich mein Glück versuchen" (compare v. 2, l. 4), or "I must quickly try my luck." M. 24 (v. 1), "frischer" (compare v. 1, l. 8, "neuer"), or "fresh." Mm. 25–30 (v. 1), "Heute die und dann die andre, / das ist so die rechte Art" (compare v. 1, ll. 9–10), or "One [girl] today, and then the other, that's the right style!" Mm. 37–38, "für versehnte Träume" (compare v. 3, l. 2, "für der Sehnsucht Träume"), or "for thwarted dreams." Mm. 57–59, "halt ich doch mir frischen Muth" (compare v. 3, l. 8), or "but I'll keep [up] my lively courage." M. 105, "will" (compare v. 5, l. 2, "kann"), or "will, want, or wish to."

Comment on text. V. 3, l. 5, "Doppelsprache," lit., "double-speech"; it does not contain the duplicity of English's "double talk."

III. Der Gleichmüthige

1. Nun, ich bin befreit,
     Wie behäglich!
Mir ist Zärtlichkeit
     Unerträglich!
Treibt sie Keine lau,
Werd' ich ohne Frau
Ruhig alt und grau.

2. Hätt' sie wohl gemocht
     So bei Festen,
Alle Puddings kocht
     Sie am besten!
Doch die Lust ward matt,
Denn am Ende hatt'
Ich die Puddings satt.

3. Sie verliebte sich
     Einst bei'm Essen;
Alles ging und ich
     War vergessen,
Weil ich köstlich schlief,
Bis sie wach mich rief,
Und ich mit ihr lief.

4. Sie gefiel mir gut
     Bei dem Wandern,
Und weil gern man thut
     Wie die Andern:
Bot ich mich zum Mann,
Und sie nahm es an
Eh' ich mich besann.

5. Doch das gab ein Joch
     Und ein Laufen!
Was nach Ausland roch,
     Sollt' ich kaufen,
Und Tag aus, Tag ein,
Und bei Mondenschein
Auch noch zärtlich seyn.

6. Ohne Ruh' und Rast
     Musst' ich küssen,
Das ist Höllenlast:
     Küssen müssen!
D'rum recht eisighart
Hab' ich sie genarrt,
Bis mein Wunsch mir ward.

7. Aus dem Hause warf
     Sie mich gestern,
Und beliebte scharf
     Noch zu lästern:
"Hätt' ich nicht viel Geld,
Wär' ich Schüsselheld
Gar nichts nutz der Welt!"

8. Doch mich macht der Hieb
     Nimmer grämlich,
Denn die Liebe lieb'

III. The Phlegmatic [Lover]

There now, I've been set free,
     how nice!
To me, affection is
     unbearable!
If no women can practice moderation,
then I'll peacefully grow old and grey
without a wife.

[I] would have liked her well
     at festivals,
she cooks the best
     puddings!
But my desire flagged,
because I finally had
my fill of puddings.

Once, she fell in love
     over dinner;
things went along and I
     was forgotten,
While I slept wonderfully,
'till she woke me up
and I went [along home] with her.

She was rather pleasing
     on walks,
and because one likes to do
     as others do:
I offered my hand in marriage,
and she accepted
before I came to my senses.

But that gave [me such] a burden
     and [such] a run-around!
Anything that smacked of foreign lands,
     I was supposed to buy,
and day in, day out,
and [even] by the light of the moon,
[I had to] be affectionate as well.

I had to kiss [her]
     without respite,
That's an infernal burden:
     to have to kiss!
Consequently, I fooled her
[into thinking I was] downright frigid,
until I got my wish.

Yesterday, she threw me
     out of the house,
and even enjoyed sharply
     maligning me:
"If I didn't have a lot of money,
I, the great glutton,
would be of no use to the world!"

Still, the gibe doesn't
     make me peevish,
because I love

Ich bequemlich;	love to be comfortable;
Treibt sie Keine lau,	if no woman can practice moderation,
Werd' ich ohne Frau	then I'll simply grow old and grey
Ruhig alt und grau!	without a wife!

Comments on music setting. M. 7, "eine" [*sic*], which has been emended to "Keine" in the edition; there is space for the "K," and the repetition of these three lines at the end (v. 8, ll. 5–7) uses "Keine." V. 2, l. 3, "Plumperpuddings" (compare text, "Alle Puddings"), lit., "plump" puddings; the term emphasizes his preference for plain, heavy peasant fare. V. 5, l. 4, "musst'" (compare text, "sollt'"), or "had to." V. 5, l. 4 ends with a period; a comma has been used in the edition.

Comments on text. V. 1, l. 5, "lau," lit., "lukewarm." V. 2, ll. 3–4, lit., "she cooks puddings the best [of all]"; puddings here could be borrowed from the British use, implying not only puddings but all desserts. V. 4, l. 2, "Wandern" here implies strolling along in a park, as on a constitutional, rather than the more extended wandering or hiking in the countryside more typically associated with Romantics.

IV. Der Liebewüthige	IV. The Choleric [Lover]
1. "Verrathen! Verschmähet!	"Betrayed! Rejected!
Wer drängte mich aus?	Who has usurped me?
Auf, Diener, umspähet	Up, servants! Scout around
Heut Abend ihr Haus;	her house this evening;
Und wagt zur Megäre	and if a single man
Ein Einz'ger den Blick,	dares glance at that vixen,
So fragt: wer er wäre?	then ask: who might he be?
Und brecht ihm's Genick!"	and break his neck!"
2. Don Marco trieb Alle	Don Marco exhorted all
Recht wachsam zu seyn,	to be most vigilant,
Dann stürmt' ihn die Galle	then vented his temper
Bergauf und Thalein;	up hill and down dale.
Er fluchte nun trabend	He swore, then lit out
Hinein in die Luft,	without thinking,
Und passte am Abend	and spent the evening
Noch selbst auf den Schuft.	[going] after the scoundrel himself, as well.
3. Mit Hast spioniret	With haste, the servants
Das Dienervolk stumm,	silently stake out [the house];
Und starr vigiliret	and Don Marco obstinately
Don Marco rings um;	keeps watch all around.
Wie schleichend geschäftig	As he, busily furtive,
Im Dunkeln er wallt,	flits in the dusk,
Gebieten recht kräftig	six fists vigorously
Sechs Fäuste ihm "Halt!"	order him to "Halt!"
4. "Wer sind Sie?" Nach Regel	"Who are you?" they cry
Klingt dies zum Gezerr;	as ordered, in the tug-of-war.
"Ihr Lümmel, ihr Flegel,	"You louts, you boors,
Ich bin euer Herr!"	I am your master!"
Und wie ihn am Toben	And as the servants recognize
Die Diener erkannt,	him by his ranting,
Spricht Clara von oben:	Clara says from above,
"Das ist ja scharmant!"	"Now, that's charming!"
5. "Die Eifersucht hordet	"Jealousy already
Schon Söldner heran,	musters mercenaries,
Der Argwohn ermordet	distrust murders
Was Liebe gewann;	what love has won!
D'rum will ich vernünftig	Therefore, I will sensibly
Mich hüten vor Leid,	protect myself from grief;
Nun quälen Sie künftig	now trouble yourself
Sich selber gescheidt!"	[to be] sensible in the future!"

6. Nichts halfen Sonette	Sonnets about [his] grief and his grave
Von Gram und von Grab,	were in vain,
Da riss er vom Brette	so he snatched his rifle
Die Flinte herab;	off the shelf;
Er jagte mit Rasen	he went hunting in a rage
Zum Walde hinaus,	out into the woods,
Und schoss—einen Hasen	and shot—a hare
Zu lärmendem Schmaus.	as a riotous feast.

Comments on music setting. Mm. 44–48, "Don Marco begieret / die Thüren rings um" (compare v. 3, ll. 3–4), or "Don Marco prowls / from door to door." Mm. 48–56, "Wie schleichend und sinnig / im Dämmern er wallt / gebieten recht innig / sechs Fäuste ihm: Halt!" (compare v. 3, ll. 5–8), or "As, furtive and judicious, / he flits in the dusk / six fists ardently / order him to Halt!" Mm. 83–87, "drum hab ich vernünftig / den Leichtsinn bereut" (compare v. 5, ll. 5–6), or "Therefore, I have sensibly / regretted my folly!" Mm. 90–91, "gescheut," a dialect form of "gescheidt" (see v. 5, l. 8).

Comments on text. V. 2, l. 3, lit., "then his bile stormed him," which reflects the philosophy underlying this cycle, that the balance of bodily fluids controls one's temperament; in this case, an excess of yellow bile, or choler, results in a stormy temper. V. 2, ll. 5–6, lit., "He swore then, trotting up into the air." V. 4, ll. 5–6, grammar is altered to fit the rhyme scheme; it should read, "Und wie ihn am Toben / die Diener erkennen."

Glossary of Deities and Characters

Adonis is a young man loved by Aphrodite; he was killed while hunting but returned from Hades.

Aether is the heavens personified, the "ether" or rarefied air being distinct from the air that lies closer to earth.

Asclepius/Aeskulap is a Greco-Roman god of healing and medicine.

Amor, also known as Cupid, is the Roman god of erotic love; his Greek counterpart is Eros, son of Aphrodite.

Aphrodite is the Greek goddess of love and beauty; her Roman counterpart is Venus and her male counterpart is Eros, her son. Her symbols are the myrtle tree and the dove.

Astraea/Asträa, the "star-bright" daughter of Eos and Astraeus, whose name means "starry," is the goddess of justice. She lived on earth during the golden age of the gods. When that age passed, she became one of the stars in the constellation Virgo. In the opening stanza of "The Dame's Violet" in *Sechszehn Blumen*, Scholz seems to depict Astraea as the goddess of dusk, but I found nothing to support that usage.

Aurora is the Roman goddess of dawn; her Greek counterpart is Eos.

Bacchus/Bachus is the Roman god of wine, sometimes confused with Liber (see below). He presides at the fall wine-making festivals; his Greek counterpart is Dionysus.

Beatrice was a Florentine woman immortalized in Dante's works; she symbolizes the ideal woman.

The *Bourbon Throne / Bourboniden Thron* refers to the eight dukes of Bourbon (1270–1527), titled French nobility of the House of Bourbon. Because Scholz places the Bourbon throne in the distant past, he was probably not referring to the House of Bourbon, one of the most important ruling houses of Europe, which was current when he wrote his cycle.

Brown, Doctor, may be the British physician John Brown (1735–88), who proposed the theory of "excitability," which classified diseases according to whether they had an over- or understimulating effect on the body. Brown prescribed stimulants or sedatives accordingly, often using wine or laudanum. He published *Elementa Medicinae* in 1780, which was widely read and well received throughout Europe. His theory was at its height of popularity in the late 1700s and early 1800s, when Scholz was writing his cycle.

Ceres is the Roman goddess of agriculture.

The *Charities/Charitinnen* are twelve Greek goddesses of beauty, grace, and charisma, i.e., the social graces; they are responsible for those things believed to enhance life.

Cupid, also known as Amor, is the Roman god of erotic love; his Greek counterpart is Eros.

Cyprus/Cypria, sometimes claimed as the birthplace of Aphrodite, is one of Aphrodite's titles; the island of Cyprus was a center for her cult.

Cytherea, more commonly known as Aphrodite, is the Greek goddess of love and beauty.

Dione is the mother of Aphrodite by Zeus.

Echo is a Greek nymph who fell in love with Narcissus; when her love went unrequited, she pined away until nothing was left of her but her voice.

Eos is the Greek goddess of dawn, more commonly known as Aurora, her Roman counterpart.

Eros is the Greek god of erotic love; he excites erotic love in gods and men with arrows and torches. His Roman counterpart is Cupid, also known as Amor.

Flora is the Roman goddess of flowers.

The *Furies/Furien* are avenging Greek deities, usually depicted as old women; they tormented criminals and inflicted illness and plagues.

Gaea, the daughter of Chaos, is the Greek goddess of Earth and mother of all creation, i.e., Mother Earth; her Roman counterpart is Terra, or Tellus.

Hetaerae/Hetären were highly cultivated courtesans in ancient Greece.

Hymen is the Greek goddess of marriage; her symbol is the myrtle wreath.

Hyperion is a Greek Titan and the father of the sun (Helios), the moon (Luna), and dawn (Aurora); his name is often used as an epithet for the sun.

Irene, the Latinized spelling of *Eirene*, is one of the three Seasons (spring, summer, and winter), daughters of Zeus. The three—Eirene and her sisters Eunomia (signifying order) and Dike (signifying justice)—are companions to Aphrodite. Eirene is the Greek goddess of conciliation and peace and is the source of the term "irenic"; her symbol is the palm.

Iris is the Greek goddess of the rainbow and a messenger of the gods.

Komos/Comus/Komus appears in later antiquity as the god of festive mirth and joy, associated with Dionysus; he is represented as a winged youth.

Liäen/Lyaeüs (lit., "He Who Frees") is an epithet for the Greek god of wine and fertility, Dionysus, also known as Bacchus, or sometimes Liber.

Liber, or Father Liber, is an ancient Roman god of fertility, usually worshiped with Ceres and Libera. Later confused with Iacchus and then fused with Bacchus and Dionysus.

Luna is the Roman goddess of the moon, night, and time; she regulates the months and seasons. Her Greek counterpart is Selené, the daughter of the Titan Hyperion and Theia and sister of the sun god Helios (Sol) and the goddess of dawn Eos (Aurora).

Morpheus is a Greek god of dreams and son of Somnus, the god of sleep. In dreams, Morpheus takes human form; his brothers, Icelos (also called Phobetor) and Phantasos, appear as animals and inanimate objects, respectively.

The *Muses/Musen* are nine sister Greek goddesses presiding over music, art, poetry, and the sciences.

The *Naiads/Najaden* are Greek water nymphs that live in and give life to bodies of water.

Narzissus/Narziss is an overly proud Greek youth who coldly rejected Echo's love; as punishment, the gods made him fall in love with his own reflection so that, like Echo, he pined away for (his own) unrequited love and was transformed into a flower.

Olympus/Olymp is a mountain in Thessaly, Greece, revered as the home of the Olympian gods, who overthrew the reigning Titans.

Phantasos/Phantasmus is a Greek god of fantasy, or dreams, and appears as inanimate objects. He is a son of Somnus, the Roman god of sleep (see Morpheus above).

Phoebe/Phoebus/Phöbe is the Greek god of sunlight, more commonly known as Apollo, his Roman counterpart; also known as Phoebus Apollo.

Proteus is a Greek sea god capable of assuming different forms.

Psyche is a princess or lesser goddess loved by Cupid; the word "psyche" comes from the Greek "breath," meaning "soul," which is her symbol.

Tellus, or Terra, is a Roman goddess of Earth; her Greek counterpart is Gaea.

The *Teutons/Teuts/(Teutonen)* are an ancient people of Germanic or Celtic origin; colloquially used to refer to all Germanic peoples.

Thetis, the mother of Achilles, is a Greek sea goddess.

Tityus/Titus, son of Gaea, or possibly of Elara and Zeus, is a Titan. Goaded on by Heré, he attempted to rape Artemis but was killed and cast into Tartarus, or Hades, where Odysseus saw him lying outstretched on the ground, his body covering nine acres, while two vultures devoured his liver for eternity.

The *Titans* are a family of giants born of Uranus and Gaea, who ruled the earth until overthrown by the Olympian gods.

Venus is the Roman goddess of productivity and fecundity, and later of love and beauty, as well; her Greek counterpart is Aphrodite.

Zephyrus/Zephyr is the Greek god of the west wind, son of Astraeus and Eos and brother of Astraea. Through Eos, Astraeus fathered the stars and the three winds—Boreas (the north wind), Notus (the south wind), and Zephyrus.

Plate 1. Karl Friedrich Müchler and Friedrich Franz Hůrka, *Die Farben* (ca. 1802), first page of "Lob der roten Farbe." Courtesy of the Staatsbibliothek zu Berlin—Preußischer Kulturbesitz, Musikabteilung mit Mendelssohn-Archiv (call no. 0. 41229).

Plate 2. Joseph Scholz and Paul Anton Wineburger, *Sechszehn Blumen* (between 1799 and 1816), title page. Courtesy of the Staatsbibliothek zu Berlin—Preußischer Kulturbesitz, Musikabteilung mit Mendelssohn-Archiv (call no. 0. 61891).

Plate 3. Karl Friedrich Müchler and Friedrich Heinrich Himmel, *Die Blumen und der Schmetterling* (1803), final engraving. Courtesy of the Staatsbibliothek zu Berlin—Preußischer Kulturbesitz, Musikabteilung mit Mendelssohn-Archiv (call no. Mus. Sig. 19,455 Rara).

Die zwölf Monate

Text by Ignaz Vincenz Franz Castelli (1781–1862)
Music by Johann Heinrich Karl Bornhardt (1774–1840)

[1.] Januar

Den er-sten Mo-nat hei-ße füg-lich man wohl den Lü-gen-mo-nat auch, denn Schmei- che- lei'n und Wün- sche plap- pern, die man nicht

fühlt, ist da der Brauch, ist da der Brauch.

Doch wenn wir

Män- ner Euch ver- si- chern, daß wir Euch stets mit Won- ne schau'n, und oh- ne

Euch nicht le- ben kön- nen, so ist es wahr Ihr hol- den

Frau'n!

[2.] Februar

Allegretto

Singstimme

Pianoforte

Gott Ko- mus füh- ret jetzt das Zep- ter durch Tanz, Mu- sik und Mum- me- -rei'n; macht er die Welt auf ein- mal när- risch; wenn's aus ist stellt sich Lang- weil' ein. Nur mag da- bei sich je- der hü- ten, daß er kein Lie- bes- fünk- chen fang': wer Frau'n zu stark ins Au- ge guk- ket, bleibt när- risch auch sein Le- be- lang.

[3.] Maerz

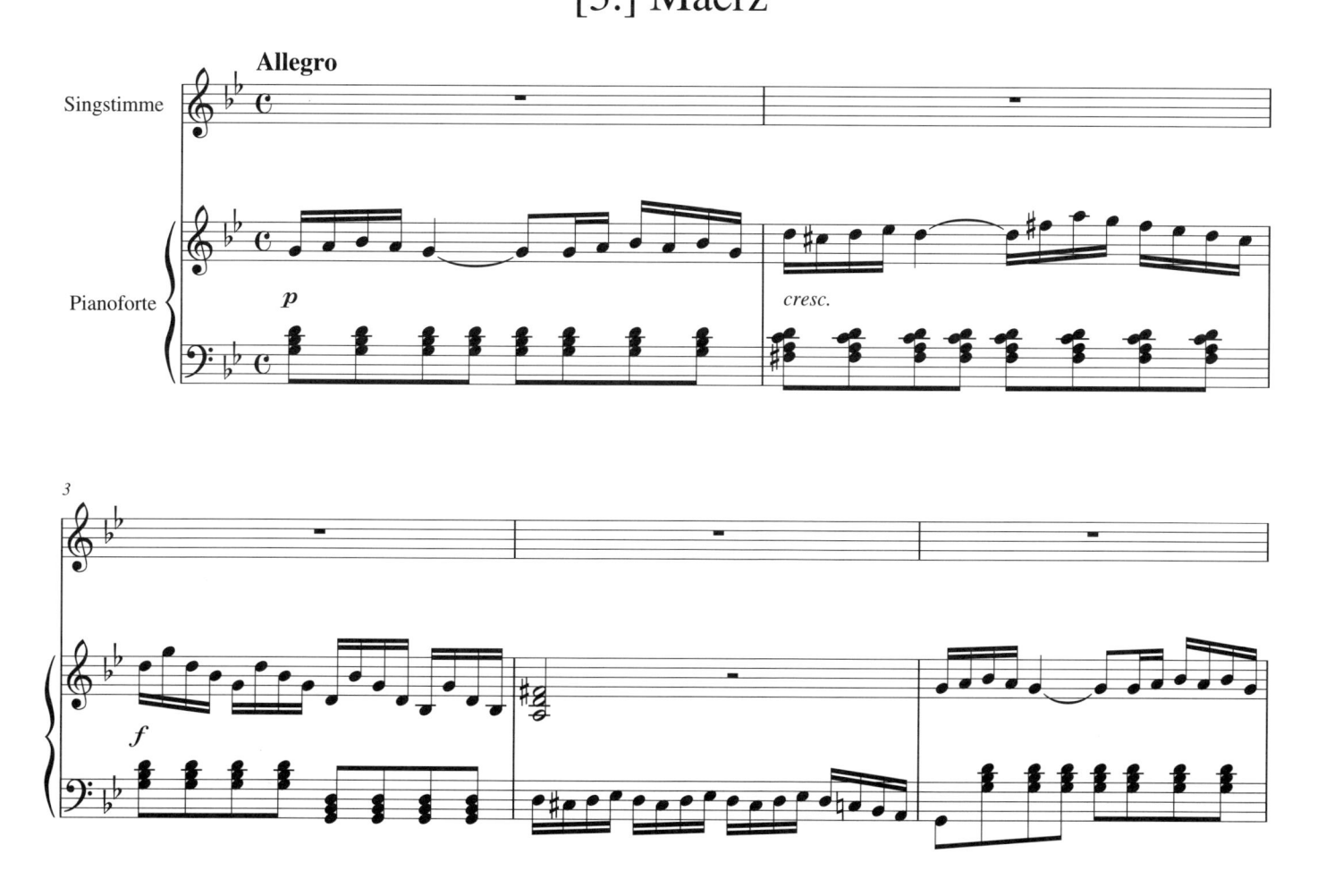

Allegro

Singstimme

Pianoforte

Noch we- hen rauh und kal- te Lüf- te, noch we- hen rauh und kal- te Lüf- te,

da blickt im ein- fach blau- en Kleid be- schei- den aus dem Schnee das Veil- chen und kün- det

Andantino

9

ei- ne schön'- re Zeit. So kün-det auch das blau- e Au- ge der gu- ten und be-schei-d'nen Frau dem Man- ne Freu- de, Trost im Lei- den, wenn um ihn stürmt das Le- ben rauh.

[4.] April

Allegretto scherzoso

Das ist der Mann, der al- le Ta- ge, al- le __ Ta- ge ein an- de- res Ge- sicht uns macht;

wir ha- ben mit ihm un- s're

Plage, weil er ohn' Ur- sach weint und lacht. Ach die- sem lau- nen- haf- ten Her- ren, Ihr Frau- en gleicht ihm gar zu sehr; wir bit- ten Euch, seid doch be- -stän- dig und quält durch Lau- nen uns nicht mehr.

[5.] Mai

Andante grazioso

Du herr- lich-ster von dei- nen Brü- dern be- lebst durch dei-nen Hauch die Flur, und Al- les prangt in fri- scher Ju- gend und Al- les at- met Lie- be nur, Al- les at- met Lie- be nur.

Seht Frau- en wie Euch je- des

Blüm- lein und je- de Mück' ein Bei- spiel

gibt, daß Ihr zur Lie- be nur ge- schaf- fen, drum öff- net Eu- er

Herz und liebt.

[6.] Junius

Ihr hol- den Frau- en! die- ser Mo- nat ist vor- zugs- wei- se Euch ge- weiht; Ihr mögt ihn Eu- ren Va- ter nen- nen, denn er er- zeugt die Ro- sen- zeit. Ihr seid die Ro- sen die- ses Le- bens und die Na-

-tur, sich stets ge- treu, gab Euch wie al- len an- dern Ro- sen auch

lei- der vie- le Dor- nen bei, lei- der vie- le Dor- nen

bei.

[7.] Julius

Der heiße Strahl der Morgensonne durchdringet selbst die tiefste Schlucht; das Werk der Liebe ist vollendet, die schöne Blüte weicht der Frucht.

Drum seid Ihr ja des Lebens Sonne, das macht das Weib zur Königin, daß sie für süße Frucht der Liebe die Blüte opfert willig hin.

[8.] August

Kna- be zum ern- sten Mann, zum fin- stern Greis. Der höch- ste Punkt führt im- mer ab- wärts; Ihr Frau- en! nehmt ihn wohl in Acht und sam- melt Euch für Eu'- ren Win- ter was Schö- nes Euch der Lenz ge- bracht.

[9.] September

Durch Wald und Flur, im Tal, auf Bergen erschallt des Hüfthorns froher Ton;

das ar- me Reh- lein will ent-wi- schen, da trifft's das Blei des Jä- gers schon:

Andantino grazioso

Ihr lie- ben Frau- en, ar- me

Rehlein! der bösen Jägerschar entflieht, die Jagd auf Eu're Tugend machet, und zielt und trifft und dann entflieht.

[10.] October

Frau- en be- tet, be- tet, da- mit der Re- ben-saft ge- deiht.

Be- den- ket, daß ein al- tes Sprich- wort mit vol- lem Rech- te de- mon- striert, daß oh- ne Ce- res, oh- ne

[11.] November

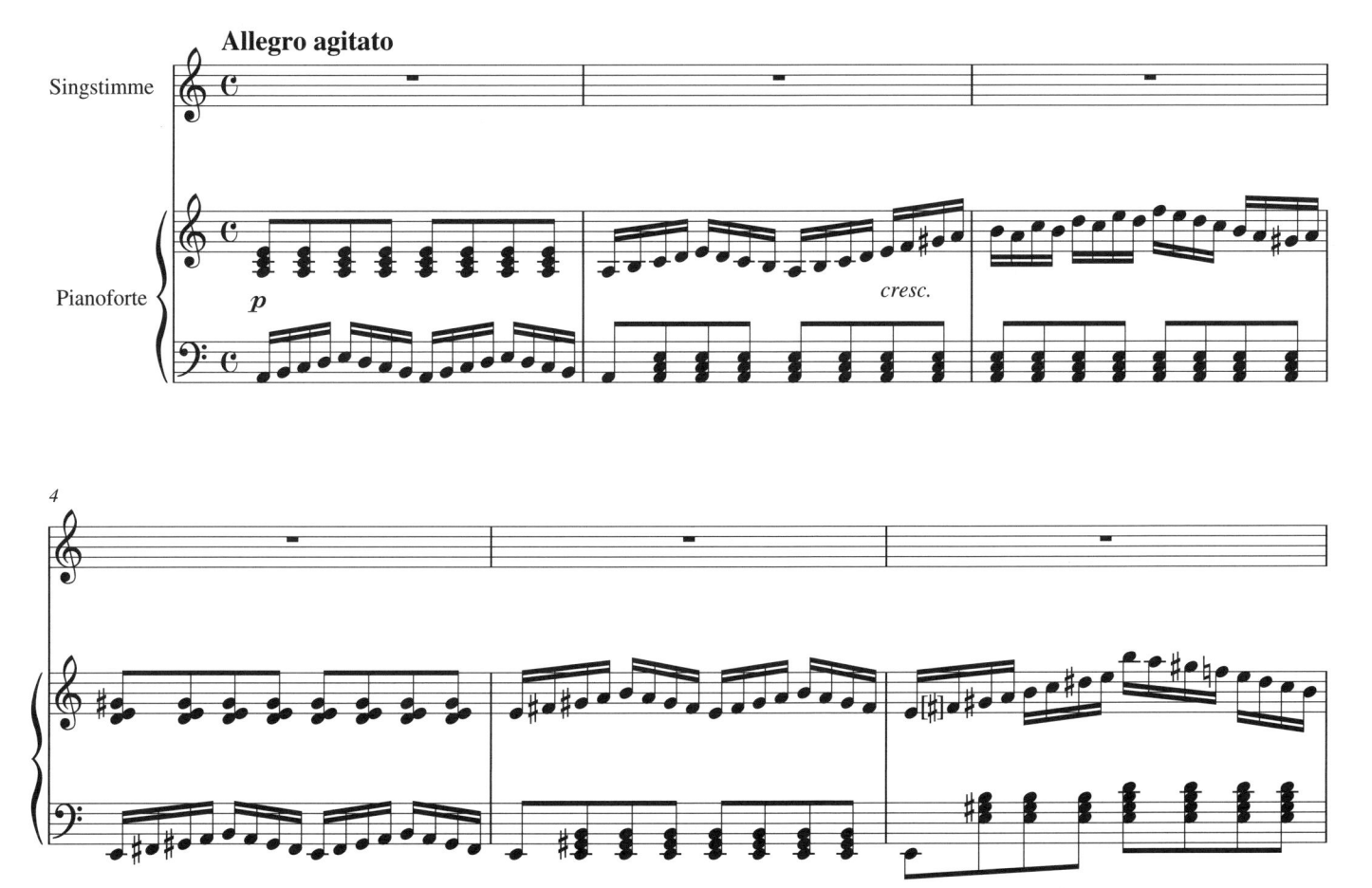

Die rau-hen kal- ten Win- de we- hen und ih- ren Schmuck ver- liert die Flur. Nicht trot- zen kön- nen Frau'n den Stür- men und ei- ne Frau ist die Na- tur;

Un poco lento

Doch seht Ihr wohl, sie weiß zu hüllen sich in der Unschuld weißes Kleid, und unter ihm wirkt sie im Stillen: folgt ihr in stürmisch rauher Zeit!

[12.] December

Je- ner kann ganz un- ge- trübt zu- rük- ke schau'n der sich sa- get: Ge- le- bet hab' ich und ge- liebt.

Andantino

Drum bit- ten wir, daß Ihr, o Frau- en! uns ja durch Prö- dig- keit nicht quält, sonst seid Ihr Schuld, wenn von uns Ei- ner das ihm be- stimm- te Ziel ver- fehlt.

Die Jahreszeiten

Text by T. L. A. Heinroth (dates unknown)
Music by Friedrich Schneider (1786–1853)

I. Winter
1. Winters Ankunft

1. Welch To- sen da drau- ßen! Welch We- hen, welch Sau- sen in stö- bri- ger Nacht! Die Flok- ken, sie ja- gen ans

13
Fen- ster ge- schla- gen! Ins Land zieht der
16
Win- ter mit stür- mi- scher Macht!
Chor
[SOPRANI]
Die
TENOR
Die
BASS
Die
f
19
Flok- ken, sie ja- gen ans Fen- ster ge-
Flok- ken, sie ja- gen ans Fen- ster ge-
Flok- ken, sie ja- gen ans Fen- ster ge-

-schla- gen! Ins Land zieht der Win- ter mit stür- men- der Macht!

2. Doch
3. Die

2.
Doch lustig! im Zimmer
da fürchten wir nimmer
den Winter-Ozean!
Uns halten die Flammen
vertraulich beisammen:
Rückt Alle, rückt näher zum Feuer heran!

3.
Die Gläser gehoben!
Wir ehren, wir loben
den köstlichen Wein!
den kräft'gen, den alten!
Des Winters Gewalten
bezwingt er und führt uns den Frühling herein!

2. Winterruhe

Mit ruhigem Vortrag

[V. 1]

V[v]. 2 und 3

1. Die Son- ne weicht nach kur- zem Lauf vom ei- si- gen Ge- -fild! Am Win- ter- him- mel steigt her- auf manch fun- kelnd Stern- ge- bild, manch

fun-kelnd Stern- ge- bild.

2. Es fleucht der
3. Es ruht und

2.
Es fleucht der Vogel in sein Nest,
der Mensch zu Hüttchens Ruh:
auch Mutter Erde deckt sich fest
mit weisser Hülle zu.

3.
Es ruht und schläft so Hain als Flur
im sichern Winterhaus:
die weite Welt doch ruht sie nur
zu neuem Leben aus!

3. Winternachtleben

(Chorgesang für Männerstimmen)

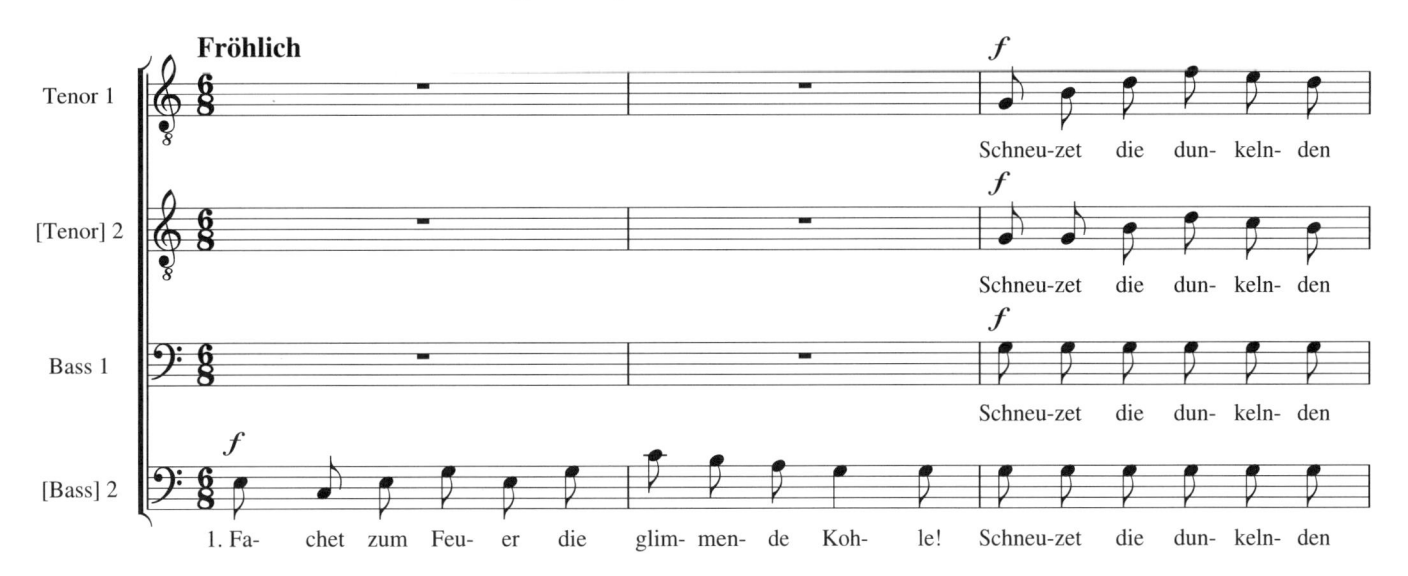

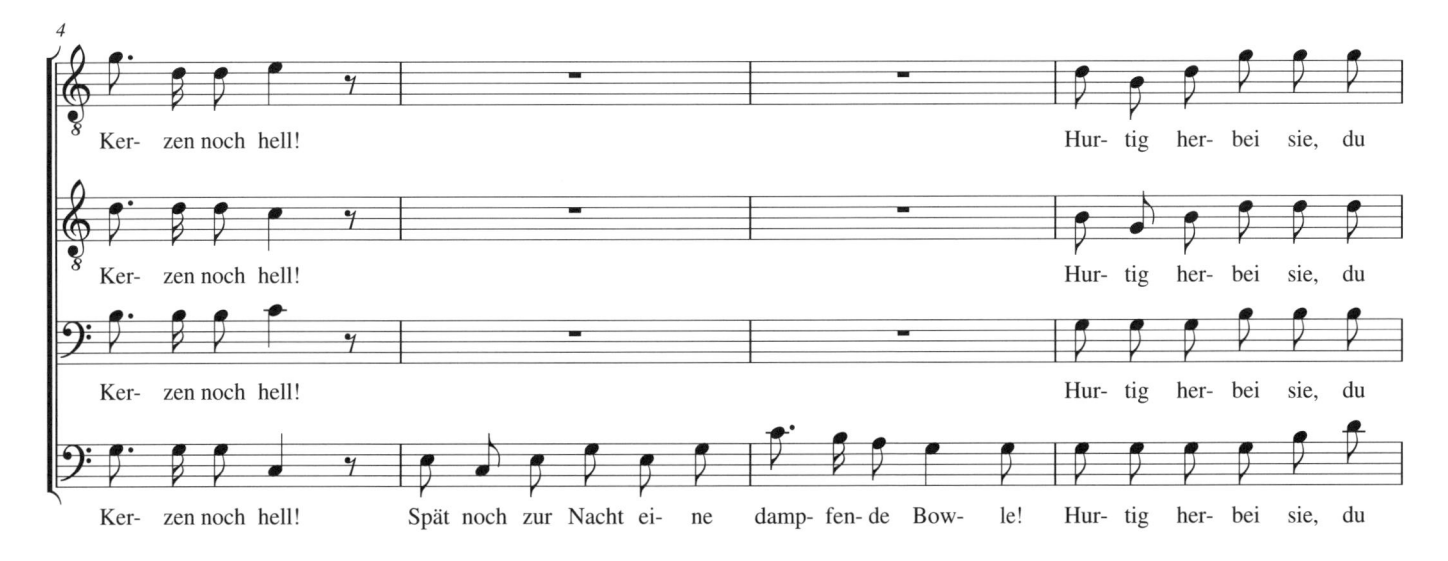

Fröhlich

Tenor 1: Schneu-zet die dun-keln-den Ker-zen noch hell! Hur-tig her-bei sie, du

[Tenor] 2: Schneu-zet die dun-keln-den Ker-zen noch hell! Hur-tig her-bei sie, du

Bass 1: Schneu-zet die dun-keln-den Ker-zen noch hell! Hur-tig her-bei sie, du

[Bass] 2: 1. Fa-chet zum Feu-er die glim-men-de Koh-le! Schneu-zet die dun-keln-den Ker-zen noch hell! Spät noch zur Nacht ei-ne damp-fen-de Bow-le! Hur-tig her-bei sie, du

2.
Munter herbei nun zum traulichen Kreise!
Eilt nicht so hastig, ihr Gäste, nach Haus!
Singt noch ein Liedchen in fröhlicher Weise!
Sorgenlos leert mir die Bowle noch aus!
Augen und Herzen macht hell sie und frisch.
Frisch auf! und spottet des Schlafers am Tisch!

3.
Winter und Nacht sie vereinen die Herzen!
Sommer und Tag sie zerstreuen den Bund!
Winter und Nacht sie entzünden mit Scherzen
Leben am Leben im fröhlichen Rund,
Leben am Leben beim traulichen Heerd.
Winternacht, sei uns willkommen und wert!

II. Frühling
1. Frühlingshimmel

1. Es schau-et vom Him-mel kein win-ter-lich Grau, kein Wol-ken-ge-wim-mel, nur lä- -cheln-des Blau!

Brust, schon at-met in Won- -ne den Früh- -ling die Brust.

2.
Es wehen die Lüfte
balsamisch und rein,
als saugten sie Düfte
der Blumen schon ein.

3.
Es strahlet die Sonne
nur Leben und Lust.
Schon atmet in Wonne
den Frühling die Brust.

2. Frühlingserde

Mit innigem Vortrag

1. Willkommen, trautes Baches Rieseln, zu dem des Hügels Quellen ziehn und scherzend über bunten Kieseln der Winterfessel rasch entfliehn, die scherzend der Winterfessel rasch entfliehn.

2.
Willkommen, junges Grün am Bache,
willkommen, junges Grün am Rain,
ihr Veilchen unterm Hirtendache,
ihr Glöckchen dort im Buchenhain!
[ihr Veilchen und Glöckchen dort im Buchenhain!]

3.
Willkommen, all du Knospenfülle
so reich am Strauch, so reich am Baum!
O, junges Frühlings zarte Hülle,
du birgst, doch du verbirgst ihn kaum!
[die zarte Hülle verbirgst du kaum!]

3. Frühlingsleben

1. Un-ter blau-em Him-mels-bo-gen, hoch und herr-lich aus-ge-spannt, kommt mit se-gens-rei-cher

Hand auf der Blu- men- düf- te Wo- gen hold der Früh- ling ein- ge- zo- gen in sein Reich, das Blü- ten- land, _____ in sein Reich, ___ das ___ Blü- ten- land.

dolce

smorzando *poco rallentando* *a tempo*

2.
Jedes Knöspchen hat erschlossen
seiner Blüte zarten Schoß!
Neues Leben ringt sich los
in den Luft- und Erd-Genossen.
Bund des Friedens ist geschlossen:
Liebe heisst des Tages Los.

3.
Liebe weht durch junge Schatten,
Liebe tönt die Nachtigall,
Liebe der Schalmei Schall,
Liebe spielt auf grünen Matten,
wo sich Taub' und Täubin gatten;
Lieb' ist Frühlings Wiederhall.

III. Sommer
1. Im Walde

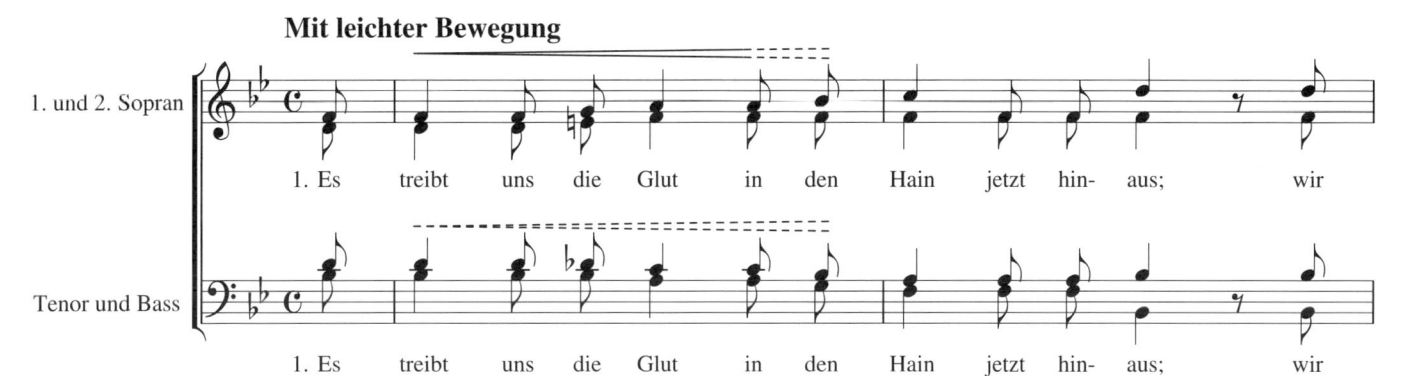

Mit leichter Bewegung

1. Es treibt uns die Glut in den Hain jetzt hinaus; wir wählen und suchen im Schatten der Buchen ein kühlendes Plätzchen, ein luftiges Haus, ein kühlendes Plätzchen, ein luftiges Haus.

2.
Hier wehen die Lüftchen, hier rieselt der Bach:
hier ist es gefunden!
Vor glühenden Stunden
beschirmt uns des Haines breitblättriges Dach.

3.
Hier lagert bekränzt euch am mosigen Hang!
Hier soll uns erfrischen
auf rasigen Tischen
die Beere des Waldes bei Scherz und Gesang!

2. Auf dem Flusse

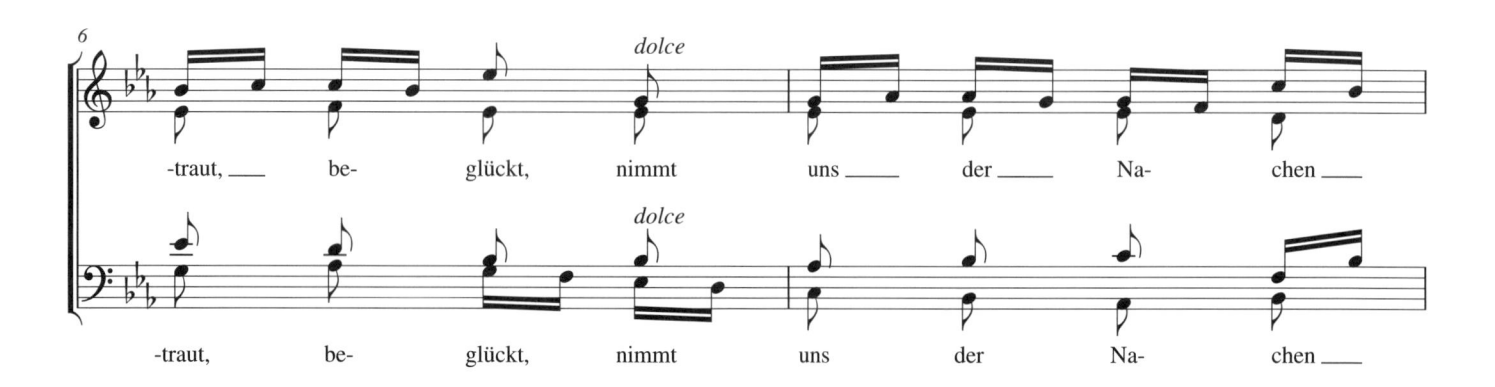

2.
Vom Strom bespült,
vom Strom gekühlt,
so schiffen wir dahin.
Der Tag erbleicht,
das Ufer weicht
und uns ist wohl zu Sinn.

3.
Wir schiffen fort
von Ort zu Ort,
vor Berg und Tal vorbei.
Das Feste weilt,
das Schiffchen eilt,
und wir sind froh und frei.

3. In der Laube

Sehr sanft

1. Lieblich weht die duft'ge Kühle durch die Sommernacht;
und der heißen Mittagsschwüle wird nicht mehr gedacht.

2.
In der trauten Laube Runde,
vom Jasmin umwebt,
sitzen wir in später Stunde
Wein- und Lied-belebt.

3.
So, von Blätternacht umdunkelt,
würzen wir das Mahl.
Lauschend durch die Bäume funkelt
sanft des Mondes Strahl.

IV. Herbst
1. Garten

In mässiger Bewegung

1. Die hol-den Ro- sen sind er- bleicht, die Li- lie hat ihr Haupt ge- neigt, ver-schwun-den ist der Früh- lings- glanz, ver-welkt ist Flo- ra's schön-ster Kranz.

Chor
SOPRANI: Ver-schwun- den ist der Früh- lings- glanz, ver- welkt ist Flo- ra's schön- ster

TENOR und BASS: Ver-schwun- den ist der Früh- lings- glanz, ver- welkt ist Flo- ra's schön- ster

2.
Nur bunte Blumen ohne Duft,
sie blüh'n auf ihrer Schwestern Gruft.
Ihr Astern blau, ihr Astern rot:
ihr kündet uns des Schönsten Tod!

3.
O Frühlingskraft, o Jugendkraft,
Die warmes Leben rings erschafft,
das süss mit Duft die Welt durchzieht:
Dich scheucht der Herbst, dein Hauch entflieht!

2. Weinberg

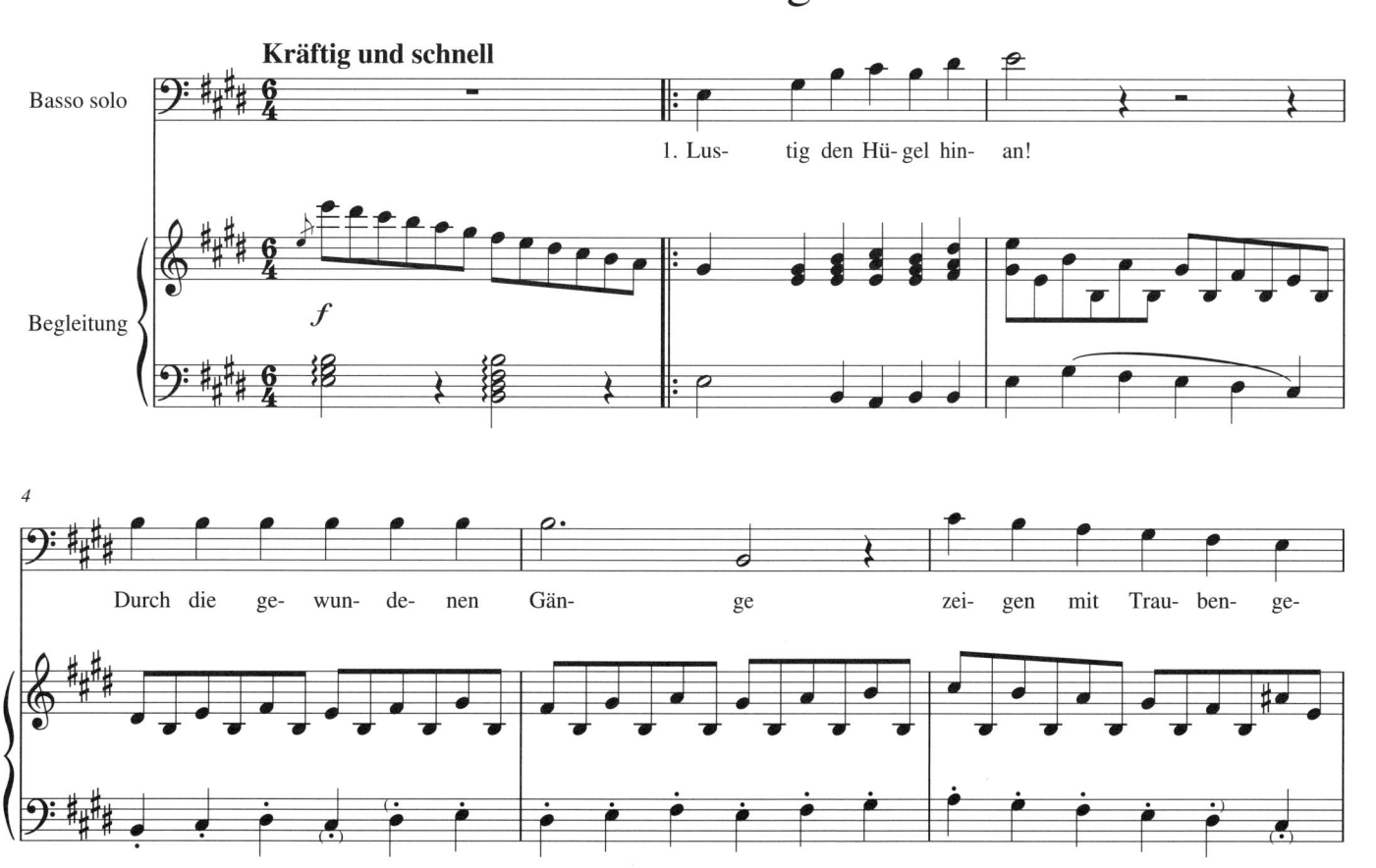

Kräftig und schnell

1. Lustig den Hügel hinan!
Durch die gewundenen Gänge zeigen mit Traubenge-

-pränge Rebengelän- der die Bahn, Rebengelän- der die Bahn!

Chor
SOPRANI
Lus- tig den Hü- gel hin- an!

TENOR UND BASS
Lus- tig den Hü- gel hin- an!

dolce
Durch die ge- wun- de- nen Gän- ge zei- gen mit Trau- ben- ge-

[dolce]
Durch die ge- wun- de- nen Gän- ge zei- gen mit Trau- ben- ge-

2.
Frisch, um die Wette den Lauf
über veralterte Stufen!
Muntere Winzer sie rufen
freundlich die Wand'rer hinauf!

3.
Trauben in schwellender Pracht,
köstlicher Lese das Beste,
schmecken wir fröhliche Gäste
hier, wo der Himmel uns lacht.

4.
Sende, du Sonne, den Strahl,
sende das heitere Leben,
uns in der Traube gegeben,
auch für das Leben zumal!

3. Herbstöde

Langsam, mit vielem Gefühl

1. Durch Herbstes-lüfte, durch Nebel-düfte geht Wand'rers Tritt. Die kahlen Raine, die öden Haine durcheilt sein Schritt.

2.
Kein Leben außen;
die Winde sausen
durch dürres Laub.
Die Blätter fallen
aus Wipfel-Hallen,
des Winters Raub.

3.
An Heerdes Flammen
drängt jetzt zusammen
sich Lebenslust.
Hinab zum Tale!
Zum frohen Mahle!
An Freundes Brust!

Die Farben

Text by Karl Friedrich Müchler (1763–1857)
Music by Friedrich Franz Hůrka (1762–1805) (nos. 1–5, 7)
and Friedrich Heinrich Himmel (1765–1814) (no. 6)

1. Lob der weißen Farbe

1. Zartes Weiß, die Feier meiner Lieder will ich dir aus voller Seele weih'n; möchte sie so fleckenlos und rein, wie des königlichen Schwans Gefieder, wie der Schnee auf hohen Alpen sein, wie der Schnee auf hohen Alpen

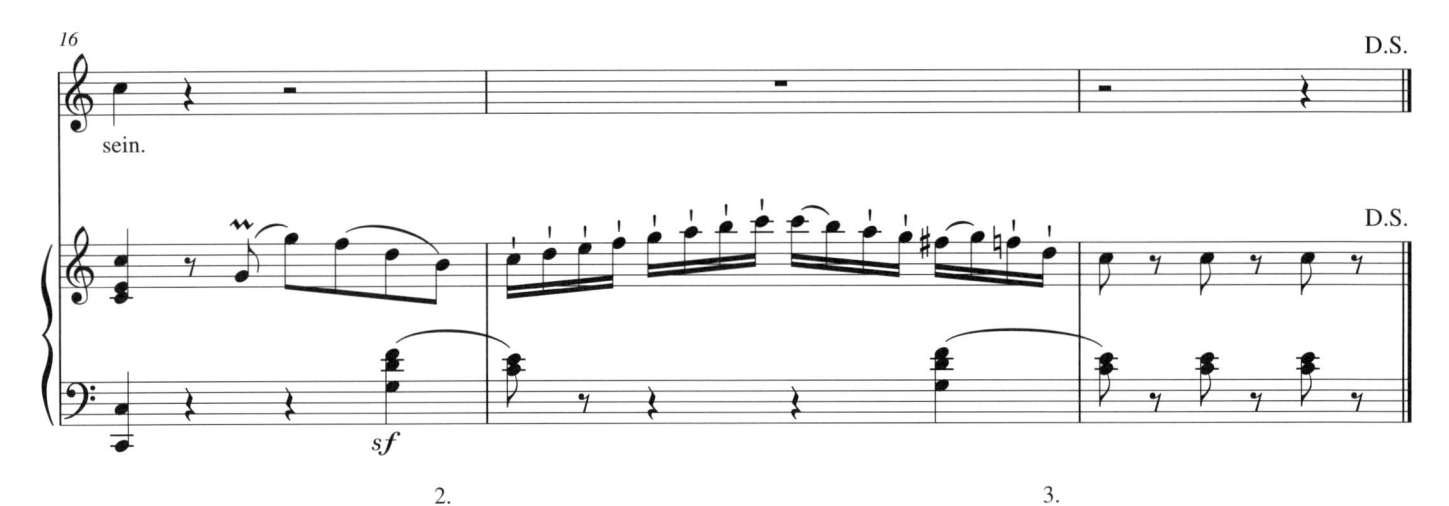

2.
Wohl dem Manne, der in seinem Herzen
Heil'ge Unschuld, deine Farbe trägt;
Wenn Verfolgung ihn in Ketten schlägt,
Kann er noch mit diesen Ketten scherzen,
Weil ein Gott mit rechter Waage wägt.

3.
Wohl ihm, harret sein am Traualtare
Die Geliebte, wie der Friede mild,
In ein weißes Brautgewand gehüllt,
Einen Lilienkranz im blonden Haare,
Ihrer engelreinen Seele Bild.

4.
Daß des Vaters Tugenden nicht sterben,
Werden Kinder seiner Ehe Glück;
Wie der Mond den hohen Sonnenblick,
Eines ungetrübten Abends Erben,
Strahlen sie des Greises Licht zurück.

5.
Er erbebt nicht an des Grabes Rande,
Denn er fühlet seines Herzens Wert;
Und der Tod, der seinen Köcher leert,
Wird ein Genius im Lichtgewande,
Der die Fackel lächelnd niederkehrt.

2. Lob der roten Farbe

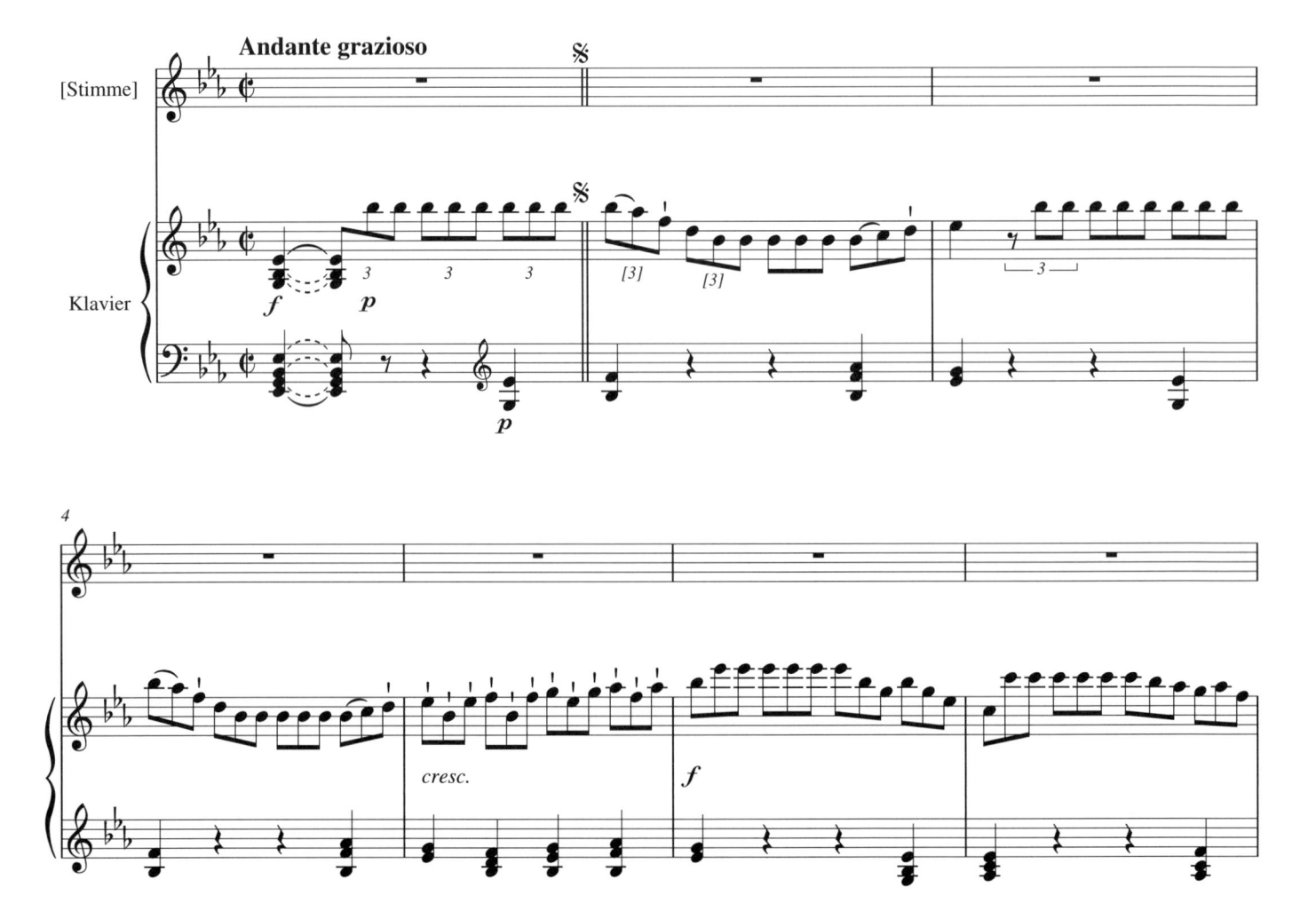

1. Dir ge- büh- ren mei- ne Hul- di- gun- gen, da- rum sei dir auch dies Lied ge- sun- gen. Bild der Lie- be, wun- der- schö- nes Rot, wel- che Far- be kann sich dir ver- glei- chen? Dei- nem Schim- mer muß die schön- ste wei- chen; ge- gen dich sind al- le,

alle tot, gegen dich sind alle, alle tot.

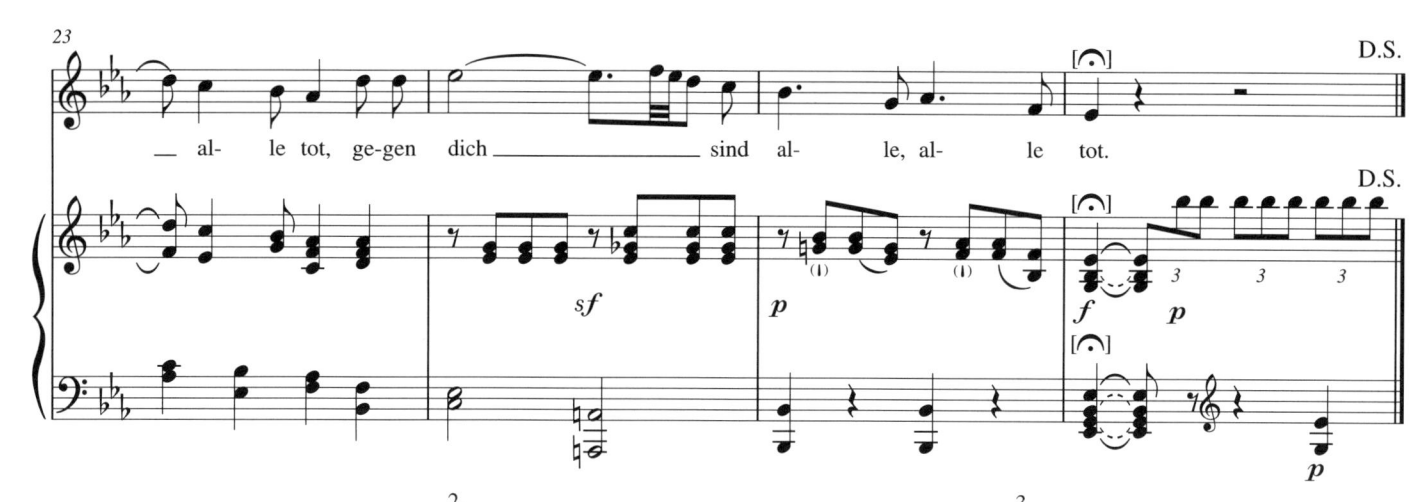

2.
Wann in Nacht das Heer der Sterne schwindet,
Wann Aurorens Blick den Tag verkündet,
 Phöbus sich aus blauer Flut erhebt,
Färbt sein Antlitz den getrübten Äther
Triumphierend rot, und immer röter,
 Bis er flammend über Wolken schwebt.

3.
Purpur ward der Schmuck der zarten Rose,
Von Cytheren in Adonis Schoße,
 Einst mit ihrem Götterblut benetzt,
Und der Stolz von allen Blumenbeeten
Malt uns nun der ersten Lieb' Erröten,
 Hat uns Amors Pfeil die Brust verletzt.

4.
Purpurrosen schmücken Hymens Lauben,
Purpurn glänzen Libers Nektartrauben,
 Purpur färbt des Mädchens zarten Mund,
Und die sanfte Röte ihrer Wangen
Macht dem holden Jüngling das Verlangen
 Ihres liebekranken Herzens kund.

5.
Selig, wem Liäens Traube glänzet,
Amors Hand die Stirn mit Rosen kränzet,
 Hymens Fackel rote Flammen strahlt,
Wem nicht Sorgen seine Freuden töten,
Wem des Mädchens banges Schamerröten
 Noch das Bild der zarten Unschuld malt.

6.
Selig, wann er dann zu ew'gem Bunde
Von des trauten Mädchens Rosenmunde
 Früh den Kuss der Treu' und Liebe küsst;
Sagt ihm das Erröten ihrer Wangen,
Und ihr Blick voll zärtlichem Verlangen,
 Daß sie treu, und daß er glücklich ist.

3. Lob der blauen Farbe

1. Von allen Farben auf der Welt,
mir doch am meisten Blau gefällt;
blau ist des Himmels lichter Bogen,
hat ihn kein Nachtgewölk umzogen.

2.
Blau ist des holden Veilchens Kleid,
Wann es sich voll Bescheidenheit
In dunkelgrüne Blätter hüllet,
Und doch die Luft mit Balsam füllet.

3.
Blau ist das Blümchen, welches spricht:
"Ich bitte dich, vergiss mein nicht!"
Das sich die Freundschaft ausersehen,
Für Liebe, Liebe zu erflehen.

4.
Aus blauen Augen strahlet rein
Der Huld und Liebe milder Schein,
Drum haben immer auch vor allen
Nur blaue Augen mir gefallen.

5.
Blau ist schon seit der Fabelzeit
Die Farbe der Beständigkeit,
Das Rot der Liebe zu erheben,
Und schöne Dauer ihm zu geben.

6.
Drum soll die blaue Farb' allein
Stets meine Lieblingsfarbe sein;
Drum will ich nur in Blau mich kleiden
Und mich an blauen Augen weiden.

7.
Und führt mich Hymen einst zur Trau,
Sei meine Braut geschmückt in Blau;
Wünsch' ich aus himmelblauen Augen
Der Treue schönsten Lohn zu saugen.

4. Lob der gelben Farbe

Allegro maestoso

1. Der gelben Farbe bin ich hold, drum sei ihr auch dies Lied gezollt; viel schönes kenn' ich in der Welt, das doppelt Reiz durch Gelb erhält.

2.
Gelb ist das Gold, und wie bekannt,
Ersetzt es Tugend und Verstand,
Erkaufst du dir für blankes Gold
Vergnügen, Ruhm, selbst Minnesold.

3.
Doch darum sing' ich freilich nicht
Der gelben Farb' ein Lobgedicht:
Wer trifft des Goldes Talisman
Wohl je bei einem Dichter an?

4.
Doch gelb ist auch der Sonne Licht,
Wenn sie hervor aus Wolken bricht,
Wenn sie im Lenz der Wiese Kleid
Mit bunten Blümchen überstreut.

5.
Gelb, wie die gold'ne Ananas,
Gelb, wie in vollem Deckelglas
Der Wein, den Nierenstein gebahr,
Ist meines Liebchens blondes Haar.

6.
Und Heil dem vaterländ'schen Rhein;
Er gibt uns reichlich edlen Wein,
Gelb, wie der Morgensonne Strahl,
Glänzt er im schäumenden Pokal.

7.
Heil diesem Wein!—Er schenkt uns Mut,
Er wärmt des Greises kaltes Blut,
Er flammt den Jüngling und den Mann
Zu kronenwerten Taten an.

8.
Auch kenn' ich noch in braunem Haar
Ein zartes gelbes Rosenpaar;
O, solltet ihr's nur einmal seh'n,
Ihr riefet alle: "Gelb ist schön!"

5. Lob der grünen Farbe

Allegro

1. Singt rot und blau und gelb und grau, schwarz, feu-er-farb, — und weiß, ——— schwarz, feu-er-farb, — und weiß; singt car-mo-sin, ich

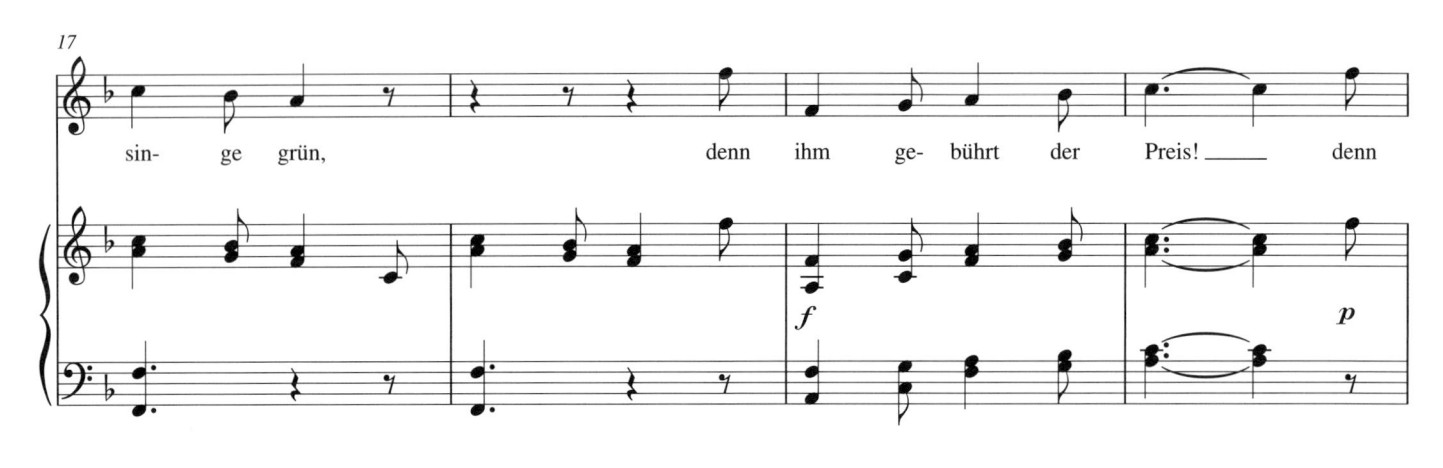

2.
Seht die Natur!
Die Blumenflur
Schmückt sich im Lenz mit Grün,
Wenn hin zum Tanz
Beim Mondenglanz
Die Hirten fröhlich ziehn.

3.
Im grünen Wald,
Dem Aufenthalt
Der Unschuld, singt allein
Die Nachtigall
Dem Wiederhall
Melodisch silberrein.

4.
Des Mädchens Haar
Am Brautaltar
Schmückt grünes Myrtenreis;
Ein grünes Blatt
Lohnt Heldentat,
Lohnt Dichtergeist und Fleiß.

5.
Der Göttin, die
Des Lebens Müh'
Durch schönen Traum versüßt,
Ist grün geweiht,
Grün ist das Kleid,
Das flatternd sie umfließt.

6.
O Göttin, sei
Mir immer treu,
Bis an des Grabes Rand;
Ich folge gern,
Glänzt nur von fern
Mir tröstend dein Gewand.

[6.] Lob der violetten Farbe

Gemässigt

1. Farbe, die Cytherens Götterhand einst erschuf aus Blau und Morgenröte, und damit des Veilchens Schmuck erhöhte, als es farbelos im Grase stand.

2.
Dir, nur dir ertön' ein Feierlied,
wie ich keiner Farb' es noch gesungen,
Bild der Treue, die mein Herz durchdrungen,
Bild der Liebe, die mein Herz durchglüht.

3.
Als ich, Jenny, dich zuerst erblickt',
war dein Haar, das sanft die Stirn umflossen,
mit Violen, die sich kaum entschlossen,
schön, als wär's ein Diadem, geschmückt.

4.
Heilig soll mir diese Farbe sein,
löscht' sich auch im raschen Strom der Zeiten
Amors Fackel,—all' die Seligkeiten
der Erinnerungen bleiben mein!

5.
Ewig, ewig schlägt mein Herz wie heut',
glühn für mich auch nicht mehr Amors Kerzen,
jedes Veilchen spricht zu meinem Herzen:
ohne Freundschaft keine Seligkeit!

[7.] Lob der schwarzen Farbe

1. Schwarz der Nacht, von dir umgeben, zittert nur der Bösewicht; wer mag schaudern, wer mag beben wem sein Herz kein Urteil

2.
Wenn am segnenden Altare
Ehrfurchtsvoll die Andacht kniet;
Wenn an des Geliebten Bahre
Jedes Auge niedersieht;
Wenn du weinst wo Freunde starben,
Dann verlöschen and're Farben
Dann bleibt heil'gem Schmerz geweih't
Schwarz der Wehmut Feierkleid.

3.
Nicht im leuchtenden Gewande
Bist du stille Trau'r gehüllt,
Schwarz verweilest du am Strande
Deiner Trennung, denkst das Bild,
Denkst das Haben, denkst das Missen,
Malest es in Schattenrißen,
Denkst was war, was wird gescheh'n,
Ahnest frohes Wiederseh'n.

4.
Nacht, durch deine Einsamkeiten
Schimmert eines Weisen Pfad,
Und aus deinen Heimlichkeiten
Sprießet manche große Tat!
Schwarz, aus deinen Finsternissen
Möge Menschenglück entsprießen:
Dann wird Liebe und Vertrau'n
Sich bei Völkern Hütte bau'n.

Sechszehn Blumen

Text by Joseph Scholz (1773–1811)
Music by Paul Anton Wineberger (1758–1822)

[1.] Das Stiefmütterchen

-fun- den, oft hat mich sein An- blick ent- zückt.

2. Nicht

2.
Nicht stolz auf die schimmernde Hülle,
Erkeimt in bescheidener Stille,
   Das Blümlein das jedem gefällt.
Fünf Blätter nur zieren die Kleine,
Drei Farben im schönen Vereine,
   Hat Flora für sie sich erwählt.

3.
Die gelbe den Argwohn bedeutet,
Der immer die Liebe begleitet,
   Wenn Treue das Herz nicht bewacht;
D'rum ward von der Göttin aufs Neue
Der Unschuld, ätherische Bläue
   Gesellet zu schützender Macht.

4.
Oft pflückt' ich die lieblichen Blüten
Und deutete dann ihre Mythen
   Der Holden, die lieb ich gewann.
Es sprachen die lehrenden Farben,
Die unser Vertrauen erwarben,
   Dann freundlich und tröstend uns an.

5.
Weswegen den drolligten Namen
Die zierlichen Blümchen bekamen,
   Dies Rätsel, traun, lös't ich noch nicht.
Doch sollt' ich's in Zukunft erfahren
Dann will ich es gern offenbahren;
   Jetzt end' ich mein kleines Gedicht.

[2.] Die Sonnenblume

Andante

1. Blume, die von Phöbus Glanz umflogen, über viele Blumen ragt hervor, die zur Sonne, zu des Äthers Bogen majestätisch hebt ihr Haupt empor: jener Schönheit Fülle singt mein Lied, die in deinem Kelche strahlend blüht.

    2.
Wie im Dunkel nied'rer Regionen,
 Nie des Kühnen stolzer Sinn verweilt,
Wie er hin zu lichterfülltern Zonen
 Sehnend auf des Geistes Schwingen eilt:
So, o Sonnen-Blume, strebt dein Blick
Auf dein hohes Ideal zurück.

    3.
Schmetterling und Biene summen lüstern
 Um den Kelch, aus welchem Nektar quillt;
Sie umgaukeln dich mit leisem Flüstern,
 Süßer Wonne-Rausch hat sie erfüllt.—
Du bist dem Inseckt auf stiller Flur,
Sonnen-Strahl belebender Natur!

    4.
Haucht um dich, du segenschwang're Blume,
 Auch kein Wohl-Geruch den zarten Duft;
Schimmern doch in Floras Heiligtume
 Wen'ge schöner durch die Sommer-Luft.
Wie am blauen Himmel Eos lacht,
Winkt, o Blume, deine stolze Pracht!

    5.
Mag auch deiner Schönheit Reiz entschweben,
 Wenn des Herbstes Stürme feindlich drohn,
Du erwachst im Lenz zum neuen Leben;
 Alles kehret wieder, was entflohn!—
Und der Sonne mächtige Gewalt
Ruft zurück die liebliche Gestalt.

[3.] Das Vergissmeinnicht

1. In feuchten Schatten-Gründen, entfernt vom Sonnen-Licht, lässt sich ein Blümchen finden, es heißt: Vergissmeinnicht.

2. Un-

2.
Unschuldig, sanft, bescheiden,
Blüht still es und versteckt,
Und scheint den Blick zu meiden
Der freudig es entdeckt.

3.
Den zarten Kelch umziehet
Kein süßer Balsamduft
Und seine Farbe glühet
Nicht schimmernd durch die Luft.

4.
Es schmückt des Äthers-Bläue
Das Blümchen, ach, so mild!
Ein Sinnbild ew'ger Treue
Hat sich in ihm enthüllt.

5.
Die kleine holde Blume,
Die ohne Prunk gefällt,
Hat sich zum Heiligtume
Empfindung ausgewählt.

6.
Der Freundschaft und der Liebe
Ist sie allein geweiht,
Daß die Erin'rung bliebe
Der schön-verlebten Zeit.

7.
Es reicht, ist sie gefunden,
Dann die geliebte Hand
In bangen Trennungs-Stunden
Sie uns als Minne-Pfand.

8.
Mit warmer Liebe sorgen
Wir für das Blümchen nun
Und lassen es verborgen
An unserm Herzen ruhn.

9.
Dort mahnt es an die Stunde
Des Abschieds; zärtlich spricht,
Wie aus geliebtem Munde,
Es sanft: Vergissmeinnicht!

[4.] Die Nelke

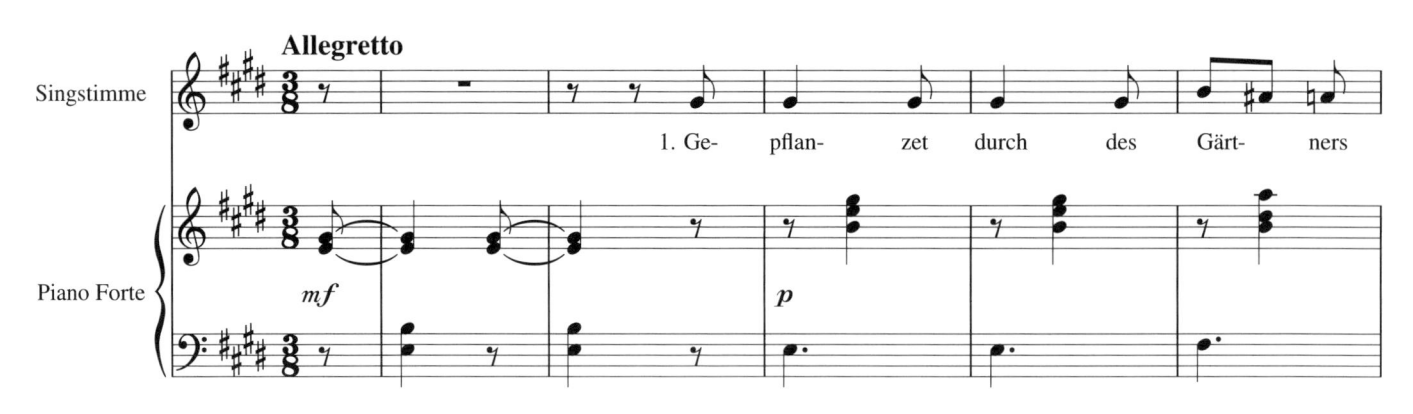

Allegretto

1. Gepflanzet durch des Gärtners Hand, und treu von ihm bewacht mit kluger Sorgfalt und Verstand, erblüht der Nelke Pracht.

2.
Wie Iris Bogen, glänzen bald
Die Farben hell und rein,
Bald hüllt die liebliche Gestalt
Ein traurig Dunkel ein.

3.
So würzig, wie aus ihr, ergießt
Sich keiner Blume Duft;
Und weit umher, wo sie entsprießt,
Füllt Wohlgeruch die Luft.

4.
Ist oft mit wenig Blättern nur
Der Nelke Kelch umlaubt.
Gesellt die Kunst sich der Natur,
Und schöner prangt ihr Haupt.

5.
Die Kunst gebeut, und üppig schwillt
Und ründet sie sich dann;
Vollendet zeigt sich nun ihr Bild,
Das höhern Reiz gewann.

6.
Des Menschen Geist der Nelke gleicht;
Gelähmt bleibt seine Kraft,
Wenn ihm nicht die Erziehung zeigt
Den Pfad zur Wissenschaft.

7.
Doch, wenn er sich durch sie erhebt
Und Psyches Flügel schwingt,
Er mutig nach dem Lichte strebt
Und Weisheit sich erringt.

8.
Das Schöne, das verborgen wohnt,
Lockt Fleiß und Kunst hervor,
Wie beide der Erfolg belohnt;
Dies zeigt der Nelken Flor.

[5.] Die Nachtviole

1. Es sinkt Asträa von den Bergen nieder, ihr brauner Schleir umhüllet Tal und Flur; der Hain verstummt, es schweigen seine Lieder, entschlummern will die lebende Natur.

2.
Schon glänzet an des Himmels hohem Bogen,
  Im dunklen Blau, der Sterne leuchtend Meer;
Auf sanftbewegten silberhellen Wogen,
  Schwebt Luna majestätisch still einher.

3.
Jetzt schwimmen durch die lauen Abend-Lüfte,
  Getragen auf der Weste leichtem Flug,
Der Nacht-Viole süße Balsam-Düfte,
  Und streuen um uns süßen Wohl-Geruch.

4.
Wenn Flora wandelt in der Töchter Kreise,
  Verweilt auf dieser Blume gern ihr Blick,
Denn dankbar schweben ihre Düfte leise
  Und liebevoll von ihr auf sie zurück.

5.
Ihr gilt mein Lob, die in bescheidner Hülle,
  Vom goldnen Farben-Schimmer ungeschmückt,
Im leisen Wehn der lauen Abend-Stille
  Mit eignem Reiz uns wunderbar entzückt!

6.
Ist auch ihr Wohl-Geruch dem Sinn entschwunden,
  Wenn Phöbus früh an Thetis Brust erwacht,
Doch kehrt zurück er in den Abend-Stunden
  Und wehet würzig durch die Sommer-Nacht.

7.
Die zarte Nacht-Viole sei vor allen
  Die liebste mir, auf Floras Blumen-Flur!
Bescheiden, anspruchlos muss sie gefallen,
  Denn schmucklos ist am schönsten die Natur!

[6.] Die Lilie

webt; die durch des Sommer-Abends laue Lüfte, so würzig haucht die süßen Balsam-Düfte!

2.
Wie wenn des Mondes sanftes Licht
  Die Blumen-Flur umzieht,
So strahlt des Mädchens Angesicht,
  Wo deine Farbe blüht.
Sie weichet nie, küsst auch die schönen Wangen
  Des holden Scham-Errötens leises Bangen.

3.
Die Blume königlicher Pracht,
  O, Lilie, bist Du!
Geweihet zum Symbol der Macht,
  Umschwebt dich stolze Ruh.
Du warst es, welche Könige bekränzte,
  Als einst der Bourboniden Thron noch glänzte!

4.
Im grauen Altertume wies
  Die Dichtung auf dich hin,
Wenn sie der Tugend Würde pries
  Und unschuldsvollen Sinn.
Es wählte die Natur ein irdisch Zeichen,
  Das Himmlische der Tugend zu vergleichen.

5.
Von heil'ger Unschuld treu bewacht,
  Und makellos und rein,
Beschützet durch der Tugend Macht,
  Soll unser Seele sein!
Dann gattet liebend sich der Herzens-Güte
  Die Lilie mit ihrer Schönheits-Blüte.

[7.] Die Kamille

1. Ich kenn' ein Blümlein klein und zart, es ist von ganz besondrer Art, kein gleiches wird gefunden, kein gleiches wird gefunden. Ka-

-mil- len- blüm- lein ist's ge- nannt und wird ge- liebt im gan- zen Land, von Kran- ken und Ge- sun- den, von Kran- ken und Ge- sun- den.

2.
Den Magen-Schmerz, das Podagra,
Das Fieber und die Kolika
  //: Vertreiben die Kamillen. ://
Drum, Kranke, trinkt Kamillen-Tee!
Traun, dann verlässt euch jedes Weh
  //: Und trollt sich fort im Stillen. ://

4.
Zu Olims grauen Zeiten gab
Den Kranken sie schon Äskulap,
  //: Der Ahnherr der Dockteren ://
Und, glaubt es meinem Dichter-Schwur,
Es ging bei der Kamillen-Kur
  //: Kein Kranker ihm verloren! ://

3.
Den Frauen und den Mädchen ist
Dies Blümelein zu jeder Frist,
  //: Vor allen zu empfehlen, ://
Wenn Nerven-Krampf und Hysterie,
Und Herz-Gespann und Kopf-Weh sie
  //: Mit Höllen-Martern quälen. ://

5.
Was Doctor Brown auch immer spricht,
Gott Äskulap kurierte nicht
  //: Mit Portwein und mit Schinken. ://
Dafür gebot der alte Herr,
Sah in Gefahr die Kranken er,
  //: Kamillen-Tee zu trinken. ://

6.
Drum stimmet alle mit mir ein
Und lobt das holde Blümelein,
  //: Das wohltut in der Stille. ://
Vor ihm fliegt Meister Klapperbein,
Des könnt ihr alle Zeugen sein:
  //: Es lebe die Kamille! ://

[8.] Die Rose

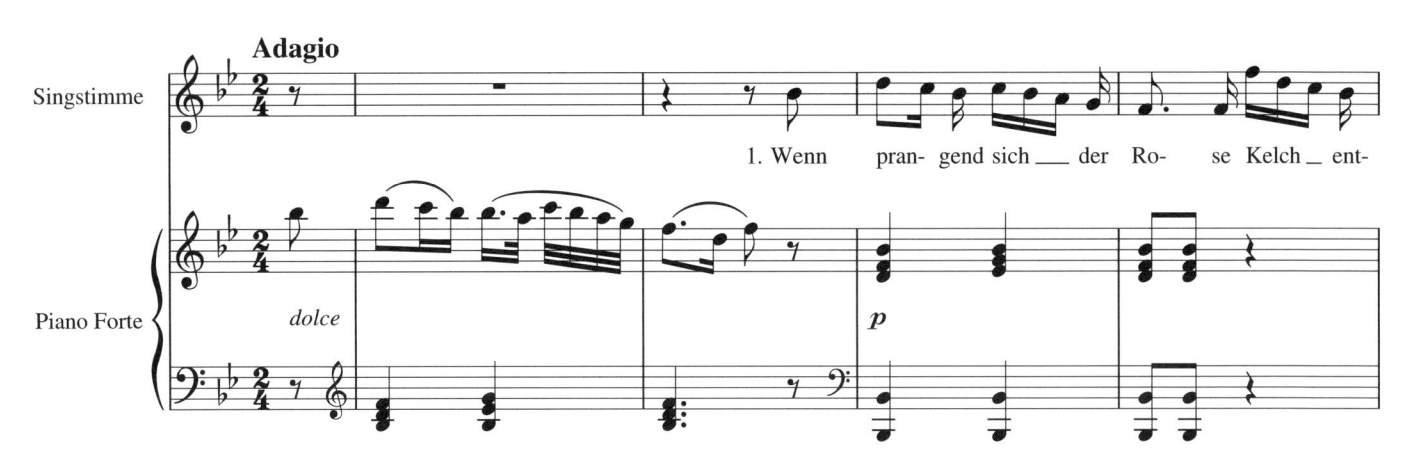

1. Wenn prangend sich der Rose Kelch entfaltet, winkt noch des Lenzes heit're Blütenzeit, von Floras Hand ward sie so schön gestaltet und liebevoll den Liebenden geweiht.

2.
Die Rose glühet auf der Jungfrau Wangen,
Wenn des Geliebten Mund um Liebe fleht
Und schüchtern sie, mit nie empfund'nem Bangen,
Was sie gefühlt, errötend ihm gesteht.

3.
Sie blühet in dem seid'nen Locken-Haare;
Vereinigt mit der Myrte dunklem Grün,
Führt sie als Braut der Jüngling zum Altare,
Wo Hymens Opfer-Flammen hell erglühn.

4.
Mit Rosen kränzt die Hoffnung unser Leben;
Die leere Zukunft glänzt in ihrem Licht
Wenn schöne Möglichkeiten uns umschweben,
Die ihre Hand in unser Schicksal flicht.

5.
Sie strahlt am Morgen, wenn Auroras Schleier
Umhüllt des Ätherslichte Purpur-Glut,
Und wenn Hyperion in stiller Feier
Am Abend sinkt in Thetis kühle Flut.

6.
Wir pflanzen Rosen auf den Grabes-Hügel,
Der uns'rer Lieben Hülle hier umschließt;
Es wehen der Erinn'rung Rosen-Flügel
Um uns, wo uns'rer Wehmut Thräne fließt.

7.
Sind ihre zarten Blätter einst gefallen,
Hat sich ihr Haupt zur Erde matt geneigt,
Wird nimmer doch der Rose Lob verhallen,
Die selbst im Welken keiner andern weicht!

[9.] Das Gänseblümchen

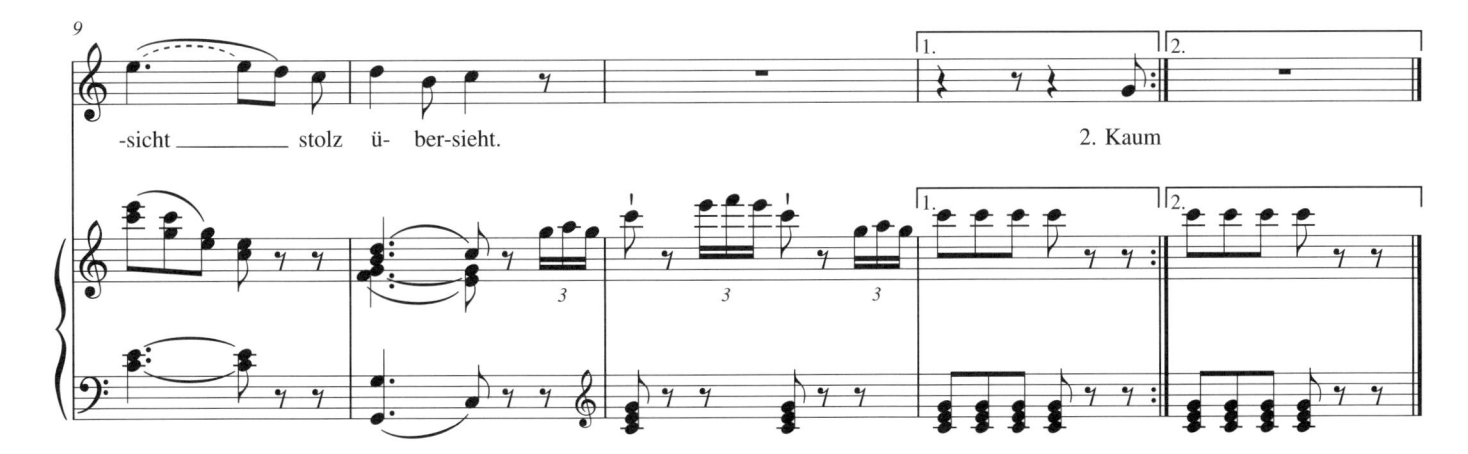

2.
Kaum schmilzt des rauhen Winters Schnee-Gewand
   Der Sonnenschein,
So trittst du schon, geführt von Floras Hand
   Ins Leben ein.

3.
Wenn kaum ein and'res Grün in der Natur
   Das Aug' entzückt,
Bist du es, holdes Blümchen, das die Flur
   Bescheiden schmückt.

4.
Du zauberst uns des Frühlings Lächeln her,
   Wenn überall
Verödet trauern, blütenlos und leer
   Noch Berg und Tal.

5.
Jetzt ist die Zeit, wo Jung und Alt dich liebt
   Und gern dich pflückt;
Doch bist du, wenn es schön're Blumen giebt,
   Nicht mehr beglückt.

6.
Dann sieht der Mensch dich mit Verachtung an;
   Des Spottes Ziel
Wirst du, die einst im Lenze Jedermann
   So wohl gefiel.

7.
So welkst du Arme, still und freudenlos,
   Vom Hohn geneckt,
Bis wieder liebend aus der Erde Schoß
   Der Lenz dich weckt.

[10.] Die Kornblume

Un poco adagio

1. Wer kennt sie nicht, die Blume, die umflossen von gold-'nen Halmen, lieblich blüht? In deren Kelch, hat er sich aufgeschlossen, ein dunkles Blau so schön erglüht? 2. Dort

auf der Flur, wo Ceres Saaten glänzen, habt ihr als Knaben sie gepflückt, und öfters euch mit selbst geflochtnen Kränzen die jugendliche Stirn geschmückt.

3.
Wenn sie verblüht, neigt sich der Ähre Segen,
  Zur Ernte reif, der Sichel hin,
Und fröhlich jauchzt der schönen Zeit entgegen
  Der Schnitter und die Schnitterin.

4.
Bald schimmert dann im bunten Ähren-Kranze,
  Ihr brennend Blau durchs falbe Stroh;
Mit ihr bekränzt, eilt hin zum Reihen-Tanze
  Die munt're Schar, beglückt und froh.

5.
Wie himmlisch glänzt ihr Blau in Mädchen-Augen,
  So hell und rein beim blonden Haar!
Es stellt der Blick, aus dem wir Wonne saugen,
  Des Herzens Blüten-Unschuld dar!

6.
Mag immer der Zyane Kelch verwelken,
  Erbleichen ihrer Farben Licht,
Wir lieben sie, wie Lilien und Nelken,
  Wie Rosen und Vergissmeinnicht!

[11.] Die Wasser-Lilie

1. Aus den Fluten keimt ein Blumen-Leben, üppig, wie aus Tellus Schoß, hervor, und aus blauen Wasser-Spiegeln heben goldne Blüten stolz ihr

Haupt—empor. Auf— der Wo-gen feuch-tem Pfad, schwimmt ihr wun-der-ba-res Blatt.

2.
Dort, wo oft die zartgeformten Glieder
Die Najad' im Gaukel-Tanz bewegt,
Wo des königlichen Schwans Gefieder
Alpen-Schnee durch Äther-Bläue trägt;
Dort im schilfumkränzten See
Wohnt die Wasser-Lilie!

3.
Wenn des Sommer-Abends Purpur-Gluten
Rosig glänzen auf dem Wellen-Schaum,
Und die Spiegel-Fläche dunkler Fluten
Wiederzeigt des Himmels weiten Raum,
Rudern wir auf leichtem Kahn
Durch die schöne Blumen-Bahn.

4.
Schweigend werfen Garn und Angel-Schnüre
Neben Wasser-Lilien wir hin,
Daß Betrug die sichern Fische führe
In die Netze, die wir um sie zieh'n.
Oft, wenn uns're List gelang,
Lohnt uns dann ein reicher Fang.

5.
So, gebohren auf den blauen Wogen,
Von der Welle zartem Schaum geküsst,
Blüht die Blume, her- und hingezogen
Von der Flut, die murmelnd sie umfließt,
Bis des rauhen Winters Hand
Auf sie wirft ein Eis-Gewand.

[12.] Die Hyazinthe

Andante moderato

1. In des Winters trüben Stunden seh'n am lodernden Kamin wir geselig uns verbunden, [ver- bun- den,]

still ____ die __ Hy- a- zin- the blüh'n.

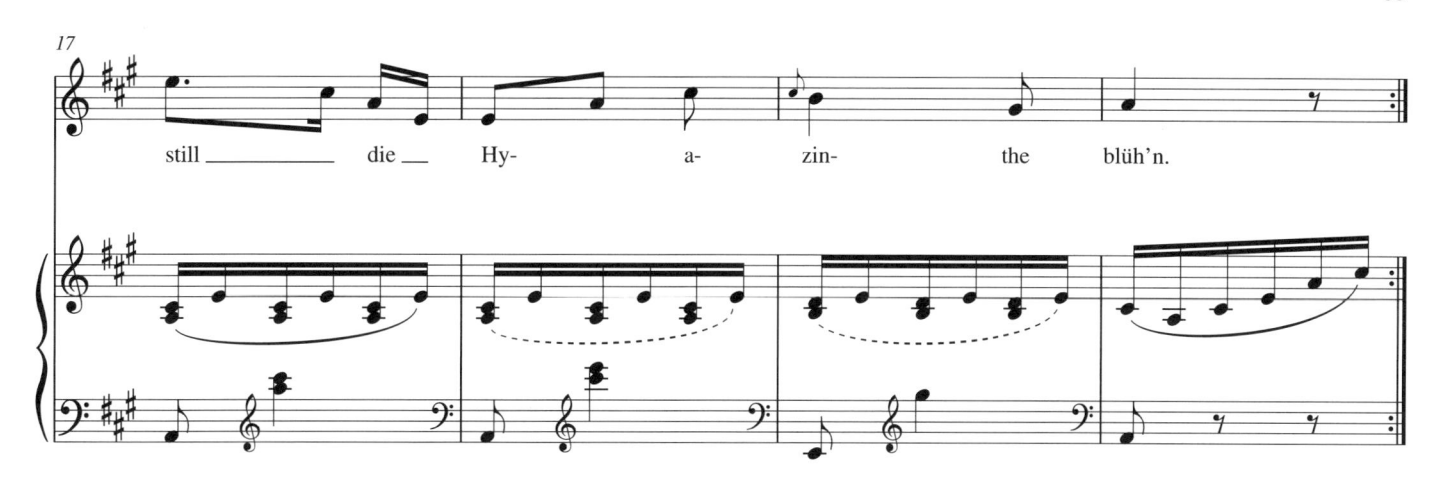

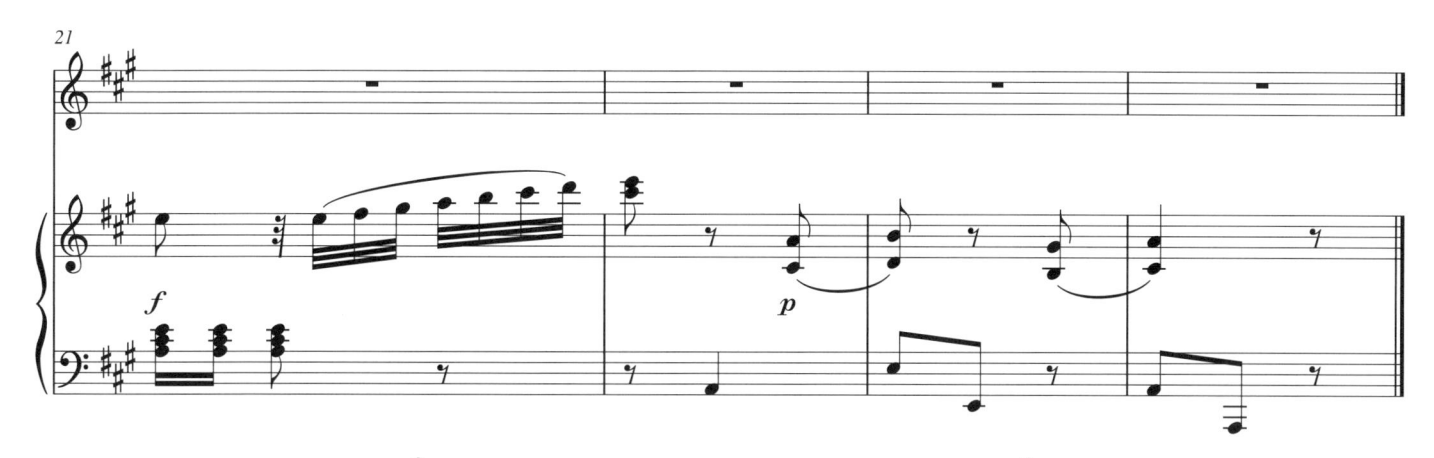

2.
Aus der Zwiebel strebt ihr Leben
   Schnell und wunderbar hervor;
Unterm Drohn des Nord-Sturms heben
   Ihre Blüten sich empor.

3.
Üppig ihre Kelche schwellen,
   Die des Gärtners Kunst gefüllt;
Zarter Ambra-Düfte Wellen,
   Schweben um sie leis' und mild.

4.
Proteus wechselnde Gestalten
   Gleiten über sie dahin,
Doch die Form hat sich erhalten
   Und der Wechsel wird Gewinn.

5.
Bald umziehen Rosen-Gluten,
   Bald des Himmels Blau ihr Haupt,
Bald hat Flora gar der Fluten
   Weißen Schaum für sie geraubt.

6.
Bald umstrahlt im gold'nen Scheine
   Brennend gelb ihr volles Blatt,
Bis im lieblichsten Vereine,
   Jeden Farben-Schmuck sie hat.

7.
Sorgsam pflegen wir das Leben,
   Das aus ihren Blumen lacht,
Denn die Hyazinthen geben
   Frühlings-Reiz der Winter-Nacht!

[13.] Die Mohn-Blume

2.
Kennt ihr sie wohl, die Blume, die, geweihet
Von Götter-Hand, uns diesen Trost verleihet,
Den Einzigen, dem wir nicht widersteh'n
Und ach, um den wir alle sehnend fleh'n?
Ihr kennet sie! Seht, liebend ließ Natur
Für uns erblühn den Mohn auf stiller Flur!

3.
Ihr kennt ihn doch? Wenn Krankheit oder Kummer
Verscheuchten einst von euch den sanften Schlummer,
Wenn eu'ren Sinn kein gold'ner Traum umschlich,
Und jeder Trost aus eu'rer Nähe wich:
Was gab euch Ruh? Dann warf von seinem Thron
Gott Phantasus auf euch den Schlummer-Mohn!

4.
Kennt ihr das Glück, das oft ein Traum gewährte,
Der das Gemüt mit zarter Hoffnung nährte,
Der schmeichelnd kos'te, wenn des Schicksals Hand
Uns Dornen in das Blüten-Leben wand?
Ihr kennt es wohl! Euch gab es öfters schon
Die Blume, die den Schlaf erzeugt, der Mohn!

[14.] Das Veilchen

Allegretto

1. Holdes Blümchen, sei willkommen auf der öden Flur! Du erwachst schon, wenn noch leise schlummert die Natur.

2.
Wenn noch feindlich
Hain und Hügel
  Decket Winternacht,
Und von Floras
Zarten Kindern
  Wenig sind erwacht.

3.
Eh' noch Phöbus
Feuerblicke
  Auf die Erde seh'n,
Eh' noch laue
Frühlings-Lüfte
  Um die Wangen weh'n.

4.
Schöne Hoffnung
Näher Freuden,
  Die der Lenz gewährt,
Hat, o Veilchen,
Dein Erscheinen
  Liebend uns beschert!

5.
Mädchen-Lächeln,
Jünglings-Wonnen
  Hast du mitgebracht,
Ahnend seh'n wir
Nun des Maies
  Volle Blüten-Pracht!

6.
Veilchen-Kränze
Reicht die Jungfrau
  Dem Geliebten hin,
Blumen-Sprache
Wählt die Treue,
  Lieb' verrät den Sinn!

7.
Schwärmerische
Augenblicke
  Reiner Seligkeit!
O erheitert
Oft hienieden
  Uns're Lebens-Zeit.

8.
Ewig blühe,
Liebes Veilchen
  Nie vergess' ich dein!
Treuer Liebe,
Schöner Hoffnung
  Sollst geweiht du sein!

[15.] Die Tulpe

1. Die Schönheit bleibt auch ohne Seele schön: wir weilen gern bei
2. Doch das Gefühl muss ojeden Reiz erhöhn! Bis in des Herzens

lieb- li- chen Ge- stal- ten; der glüh'n- de Blick
tief- ver- borg'- ne Fal- ten dringt sei- ne Macht

gern bei lieb- li- chen Ge- stal- ten; der glüh'n- de
Her- zens tief- ver- borg'- ne Fal- ten dringt sei- ne

Blick will e- wig nicht er- kal- ten, die
Macht mit zau- b'ri- schen Ge- wal- ten, und

will e- wig nicht er- kal- ten, die
mit zau- b'ri- schen Ge- wal- ten, und

zar- te Form be- wun- dernd an- zu- seh'n.
lässt dort sanft den Göt- ter- O- dem

zar- te Form be- wun- dernd an- zu- seh'n.
lässt dort sanft den Göt- ter- O- dem

weh'n. 3. Schön bist du,

weh'n.

Tul- pe! Schön bist du, Tul- pe!

3. Schön bist du, Tul- pe!

Dei- ner Rei- ze

Dei- ner Rei- ze Schim- mer er-

Schim- mer er- hellt mit stol- zer Pracht den Blu- men- Hain.

-hellt mit stol- zer Pracht den Blu- men- Hain.

Doch kön- nen wir dir nur Bewund'- rung weih'n.

Doch kön- nen wir dir nur Bewund'- rung weih'n.

4. Drum glaubt es, Mäd- chen! Drum glaubt es,

4. Drum glaubt es,

Mäd- chen! Blo- ße Schön- heit nim- mer wird

Mäd- chen!

euch ____ der Lie- be dau- ernd Glück ver-

Blo- ße Schön- heit nim- mer wird euch der

-leihn, denn

Lie- be dau- ernd Glück ver- leihn, denn

wisst, der Mann liebt Schönheit nie allein, denn

wisst, der Mann liebt Schönheit nie allein, denn

wisst, der Mann liebt Schönheit nie allein, liebt

wisst, der Mann liebt Schönheit nie allein, liebt

Schönheit nie allein.

Schönheit nie allein.

[16.] Der Lavendel

1. Ein Liedchen dir zu singen, Lavendel-Blümelein, muss traun, soll es gelingen, kurz und erbaulich sein. Dich streut die Göttinn Mode verschwendrisch durch die Luft, im

Le- ben und im To- de flieht nie dein Bal- sam- duft.

2.
Lavendel-Düfte wehen
   In Logen und Parterr,
Wo wir Beaumonde sehen
   Um Herrn und Damen her.
Beim Ball, bei Maskeraden,
   Im raschen Walzer-Flug,
Ja selbst auf Promenaden
   Küsst uns dein Wohl-Geruch.

3.
So manches holde Weibchen
   Durch dich süß parfümiert,
Ward wie ein Lirres Täubchen
   Im finstern aufgespürt.
Dein Spiritus beseelet
   So manchen dummen Tropf;
Du gibst den Geist, der fehlet,
   Dem leeren Titus-Kopf!

4.
Beaten und Hetären,
   Schön, hässlich, warm und kalt,
Sie halten dich in Ehren;
   Dich liebet Jung und Alt!
Dich musst' ich hier besingen,
   Du holdes Blümelein!
Mag auch mein Lied verklingen,
   Du wirst unsterblich sein!

Die Blumen und der Schmetterling

Text by Karl Friedrich Müchler (1763–1857)
Music by Friedrich Heinrich Himmel (1765–1814)

[1.] Zueignung an Deutschlands Töchter

Froh, tändelnd

1. Euch ihr Guten, Euch ihr Schönen, die ihr zart wie Blüten seid, Euch sei

unter sanften Tönen dieser Blumenkranz geweiht. Aus dem Mutterschoß der Erde sproßten sie an Anmut reich: deutsche Mädchen, jedes werde diesen hol- den Blu- men gleich.

2.
Wie das Veilchen, blüht bescheiden,
   Wie das Maienblümelein
Frost erduldet, traget Leiden,
   Hüllend Euch in Demut ein.
In der Lilien weißem Kleide,
   Wie der Rose Knospe schön,
Mögt Ihr einst im Festgeschmeide
   An dem Brautaltare steh'n.

3.
Auf der Pfirsichwange male
   Die Gesundheit Rosenlicht;
Aus dem off'nen Auge strahle
   Sanftmut wie Vergissmeinnicht.
Fest wie Ephen rankt, umgürte
   Sittsamkeit die keusche Brust;
Dann nur blühet Hymens Mirte
   Euch zu dauerhafter Lust.

[2.] Das Schneeglöckchen

Mit ruhigem Vortrag

1. Wenn noch Eis die Flu- ren drückt, sich noch kei- ne Schwal- be zei- get, noch kein Halm der Erd' ent- stei- get, und kein Knösp- chen freund- lich nickt, und kein Knösp- chen freund- lich nickt, hebst du schon dein Haupt em- por, zeigst du rein wie Win- ter- flok- ken dei- ne zar- ten wei- ßen

Glok- ken, blühst du __ schon im hell'- sten Flor, blühst _ du __ schon im hell'- sten Flor.

          2.
Holde Lenzverkünderin,
Du des Frühlings Erstgebor'ne,
Von der Unschuld Auserkohr'ne,
  Bildlich zeigend ihren Sinn.
  Sanft erduldest du den Sturm,
Und der Schnee muss in Gefahren,
Ist er gleich dein Feind, dich wahren;
  Dich zerstört kein böser Wurm.

          3.
Liebliche, dies ist dein Bild:
Mädchenunschuld, fromm, bescheiden
Blühet schöner unter Leiden;
  Das Gemüt macht Kummer mild.
  Sieh! so strahlen unterm Schnee
Heller dieses Blümchens Blätter;
Fröhlich blüht's in Sturm und Wetter
  Und sprießt mutig in die Höh'.

          4.
Bleibe diesem Blümchen gleich:
Such' in trüben rauhen Zeiten
Fried' und Freude zu verbreiten;
  Schaff' um dich ein Himmelreich.
  Es steht ganz in deiner Macht,
Wenn du im Verborg'nen blühest,
Und das Gift der Anmut fliehest,
  Schnöden Stolz und eitle Pracht.

[3.] Das Veilchen

1. Von dunk- lem Laub um- schlos- sen blüht heim- lich auf der Au, wo

wild nur Grä- ser spro- ßen, ein Blüm- chen dun- kel- -blau, _____ ein Blüm- chen dun- kel- blau, _____ ein Blüm- chen dun- kel- blau.

D.S.

2.
Es prangt nicht stolz im Garten
    Und keines Künstlers Hand
Müht sich es treu zu warten
    Mit Vorsicht und Verstand.

3.
Es schimmert nie in Kränzen,
    Die leere Prunksucht flicht,
Es strebt auch nie zu glänzen
    Durch bunter Blätter Licht.

4.
Nur einsam und bescheiden,
    Sich keines Werts bewußt,
Schmückt es der Hirten Weiden,
    Der Schäfferinnen Brust.

5.
Des Leichtsinns Tritte schweben
    Vorüber, wo es steht,
Und kürzen roh sein Leben,
    Weil es nicht keck sich bläht.

6.
Doch durch die Frühlingslüfte,
    Wenn es versteckt auch blüht,
Verstreut es Balsamdüfte,
    Wo es kein Auge sieht.

7.
O, es ist zu beneiden
    In seinem Kindersinn;
Der Einfalt reine Freuden
    Gewähren nur Gewinn.

8.
Von allen Blumen wählen
    Zu einem Lieblingsstrauß
Sich fromme Mädchenseelen
    Das holde Veilchen aus.

9.
Es ruht an ihren Herzen,
    Sinkt dort in süße Ruh,
Und schließet ohne Schmerzen
    Den Kelch auf ewig zu.

[4.] Die Myrte

2.
Dich Zarte schuf
Auf Amors Ruf
　Einst Flora für Hymens Entzücken,
Der Jungfrau Haar
Am Brautaltar
　Mit schimmernden Knospen zu schmücken.

3.
Stets bleibst du grün,
Und dauernd blüh'n
　Die Blüten der bräutlichen Krone;
Was Liebe flicht
Verwelket nicht;
　Dich schützet allmächtig Dione.

4.
Ihr Töchter Teuts!
Den höchsten Reiz
　Verleiht Euch die Krone von Myrten,
Wenn froh und frei
Euch Lieb' und Treu
　Die Stirne der Unschuld umgürten.

[5.] Die Narzisse

Schwermütig, doch nicht zu langsam

1. Horch, was tönt vom Fel- sen- han- ge trau- rig dort am Was- ser- fall, gleich dem kla- gen- den Ge- san- ge der ver- lass'- nen Nach- ti- gall, der ver- lass'- nen Nach- ti- gall.

2.
Echo seufzet, die Verschmähte,
Ach, die für Narziss entbrannt,
Schwärmerisch um Liebe flehte,
Doch nie Gegenliebe fand.

3.
Er bleibt kalt wie Meeresfluten,
Höhnend ihren zarten Sinn,
Und verzehrt von ew'gen Gluten
Welkt die Liebende dahin.

4.
Doch die mitleidsvollen Götter,
Fühlend ihres Busens Pein,
Wandeln, als gerechte Retter,
Die Verschmachtende in Stein.

5.
Und sie werden Echos Rächer,
Der Olymp hält strengen Rat:
Schrecklich büße der Verbrecher
Seine rohe Freveltat.

6.
Einst im klaren Bach erblicket
Er sein Bild mit hoher Lust,
Und der Gott der Liebe drücket
Gift'ge Pfeil' in seine Brust.

7.
Ihn ergreift ein töricht Schmachten,
Wahnsinn dunkelt sein Gemüt,
Und ihn züchtigt das Verachten,
Daß er für sich selber glüht.

8.
So, der Eitelkeit zum Raube,
Schließt sich ungeliebt sein Lauf,
Und es sprießt aus seinem Staube
Eine Blume warnend auf.

[6.] Das Vergissmeinnicht

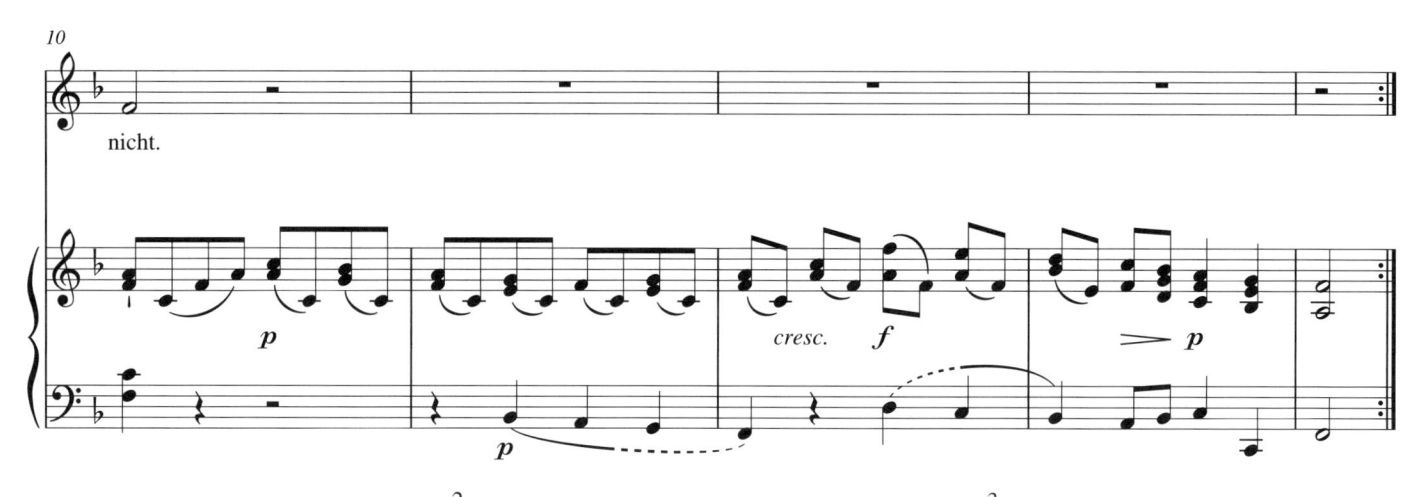

nicht.

2.
Schimmernd, wie des Äthers Bläue
  Wenn ihn kein Gewölk umflicht,
Ist es ein Symbol der Treue,
  Das zum Herzen tröstend spricht.

3.
Mild, wie Deiner Augen Sterne,
  Wie verklärter Unschuld Licht,
Ruft es warnend aus der Ferne:
  O, vergiss, vergiss mein nicht!

4.
Wann der Trennung Zähren fließen,
  Folgsam dem Gebot der Pflicht,
Soll es deinem Pfad entsprießen,
  Bittend: ach! vergiss mein nicht!

5.
Doch, geliebte Seele, höre,
  Was aus jedem Blättchen spricht:
Ach, sein Tau ist eine Zähre,
  Und sie seufz't: vergiss mein nicht!

[7.] Die Palme

Held den Lor- beer prei- sen, der um des blut'- gen Schwer- tes Ei- sen nach lan- gem

2.
Des Lorbeers dunkle Blätter sprießen
Nur dort, wo Kummertränen fließen,
   Wo schuldlos Blut die Fluren düngt;
Die Palme wächst auf stiller Haide,
Wo zu der Einfalt reiner Freude
   Die Friedensgöttin lächelnd winkt.

3.
Der Zwietracht Furien, wo die wüten
Verdorren schnell des Lebensblüten,
   Erstirbt des Herzens Zartgefühl;
Nur wo sich Fried' und Freude gatten,
Nur in der edlen Palme Schatten
   Lacht, süße Liebe, dein Asyl.

[8.] Die Rose

Gemässigt, doch heiter

1. Bild der jung-fräu-li-chen Tu-gend, die in ho-her Scham er-glüht, Bild der Schön-heit, Bild der Ju-gend, dir, o Ros'! er-tön' ein Lied, dir, o Ros'! er-tön' ein Lied.

2.
Flora schloss, um dich zu schützen
  Deine Knosp' in Dornen ein,
Um der Frevler Hand zu ritzen,
  Die mit frechem Raub dir dräu'n.

3.
Deine Purpurblüten glänzen
  In der Charitinnen Haar,
Und mit deinen vollen Kränzen
  Schmücket Hymen den Altar.

4.
Zarte Liebesgötter kosen
  Um der Knospen süßen Mund,
Und auf einem Thron von Rosen
  Herrscht Cyther' in Amathunt.

5.
Sanfter Weste Schmeichellüfte,
  Wenn die Knospen dir entblüh'n,
Rauben dir die Balsamdüfte,
  Die durch deine Lauben zieh'n.

6.
Aller Haine Sänger preisen
  Dich, du Blumenkönigin,
Du umschlingst den Kelch des Weisen,
  Und die Brust der Schäferin.

7.
Ämsig Honig suchend, gaukelt
  Hin die Bien' an deine Brust,
Und auf deinen Blättern schaukelt
  Sich der Schmetterling mit Lust.

8.
Dich bewundernd, weilt die Quelle,
  Wo dein Liebreiz sich enthüllt,
Und in jeder leichten Welle
  Spiegelt sich dein schönes Bild.

9.
Aber ach, nach kurzen Stunden
  Ist der zarten Blätter Pracht,
Ist der Zauber hingeschwunden,
  Der aus jedem Knöspchen lacht.

10.
Zephyr eilt mit raschen Flügeln
  Den verwelkten Blättern nach,
Keine Purpurblüten spiegeln
  Sich im klaren Silberbach.

11.
Vogel, Schmetterling und Biene
  Flattern, suchend dich, umher,
Doch verwandelt ist die Bühne;
  Du, o Rose, bist nicht mehr!

[9.] Wechselgesang der Blumen

Fröhlich, doch nicht zu geschwind

1. Wir Kinder des Lenzen, wir keimen und sprießen im Garten und Hain, auf grünenden Wiesen zu duftenden Kränzen uns lieblich zu reih'n, uns lieblich zu reih'n.

2. Wir krönen die Musen mit Blüten, und fröhnen Cytherens Altar. Wir zieren der Schönen, der Schönen sanft wallenden Busen, leicht flatterndes Haar, wir zieren der Schönen sanft wallenden Bu-

-sen, der Schö- nen sanft wal- len- den Bu- sen, leicht flat- tern- des Haar.

Ruhig und sanft
Solo
Das Veilchen

3. Ich lie- be nur Triff- ten, mich nährt nur der Mor- gen mit la- ben- dem Tau; ich

blü- he ver- bor- gen, doch würz' ich mit Düf- ten die la- chen- de

Au, _____ doch würz' _____ ich mit Düf- ten die

la- chen- de __ Au! _____

Sanft und ruhig
Das Vergissmeinnicht

4. An ländlicher Hütte umgürt' ich die Quelle und brüste mich nicht; an heimlicher Stelle entkeim' ich und bitte, und bitte, vergiss, ach! vergiss mein nicht, und bitte, vergiss, ach! vergiss mein nicht!

Leicht
Die Myrte

5. Wir krän- zen die Haa- re der schmach- ten- den Bräu- te, der Keusch- heit Sym- bol, _____ der Jüng- lin- ge Beu- te an

Hy- mens Al- tar, an Hy- mens Al- ta- re, ihr schön- stes I- dol, an Hymens Al- ta- re, ihr schön- stes I- dol.

Gemässigt, doch heiter

Die Rose

6. Zur Für- stin, zur Für- stin der Bee- te er- nann- te mich Flo- ra als A- mor mich nahm; mich ma- let Au- ro- ra mit lieb- li- cher Rö- te, ein Sinn- bild der Scham, ein Sinn- bild der Scham.

(sehr bedeutend)

Fröhlich, doch nicht zu geschwind

Alle

7. Wir al- le, wir grü- nen in I- ris Ge- schmei- de, in kunst- lo- ser Zier, der Schön- heit zu die- nen; der Un- schuld zur Freu- de wir hul- di- gen ihr, wir hul- di- gen ihr.

119
Wir
122
hul- di-gen ihr, wir hul- di-gen
tutti piano
125
ihr.
cresc.

[10.] Der Schmetterling

1. Von Knosp' auf Knospe schwebend, vom Duft der Blüten lebend, sich badend in des Äthers Blau, sich badend in des Äthers Blau, bestrahlt vom Sonnenspiegel, hebt er die goldnen Flügel, und

2.
Den schönen Lenz verkündend,
Der Liebe Wonn' empfindend,
   Auf Myrt' und auf Orangenbaum,
Und unter flücht'gen Küssen,
Auf Veilchen und Narzissen,
   Umgaukelt ihn des Lebenstraum.

3.
Doch wenn die Blätter fallen,
Des Herbstes Nebel wallen,
   Beschließt sich auch sein kurzer Lauf,
Sein Grab ein Kelch der Rose;
Froh steigt die fessellose,
   Verklärte Psyche himmelauf.

4.
Dies' ist des Sängers Leben;
Viel' holde Träum' umschweben
   Den reinen, frommen Kindersinn.
Weit von der Heimat Hügeln
Trägt ihn sein Geist auf Flügeln
   Ins Reich der Phantasieen hin.

5.
Die Nachtigall, die Blume
Führt ihn zum Heiligtume,
   Das nur dem Reinen sich erschließt;
Enträtselt wird ihm vieles
In Taumel des Gefühles,
   Wenn süßer Wehmut Thräne fließt.

6.
Der Erde Druck entbunden,
Blickt in geweihten Stunden
   Sein Seherauge himmelwärts,
Gleichfühlenden verkündet
Sein Lied, was er empfindet,
   Und flieht die Jugend, bricht sein Herz!

*Die Temperamente bei dem
Verluste der Geliebten*

Text by Wilhelm Gubitz (1786–1870)
Music by Carl Maria von Weber (1786–1826)

[1.] Der Leichtmütige

1. Lust ent- floh und hin ist hin! Blan- da will mich nicht mehr lie- ben!
Ich wär ihr, so wahr ich bin! noch acht Ta- ge treu ge- blie- ben, kam ihr'
Hoch- zeit nicht zu Sinn; da- für hat mich Gott be- wahrt!
Le- be wohl, mein Kind! ich wan- d're schon zu

2. Schei- den macht mein Herz nicht schwer; wei- nen kann ich nicht noch flu- chen.
Doch da kommt ein Mäd- chen her; schnell muss ich mein Glück ver- su- chen, oh- ne
Lieb' ist all mir leer! Sprö- des Kind, wirf ab dein Joch,
lass' von Him- mels- kost mich nip- pen, eh' wir

frischer Liebesfahrt! Heute die und dann die and're: das _____ ist _____
bleichen, lebe noch! Mädchen reiche mir die Lippen, denn _____ ge-

so _ die _ rech- te _ Art!
-küsst wirst du _ ja _ doch!

3. Sieh' man darf sich im Genuss für _____ versehnte _ Träume _ rächen.

Lass der Seelen Genius aus dem Schlag der Herzen sprechen:

Dop-pel- spra-che ist der Kuss! Ah, du magst mich nicht? Nun gut! kann ich's auch nicht gern er- tra- gen, halt' ich doch mir fri- schen Mut; mor- gen will ich wie- der fra- gen, hast viel- -leicht dann wär- mer Blut.

4. Lie- ben muss man schö- nes Kind! Soll der- einst ich see- lig wer- den, was schon hier recht gut be- ginnt frag' ich gleich den Herrn der Er- den, ob die En- gel weib- lich sind! Wenn er et- wa "Nein!" nun spricht, sag' ich keck und voll Ver- trau- en: "Herr, dein

Reich gefällt mir nicht, denn ein Himmel ohne Frauen ist die Sonne ohne Licht!"

5. Hebt die Treue hoch empor, quälend Glück will ich euch schenken. Schwatzt nur mir Moral nicht vor; bei der

Lie- be will ich den- ken wenn ich den Ver- stand ver- lor.

Al- le We- sen huld'- gen ihr:

con anima *scherzando*
Lie- be ist das Herz vom Le- ben, nur durch

Lie- be sind wir hier, Lie- be will ich wie- der ge- ben:

137

[2.] Der Schwermütige

Lie- be Klän-ge schwan- gen sie- gend mich zum Him- mel ein.

3. Ach, die Won-nen all' zer- klan- gen, e- wig kann nicht Früh- ling sein! Traum und Treu- e sind ver-gan-gen, aus-ge-löscht der Heil'- gen- schein!

4. Fern von ihr muss ich ver- ban- gen, von der
Welt ist nichts mehr mein; glü- hend fas- set all' Ver- lan- gen nur der Hoff- nung Lei- chen- stein,
nur der Hoff- nung Lei- chen- stein. 5. Doch zum To- des En- gel
dran- gen mei- nes Her- zens Oed' und Pein; lie- bend

bald von Erd' um- fan- gen wird der Him- mel wie- der mein, wird der Him- mel wie- der mein.

[3.] Der Liebewütige

Allegro furioso

1. "Ver- ra- ten! Ver- schmä- het! Wer dräng- te mich aus? Auf! Die- ner, um- spä- het heut'

[sempre staccato]

Abend ihr Haus; und wagt zur Megäre ein Einz'ger den Blick, so fragt: wer er wäre? Und brecht ihm's Genick!"

2. Don Marco trieb alle recht wachsam zu sein, dann stürmt' ihn die

Gal- le Berg auf und Tal ein. Er fluch- te nun tra- bend hin- ein in die Luft und pas- ste am A- bend noch selbst auf den Schuft.

3. Mit Hast spi- o- nie- ret das Die- ner- volk stumm;

Don Mar- co be- gie- ret die Tü- ren rings um. Wie schlei- chend und sin- nig im Däm- mern er wallt, ge- bie- ten recht in- nig sechs Fäu- ste ihm: "Halt!" 4. "Wer sind Sie?" nach

Re- gel klingt dies' zum Ge- zerr. "Ihr Lüm- mel! Ihr Fle- gel! Ich bin eu- er Herr!" Und wie ihn am To- ben die Die- ner er- kannt, spricht Kla- ra von o- ben: "Das ist ja schar- mant!" 5. "Die Ei- fer- sucht horch! det schon Söldner heran; der Argwohn ermordet was Liebe gewann: drum hab' ich vernünftig den Leichtsinn bereut; nun quälen Sie künftig sich selber gescheut!"

Tempo primo

6. Nichts halfen Sonette von Gram und von Grab,

da riss er vom Bret- te die Flin- te her--ab; er jag- te mit Ra- sen zum Wal- de hin--aus, und schoss ei- nen Ha- sen zum lär- men- den Schmaus.

[4.] Der Gleichmütige

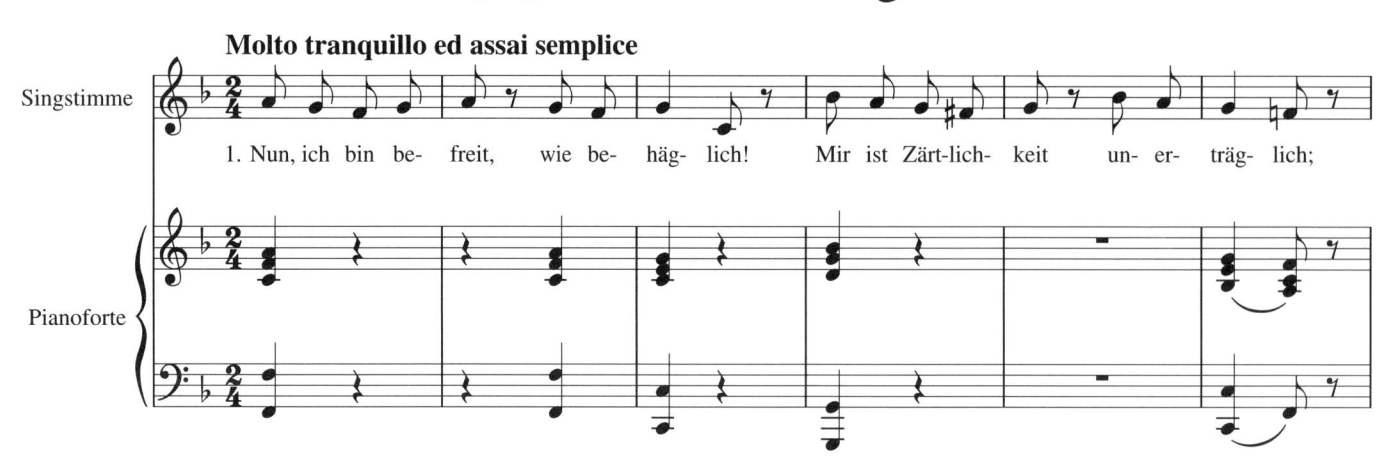

Molto tranquillo ed assai semplice

1. Nun, ich bin be- freit, wie be- häg- lich! Mir ist Zärt-lich- keit un- er- träg- lich; treibt sie Kei- ne lau, werd' ich oh- ne Frau ru- hig alt und grau.

2.
Hätt' sie wohl gemocht
 So bei Festen.
Plumperpuddings kocht'
 Sie am besten.
Doch die Lust ward matt,
Denn am Ende hatt'
Ich die Puddings satt.

3.
Sie verliebte sich
 Einst beim Essen;
Alles ging und ich
 War vergessen.
Weil ich köstlich schlief,
Bis sie wach mich rief
Und ich mit ihr lief.

4.
Sie gefiel mir gut
 Bei dem Wandern,
Und weil man gern tut
 Wie die Andern,
Bot ich mich zum Mann,
Und sie nahm es an,
Eh' ich mich besann.

5.
Doch das gab ein Joch
 Und ein Laufen!
Was nach Ausland roch
 Musst' ich kaufen,
Und Tag aus Tag ein,
Und bei Mondenschein,
Auch noch zärtlich sein.

6.
Ohne Ruh' und Rast
 Musst' ich küssen;
Das ist Höllenlast,
 Küssen müssen!
Drum recht eisig hart
Hab' ich sie genarrt,
Bis mein Wunsch mir ward.

7.
Aus dem Hause warf
 Sie mich gestern,
Und beliebte scharf
 Noch zu lästern:
"Hätt' ich nicht viel Geld,
Wär ich Schüsselheld
Gar nichts nutz der Welt!"

8.
Doch mich macht der Hieb
 Nimmer grämlich,
Denn die Liebe lieb'
 Ich bequemlich;
Treibt sie Keine lau,
Werd' ich ohne Frau
Ruhig alt und grau.

Critical Report

Editorial Methods

In general, aspects that do not alter the performance of the music (barlines, for example) have been modernized; aspects that might influence performance (such as irregular beaming) have been retained. I have chosen not to translate the following music into a fully modern edition for two reasons. First, I have tried to respect the sources' notation, limiting my role to clarifying what might be confusing, correcting errors, suggesting solutions to problems (such as discrepancies between parallel passages or how to modify scansion for subsequent verses), and noting quirks and subtleties that might easily be overlooked. Second, composers' writing was influenced by their orthography and translating their systems to our own risks losing subtleties of meaning that do not translate well.

Format

Titles, subtitles, and song titles follow the sources, except that periods have been removed. Only the twelve songs of *Die Jahreszeiten* and the original five songs of *Die Farben* (using "No. 1," etc.) are numbered in the sources; all other numbers have been added in brackets. The songs in *Die Farben* have been ordered as discussed in "Poets, Composers, Publishers, and Cycles" (see table 7).

Placement, spelling, and alignment of tempo and performance indications have been modernized. Only currently standard abbreviations have been retained; the rest have been spelled out. Spelling has been regularized and non-abbreviation periods deleted. Tempo indications have been regularized, so that initial words are capitalized and subsequent words are in lowercase; performance indications have been changed to all lowercase.

Braces, brackets, barlines, and repeat marks have been modernized. First, second, and third endings have been written out where necessary, with any attendant repeat bars added; original markings thereby replaced are removed. *Dal segno* instructions and markings have been converted to *D.S.*—placed above staves—and modern signs have been employed. Repeat marks have been added to final bars of songs that have multiple verses but no internal repeats or *dal segno* directives. Midmeasure repeat marks in *Sechszehn Blumen* have been shifted onto barlines and consequent changes made to other affected measures. Tag measures for the third verse of "Winternachtleben" in *Die Jahreszeiten,* indicated in the source by "Vers 3" written over the repeat marks of measure 13, have been written out as mm. 17–20 in the edition.

The page numbers of the original cycles reflect their individual publication formats and have been superseded by the ordering of cycles in the present edition. Measure numbers have been added.

Clef changes are numerous in this music. Most have been retained, but awkward changes have been omitted or moved for ease in reading and reported in critical notes. Clef changes meant to emphasize aspects of the music are discussed in "Notes to Performers." Treble clefs specified for tenor voice(s) have been silently emended to treble-8 clefs. Right- and left-hand piano parts have been separated into their own staves. Omissions and errors in the order and placement of key signatures have been emended.

Part names in the sources have been retained, except that non-abbreviation periods have been removed and orthographic shorthands (the macron over "m" to indicate "mm" and "u." for "und") have been realized. Added part names are enclosed in brackets; all other changes are reported in critical notes. In "Wechselgesang der Blumen," part names such as "Alle" and "Das Veilchen," etc., which precede the voice's underlaid text in the source, are placed above the vocal staff.

Notation

Except as explained below, notation appears as in the sources and all editorial deletions are reported in critical notes. Editorial slurs, ties, and hairpins are dashed; editorial articulations are placed in parentheses; and editorial letter dynamics are set in bold type; all other editorial additions are enclosed in brackets.

Stemming and Beaming

Note stems have been modernized. Stemming that denotes contrapuntal voice leading or a chorale style has been retained. Occasionally, a source alternates between stemming contrapuntal voices together and apart, or, in the piano, between common stemming and opposing stems; these passages have been regularized in the edition.

Beaming in music of this period is somewhat problematic. It no longer consistently denotes slurring, nor does it yet consistently denote metric division: it lies somewhere in between, its use and meaning in transition. Some exceptions from modern standardized beaming are the result of either orthographic considerations—keeping the beams in the staff, for example—or of the casual editing typical of publications geared for popular consumption.

A great many exceptions, however, seem musically significant. In Bornhardt's "Januar" of *Die zwölf Monate*, for example, compare beats 3–4 of measure 3 to beats 1–2 of measures 26 and 30. Is measure 3 an anomaly, or does the irregular beaming emphasize the contrast between the disjunct *forte* opening and the smoothly repeated *piano* chords? Notice also how the break in beaming of "Januar's" measure 10, beat 1, reinforces the separation of phrases. Finally, notice the final measures of the same piece, in which the tail of a motive repeats to lead into a cadence. Beaming contributes nuances of interpretation: the three eighth-note pickups in measure 33 are beamed together; the beaming in measures 34–35 reinforces the aural spaces between beats 1 and 2 and connects the group on beats 3–4; and in measure 36, the tail of the motive is suddenly beamed differently, signalling the cadence. In fact, a change in beaming—as with a change in articulation—often signals a cadence.

Beaming may suggest an intermediate level of connection, somewhere between *legato* and *détaché* notes; it almost certainly suggests a subtle grouping that conveys meaning. This reading carries widespread implications affecting every nuance of phrasing and touch, from the shaping of long phrases to the minute emphases and separations that distinguish beats.

The information currently available on orthography of the early nineteenth century indicates only that the system was in transition; it does not suffice to distinguish between orthographic beaming and beaming that is musically significant. Nor does it clarify the beginning and end of that transition. Because research is still inconclusive, the beaming in this edition appears as in the sources, inconsistencies included (unless cited in critical notes), in an effort to provide material for further research. Cross-beams that span less than a tenth, however, have been changed to straight beams.

Slurs, Ties, and Articulations

Where figures have both ties and slurs, the slurs have been extended to include the ties. Most vocal slurs in the sources duplicate declamatory beaming; these have been omitted. Declamatory slurs that connect unbeamed notes and slurs that appear to indicate interpretation have been retained.

The notation of slurs and ties has been modernized. Where necessary, ties are extended tacitly to connect the relevant notes. The occurrence and meaning of slurs, however, is another matter. Even more than beaming, slurring implies nuances in touch and emphasis that can transform the same group of notes from one gesture to another. Compare measures 2–3 with measures 32–34 in Bornhardt's "Januar." Although both involve three eighth-note upbeats leading to downbeats, they present very different gestures. In measures 2–3, the slur crosses the barline—unusual in itself—and closes on a downbeat, which leads smoothly into the repeated chords, thereby suspending the emphatic beat set up in the opening measures and underscoring the two-faced nature of the "Month of Lies." In measures 32–34, the even, strongly metrical weak-strong-weak-strong reestablishes the beat following a fermata and stresses the downbeat, emphasizing the crucial word "wahr" and underscoring its irony: is the text true, or is it only another example of January's lies?

These excerpts reveal how crucial slurring is to the performance and interpretation of this music. Unfortunately, slurring is even more irregular than beaming. In Bornhardt's "Mai," for example, the upbeat slur that sets off the sigh so well in measures 2–3 is absent in the rest of the song, and the slur on the sigh motive, which seems so critical to its character, disappears in the postlude. The sources often employ a notational shorthand, called initial markings in this edition, where the composer indicates articulation for the first occurence of a passage, sometimes even just for one part, expecting the performers to apply those marks where appropriate. Identifying "where appropriate" is often difficult. Consequently, most slurs appear as in the sources.

Staccatos, accents, etc. are used even more irregularly than slurs and can only be dealt with case by case. In general, the character of a motive is determined by its initial markings. The disappearance of *legato* and especially *staccato* marks often signals the arrival of cadences; I have retained this feature as an integral part of the style. Staccato strokes and staccato dots have been retained as found in the sources except as noted in the critical note to "Der Leichtmütige" (m. 6).

Dynamics

Source dynamics appear in bold italics; editorial dynamics, in bold regular font. In general, dynamics are used more as signposts for special events than as a map. There has been no attempt to complete a map of the dynamics; performers must interpret specifics from the overall view. Rare in vocal parts, dynamics for singers are discussed in "Notes to Performers."

In piano parts, duplicate dynamics (one for each hand) have been omitted and the remaining ones placed between the staves. Most dynamic marks alternate *forte* and *piano,* indicating level shifts rather than gradual changes. Piano preludes usually begin *forte* or *mezzo forte,* dynamics that become *piano* or *mezzo piano* when the voice enters. *Mezzo, fortissimo,* and *pianissimo* markings are few in the sources, and quite a number of songs indicate no dynamics at all because there is no deviation from the "normal," i.e., *mezzo,* range. Spelling and abbreviations have been modernized.

Hairpin crescendo or decrescendo marks appear in the sources in a variety of uses: (1) as a gradual dynamic change, as is common today, that can pertain either to both hands (Himmel, *Die Blumen und der Schmetterling,* "Das Schneeglöckchen," m. 10) or to just one (mm. 3–4), depending on placement; (2) to indicate the stressed-unstressed articulation associated with the sigh motive

(m. 2); and (3) as the rapid decay of a held chord, usually marked sforzando (m. 18). In this edition, the latter is referred to as a decay decrescendo. There is a clear distinction between uses: the gradual dynamic change covers several notes; the stressed-unstressed sigh articulation occurs between two notes of one part; and the decay decrescendo follows a held chord, ending before the next note. All three uses have been retained. Although decay decrescendos cannot be performed, per se, on the piano, they serve as a reminder to refrain from sustaining the chord with a pedal. More importantly, the piano part was intended to serve as a generic part, in that not only does the vocal part take its cues from the piano part, but any number of different instruments may play with or instead of the piano, including instruments that can perform a decrescendo on a held note. The placements of hairpins have been slightly adjusted where necessary; more substantial adjustments are covered by critical notes or by partial dashing.

OTHER ISSUES

The symbol for quarter rests has been modernized. Extraneous rests, as in empty staves where one hand in the piano part has been notated in another staff, have been deleted. Fermatas over the final barlines of all the songs in *Sechszehn Blumen* have been deleted; all others have been retained and their placement modernized. To avoid confusion with slurs, curved lines indicating groupettes have been deleted and reported in the critical notes. Numeric labels, which usually appear at the note head end, have been moved to the beam or stem end. Redundant accidentals within a measure and extraneous accidentals intended to remind performers to correct previous distant accidentals have been omitted. Cautionary accidentals have been added in parentheses. Unambiguous notational shorthands (slashed stems, unstemmed dots for pitches, repetition signs, etc.) have been realized.

Appoggiaturas are by far the most common ornaments, followed by trills. In general, ornaments appear as in the sources, the numerous irregularities included. Ornaments in Weber's *Die Temperamente* have been rendered as the modern slashed grace note and all changes are reported in critical notes. Ornamentation in early nineteenth-century lieder in general and in individual cycles and songs is discussed under "Notes to Performers."

Where practical, passages marked to be played up or down an octave have been written at pitch and noted in critical notes. The modern *octava* sign is used throughout and *loco* indications have been deleted, except as a reminder after extended *octava* passages. Directives within the scores are written in lowercase.

Vocal Text

No original editions of the poetry—only later editions of Castelli's *Die Monate*, Müchler's *Die Farben*, and Gubitz's *Die Temperamente*—were available for comparison. These later editions were used as guides in editing the musical texts of those cycles, but no attempt was made to reconcile the two. "Texts and Translations" reproduces Castelli's, Müchler's, and Gubitz's later editions and the musical texts of the other cycles exactly as they appeared in the sources, with underlaid verses formatted as those printed separately.

In the music, spelling has been modernized and orthographic shorthands have been realized. Capitalization has been regularized and emended to match punctuation but otherwise remains as in the sources, with underlaid first verses capitalized as in subsequent verses. Capital or lowercase use of "ihr" and "euch" remains as in the sources. In *Die Jahreszeiten, Sechszehn Blumen,* and *Die Blumen und der Schmetterling,* the three cycles for which the music served as the source for the texts (printed verbatim in "Texts and Translations"), punctuation has been emended or added for grammatical and syntactical clarity, but where it influences meaning, changes have been noted in critical notes. In *Die zwölf Monate, Die Farben,* and *Die Temperamente bei dem Verluste der Geliebten,* for which later editions of the poetry served as sources for the texts printed in "Texts and Translations," all changes to the texts printed in the music have been reported in critical notes. Missing apostrophes, however, have been tacitly added. Significant discrepancies between music sources and the available poetry sources are discussed in the comments to "Texts and Translations."

In the text underlay, word division has been modernized and hyphens added for syllabification. Where necessary, alignment of syllables to notes has been clarified, and extender lines have been modernized. Unnumbered verses have been numbered. Text added to clarify part singing appears in square brackets. Only the first verse has been underlaid, as in all the sources except the Simrock edition of *Die Farben,* which underlaid between two and four verses per song (Weber's "Der Leichtmütige" is a special case given that all verses are written out except for verses 1 and 2, which are underlaid together). Suggestions for altering the music to fit subsequent verses are offered in critical notes; the merely awkward has not been addressed.

Critical Notes and Commentary

The following notes report all textual and musical discrepancies between the sources and this edition that are not covered in editorial methods. Unless otherwise stated, notes describe rejected source readings. Locations are identified by measure (m., mm.) and beat (b., bb.) or verse (v., vv.) and line (l., ll.). References to the text underlay are cited as "text." When the music involves only one singer, the singer's part is cited as "voice." Other parts are cited as follows: pn. = piano; r.h. = piano, right hand staff; l.h. = piano, left hand staff; S = soprano; T = tenor; B = bass; Ch = choir. Notes (including appoggiaturas) are numbered consecutively within a measure; notes sounding simultaneously are numbered from bottom to top. When appropriate, chords are numbered rather than notes or beats. Pitch names are given according to the system in which c' refers to middle C.

Die zwölf Monate

[1.] Januar

M. 22, text: semicolon after "Brauch." M. 24, r.h., note 8: g′ (compare m. 28). M. 30, text: no comma after "schau'n." M. 35, text: period after "Frau'n." M. 36, r.h., note 5: d′.

[2.] Februar

Mm. 11–12, text: no semicolon after "Mummerei'n." M. 12, r.h., note 3: e″. M. 14, text: comma after "närrisch." Mm. 23–24, r.h.: notes engraved an octave lower with *8va*. M. 24, text: comma after "fang'." M. 26, text: "kuk-ket" [*sic*]. M. 26, all parts, b. 2: 8th notes on "-ket" followed by 8th rests under the fermatas.

[4.] April

M. 11, text: no semicolon after "macht." M. 20, b. 3 through m. 21, r.h.: notes engraved an octave lower with *8va*. M. 23, r.h.: note 1 lacks augmentation dot. M. 24, text: comma after "sehr." M. 26, text: no comma after "Euch."

[5.] Mai

M. 1, b. 1, pn.: *con Sordin.* M. 4, b. 3, pn.: *senza Sordin.* M. 9, r.h., note 4: d′. M. 11, chord 2 through m. 12, chord 2, r.h.: notes engraved an octave lower with *8va*.

[6.] Junius

Mm. 4–5, text: comma after "geweiht." Mm. 15–16, text: no comma after "Natur."

[7.] Julius

M. 8, text: comma after "Schlucht." M. 16, bb. 1–2, r.h.: notes engraved an octave lower with *8va*.

[8.] August

M. 8, text: no semicolon after "Spitze." M. 12, b. 1, r.h.: notes engraved an octave lower with *8va*. M. 17, text: no period after "Greis"; lowercase "der." M. 19, text: comma after "abwärts." M. 21, bb. 1–2, l.h.: half note and quarter rest.

[9.] September

Anacrusis, r.h.: quarter note. M. 16, text: comma after "Ton." M. 18, r.h., note 2: g′. M. 26, text: period after "schon." M. 34, text: no exclamation mark after "Rehlein." Mm. 35–36, text: no comma after "entflieht."

[10.] October

M. 14, r.h., note 7: f♯′. M. 16, voice, note 2: 8th note. M. 24, text: no comma after "Bedenket." M. 29, text: no comma after "Ceres."

[11.] November

M. 18: tempo indication (moved to m. 17 anacrusis in edition). M. 27, text: semicolon after "Stillen." M. 28, b. 1, text: "ihm" [*sic*], which would refer to the dress rather than nature. M. 31, r.h., notes 1–2 and 4–5: compare slurs to m. 18.

[12.] December

M. 35: tempo indication (moved to m. 34 anacrusis in edition). M. 40, text: no exclamation mark after "Frauen." M. 41, r.h., notes 1–2: slurred, probably misplaced; see m. 42 and compare with voice part.

Die Jahreszeiten

I. Winter

1. Winters Ankunft

M. 1, b. 1, l.h.: *sempre staccato* (moved to m. 3 in edition, and all subsequent intermittent staccatos have been omitted). Mm. 4 and 5, r.h.: whole rests (notes engraved in l.h. staff in source). M. 16, r.h., note 12: e′. M. 25, text: "stürmender" (storming) has been retained; compare to m. 17, "stürmischer" (stormy). M. 28, b. 2, l.h.: ♯ on F space is meant for note 4.

2. Winterruhe

M. 10, pn., crescendo hairpin begins on second 8th; another crescendo hairpin follows on b. 3 (replaced by decrescendo hairpin to m. 11 in edition). M. 12, voice: half rest. V. 2, l. 1: no comma after "Nest."

3. Winternachtleben

M. 8, all parts: quarter rest at end. Mm. 13–16, all parts, all verses: the original notation is shown below; in m. 13, vv. 1–2 use notes with downward stems while v. 3 uses those with upward stems (N.B.: in the edition, the repeat bars of m. 13 have been removed and the ending for v. 3—to be sung twice—has been newly written out as mm. 17–20):

II. Frühling

2. Frühlingserde

Mm. 9–10, voice: the original notation is as follows:

[musical notation: -fliehn, die scher- zend der Win- ter- fes- sel rasch ent-]

V. 2, l. 2: colon after "Rain."

3. Frühlingsleben

M. 10, b. 1, r.h.: 8th rest. M. 16, l.h.: note 1 lacks augmentation dot. M. 18, b. 2 through m. 19, b. 1, l.h.: chords engraved in treble clef. M. 19, l.h., chord 3: quarter notes.

III. Sommer

2. Auf dem Flusse

M. 8, l.h., note 9: unclear, either e♭ or d. M. 9, S1: text moved above staff in edition.

3. In der Laube

M. 5, T, note 5: quarter note.

IV. Herbst

1. Garten

Mm. 16–17, r.h.: notes engraved in bass staff; edition moves them to treble staff and adds change to bass clef. M. 16, l.h., note 2: whole note. M. 17, r.h., note 3: half note.

2. Weinberg

M. 20, text: period after "Bahn"; compare to basso solo, m. 11. Mm. 21–22, pn.: accents centered between staves (edition moves them to l.h. chords).

3. Herbstöde

M. 12, b. 1, above r.h. staff: ⊕. M. 13, b. 2, above l.h. staff: ✻.

Die Farben

The optional guitar part included in the Simrock edition has been omitted.

1. Lob der weißen Farbe

M. 8, text: comma after "weih'n." V. 2, l. 2: comma after "trägt." V. 3, l. 2: comma after "Friede."

2. Lob der roten Farbe

Mm. 12–13, text: comma after "gesungen." M. 15, r.h., note 8: b♭' (see "Notes to Performers"). M. 16, voice, note 4: b♭'. Mm. 18–19, text: comma after "vergleichen." M. 21, text: comma after "weichen." M. 23, text: semicolon after "tot." M. 26, bb. 3–4, r.h.: dotted half note with measured-tremolo slash and "6" indication has been realized in the edition as two triplets, as it appears in the Oehmigke edition. V. 3, l. 2: no comma after "Schoße." V. 3, l. 5: no comma after "Erröten." V. 6, l. 3: comma after "Treu'."

3. Lob der blauen Farbe

M. 1, pn.: *sempre p* above r.h. staff (moved between staves in edition). M. 15, l.h., note 2: no ♮; editorial ♮ based on g♮" in the guitar part doubling that line. V. 3, l. 2: no quotation marks. V. 5, l. 2: semicolon after "Beständigkeit."

4. Lob der gelben Farbe

M. 2, text: semicolon after "hold." M. 4, text: comma after "gezollt." M. 8, r.h., note 3: a; Oehmigke edition shows g. V. 2, l. 2: comma after "Tugend." V. 3, l. 2: comma after "Lobgedicht." V. 4, l. 3: lowercase "wiese" [*sic*]. V. 6, l. 1: comma after "Rhein." V. 7, l. 1: period after "Wein"; exclamation mark in Oehmigke edition. V. 8, l. 2: comma after "Rosenpaar." V. 8, l. 4: no quotation marks.

5. Lob der grünen Farbe

M. 9, r.h.: *tr* below note 4 (set as turn in edition). M. 13, text: no comma after "feuerfarb." M. 28, l.h.: note 1 lacks augmentation dot. V. 2, l. 2: lowercase "die." V. 3, l. 1: no comma after "Wald." V. 5, l. 2: "Muh'" (no umlaut). V. 6, l. 3: lowercase "grabes."

[6.] Lob der violetten Farbe

Song no. 4 in Oehmigke edition; the duplicate first verse in the Oehmigke edition has been omitted. Systems 1 (mm. 1–7) and 2 (mm. 8–13), l.h. staff: no key signature. System 3 (mm. 14–20), voice staff: no key signature. M. 1, text: no comma after "Farbe." M. 6, b. 4, r.h.: ♯ on b' line is meant for note 5. M. 7, r.h., note 6: e'. Mm. 9–13, r.h.: curved lines indicating sextuplets have been deleted. M. 10, r.h., notes 2 and 8: d' (ledger lines missing). Mm. 11–12, text: no comma after "erhöhte." M. 12, voice, note 1 (appoggiatura): e". M. 13, r.h., note 2: d' (ledger line missing). M. 14, voice, note 7 (appoggiatura): b♭'. M. 14, bb. 3–4, r.h.: notes are half notes without measured-tremolo slash; compare to mm. 5–7, l.h. M. 16, b. 3, l.h.: whole rest. M. 17, b. 3, l.h.: ♯ on e space is meant for note 5. M. 19, l.h., note 5: no quarter note stem.

[7.] Lob der schwarzen Farbe

Published separately in Spehr edition. Mm. 9–10, text: no comma after "umgeben." Mm. 15 and 17, r.h.: curved lines indicating triplets have been deleted. M. 16, voice: note 1 has augmentation dot.

Sechszehn Blumen

The slurs on single and double appoggiaturas have been deleted.

[1.] Das Stiefmütterchen

M. 2, b. 2 through m. 3, b. 1, l.h.: notes engraved in treble staff; edition moves them to bass staff and adds change to treble clef. V. 3, l. 4: lowercase "neue."

[4.] DIE NELKE

V. 6, l. 4: "Denn" [*sic*].

[5.] DIE NACHTVIOLE

M. 1, b. 2, l.h.: f + a♭ + b♭ stemmed up, separated from e♭, stemmed down. M. 8, r.h.: 8th note (note 1) beamed separately from following 32d notes.

[6.] DIE LILIE

M. 10, text: "Gespinnste" [*sic*].

[7.] DIE KAMILLE

Mm. 3–4, l.h.: notes engraved in treble staff; edition moves them to bass staff and adds change to treble clef. M. 5, r.h., appoggiatura: possibly the victim of an ink smudge, it may have been intended as a 16th, as in m. 6. M. 14, text: the syllable "-fun-" is under note 2 (moved to under downbeat in edition). V. 2, l. 5: "velässt" [*sic*].

[9.] DAS GÄNSEBLÜMCHEN

Anacrusis, mm. 1, 10, and 11, r.h.: curved lines indicating triplets have been deleted. M. 2, l.h., chord 4: quarter notes. M. 5, r.h., note 2 through m. 6, chord 3: notes engraved an octave lower with *8va*.

[10.] DIE KORNBLUME

M. 10, text: lowercase "in." Mm. 12–13, text: "auf geschlossen" (two words). V. 6, l. 2: exclamation mark after "Licht."

[11.] DIE WASSER-LILIE

V. 3, l. 1: "Pupur-Gluthen" [*sic*].

[12.] DIE HYAZINTHE

M. 16, voice: in lower part, 8th note aligned below last two 32d notes of rising melisma, with the second syllable "-den" under the 8th note; in the edition, "-den" remains as in the source, but the 8th note has been moved as shown, with bracketed text added to match. M. 16, r.h.: no indication of treble clef before m. 17. M. 17, r.h.: two slurs, one on b. 1, the other connecting bb. 2–3; the break between the slurs makes space for printing the treble-clef chord for the l.h. M. 18, l.h., chord in treble clef: notes engraved an octave lower with *8va*.

[13.] DIE MOHN-BLUME

Mm. 5–9 (except 8th-note dyad at end of m. 9), r.h.: notes engraved in bass staff; edition moves them to treble staff and adds change to bass clef. System 2 (mm. 9–17), r.h. staff: key signature has ♭ on a' space. Mm. 14 and 18, l.h.: notes engraved in treble staff; edition moves them to bass staff and adds change to treble clef.

[14.] DAS VEILCHEN

M. 1, voice: breve rest after whole rest.

[15.] DIE TULPE

Part names: "2te Stimme" and "Fortepiano." Mm. 7–9: dash after "schön" in voice 1, period and dash after "schön" in voice 2; in order to distinguish the punctuation from extender lines, dashes and periods are replaced with colons and the following word ("wir") is made lowercase in the edition. M. 12, voice 2, note 3: quarter note. Mm. 32, 45, and 48, pn.: 8th notes separated by 8th rests are connected by beams. M. 43 through m. 45, b. 2, l.h.: notes engraved in treble staff; edition moves them to bass staff and adds change to treble clef.

[16.] DER LAVENDEL

M. 17, r.h., chord 2: ♮ is on c‴ (moved to e‴ in edition).

Die Blumen und der Schmetterling

Himmel provides remarkably detailed, as well as remarkably irregular, articulation and dynamic marks, even providing separate ones for each hand in the piano part. Duplications have been omitted; where marks apply to only one hand, they have been left within or immediately outside that part. In the piano part, Himmel often stems for two parts per staff. That stemming has been retained for counterpoint, but stemming has been changed to one part per staff to reflect chordal writing.

[1.] ZUEIGNUNG AN DEUTSCHLANDS TÖCHTER

M. 13, l.h.: two slurs, one from the grace notes to note 8 (a♭'), the other on notes 8–9; slurs combined in edition to match r.h. M. 18, b. 3, l.h.: *f fz* below staff. Mm. 28–30, r.h.: dynamics are below staff (moved above in edition). M. 31, b. 1: *f fz* below l.h. staff and *f* preceding the *fz* below the r.h. staff. M. 33, voice: whole rest.

[2.] DAS SCHNEEGLÖCKCHEN

M. 3, l.h.: notes 5–8 slurred together. M. 13, l.h.: notes 1–4 and 5–8 each slurred together. M. 14, r.h.: notes 1–4 and 5–8 each slurred together.

[3.] DAS VEILCHEN

System 5 (mm. 17–20), l.h. staff: key signature as for treble clef, beginning on middle line. System 6 (mm. 21–24), l.h. staff: key signature as for bass clef, beginning on second line. M. 19, r.h.: notes 1–6 slurred together. M. 19, r.h., note 6: possibly intended as e♭'. M. 20, r.h., note 5: f″.

[4.] DIE MYRTE

M. 11, r.h.: curved lines indicating triplets have been deleted. M. 17, l.h., chords 1–3: 8th notes. M. 18, r.h., chord 4: quarter notes. Mm. 20 and 28, r.h.: dynamics are below staff (moved above in edition). M. 25, b. 1, pn.: *p* (moved to m. 24, b. 3 in edition). M. 27, b. 1, pn.: *p* (moved to m. 26, b. 3 in edition).

[5.] DIE NARZISSE

M. 6, r.h., note 12: no fractional beam. M. 9 through m. 10, b. 1, r.h.: first two 8ths are beamed separately from the last 8th of each beat. M. 11, l.h.: no indication of bass clef before b. 2. M. 17, pn.: chords lack augmentation dots.

[6.] DAS VERGISSMEINNICHT

Anacrusis, l.h.: whole rest. M. 14, voice: whole rest.

[7.] DIE PALME

Mm. 1–3, r.h.: curved lines indicating triplets have been deleted. M. 4, r.h.: note is dotted half note (edition adds tie, 8th note, and 8th rest). M. 4, l.h.: whole rest. M. 6, b. 1, r.h.: *ff* below staff; l.h.: *fz* below staff. M. 7, r.h.: chord 2 lacks arpeggio mark.

[8.] DIE ROSE

Added articulations correspond to this song's reprise in "Wechselgesang der Blumen." M. 4, bb. 3–4, l.h.: crescendo hairpin below staff.

[9.] WECHSELGESANG DER BLUMEN

Tempo (also in m. 107): "Frölich." M. 1, r.h., note 8: a'. M. 3, bottom voice: note 4 has augmentation dot. Mm. 9–10, r.h.: the editorial dynamics are from the parallel passage, mm. 117–18. Mm. 9 and 10, l.h., note 6: f'. M. 11, r.h.: cautionary ♮ on note 9 (g") and cautionary ♭ on note 11 (e♭"). M. 14, middle voice, note 2: a'. M. 14, b. 1, r.h.: *p* (moved to m. 13 in edition). M. 17, r.h.: *p* between notes 9 and 10 (moved to note 11 in edition to coincide with entry of voice). M. 18, top voice, note 1: f". M. 21, r.h.: dyad (notes 1–2) stemmed separately from the following 16th notes. M. 21, r.h.: note 11 has ♭. M. 22, b. 2, r.h.: *p* (moved back to note 2 in edition). M. 26, l.h., note 4: f. System 10 (mm. 36–39), l.h. staff: key signature as for treble clef, beginning on middle line. M. 36, l.h., chord 1: G + g. M. 51, b. 1, l.h.: *p* below staff (moved between staves of anacrusis in edition). M. 52, b. 1, r.h.: *p* below staff. M. 55, l.h.: no indication of treble clef before m. 56. M. 58, l.h.: notes 1–4 slurred together. M. 59, voice, note 5: f'. M. 76, l.h.: note 1 lacks augmentation dot. M. 89, r.h., note 1: f♯". M. 96, r.h.: *p* below chord 1 (moved to downbeat in edition). M. 97, r.h.: *p* below chord 4 (moved to b. 3 in edition). M. 113, l.h., note 7: cautionary ♮. Mm. 117 and 118, l.h., note 6: f'. M. 118, b. 1, r.h.: *p* (moved to m. 117, note 8 in edition). M. 120, l.h., note 2: cautionary ♮. M. 122, bottom voice: note 2 lacks augmentation dot. M. 125, bottom voice: note 1 lacks augmentation dot. Mm. 125–26, r.h.: curved lines indicating triplets have been deleted. M. 128, voice: half rest; pn., both chords: half notes.

[10.] DER SCHMETTERLING

M. 1, b. 1, pn.: *pp* (moved to anacrusis in edition). M. 7, r.h.: note 12 has ♭. M. 8, l.h.: notes engraved in treble clef. M. 10, r.h.: notes 1–4 beamed separately from notes 5–8. M. 12, b. 1 through first two-thirds of b. 2, l.h.: notes engraved in treble clef; treble clef moved to precede last two notes of m. 12. M. 21, l.h., note 7: G.

Die Temperamente bei dem Verluste der Geliebten

[1.] DER LEICHTMÜTIGE

There are numerous errors and discrepancies; discrepancies in articulation between verses have not been reconciled. Tempo: "Vivace giojoso." Mm. 1–2, pn.: accents below r.h. staff (replicated editorially in l.h. in edition). M. 2, v. 2, text: comma after "schwer." M. 5, v. 1, text: period after "lieben." M. 5, v. 2, text: semicolon after "fluchen." M. 6, r.h.: notes 6 and 7 each has a stroke. M. 8, l.h., bass: note (a) is half note without measured-tremolo slash. M. 8, v. 2, text: comma after "her." Mm. 10–11, v. 1, text: no comma after "geblieben." M. 11, b. 1, r.h.: no slash on 8th-note ornament. M. 14, text: colon after "Sinn." M. 16, v. 2, text: no comma after "Kind." Mm. 17–18, v. 1, text: period after "bewahrt." M. 18, v. 2, text: no comma after "Joch." M. 19, l.h.: beaming breaks between notes 6 and 7. M. 24, v. 2, text: no comma after "bleichen." Mm. 24–25, v. 1, text: comma after "Liebefahrt" [*sic*]. M. 25, v. 2, text: period after "noch." M. 27, v. 1, text: comma after "and're." M. 29, b. 1, l.h.: chord missing; dots on the spaces for A and g. M. 30, v. 1, text: period after "Art." M. 30, v. 2, text: period after "doch." M. 42, text: comma after "Genius." M. 45, b. 1, voice and r.h.: no slashes on 8th-note ornaments. M. 45, text: comma after "sprechen." M. 48, text: no exclamation mark after "Kuss." M. 51, text: lowercase "nun." M. 52, text: comma after "gut." M. 56, l.h., note 3: G. Mm. 56–57, text: no comma after "ertragen." M. 58, l.h., note 3: G. M. 59, text: comma after "morgen." M. 60, l.h., notes 1 and 4: both e. M. 62, l.h., note 1: A. M. 63, b. 1, l.h.: chord missing; dots on the spaces for A and g. M. 69, l.h., note 5: c♯. M. 70, l.h., note 1: B. M. 76, text: capitalized "Frag'." M. 78, b. 1, voice and r.h.: no slashes on 8th-note ornaments. M. 78, text: semicolon after "Erden." M. 78, text: capitalized "Ob." M. 81, text: no exclamation mark after "sind." M. 83, text: lowercase "wenn." M. 84, text: no quotation marks. M. 90, text: no quotation mark and no comma after "Herr." M. 94, text: comma after "Frauen." M. 96, b. 1, l.h.: chord missing; dots on the spaces for A and g. M. 97, text: no exclamation or quotation marks after "Licht." Mm. 102–3, text: no comma after "empor." M. 106, text: comma after "schenken." M. 108, text: lowercase "schwazt" [*sic*]. M. 109, text: comma after "vor." M. 112, r.h.: beaming breaks between notes 2 and 3. M. 112, text: comma after "denken." M. 119, text: comma after "ihr." M. 120, r.h.: notes are half notes without measured-tremolo slash. M. 124, text: semicolon after "Leben." M. 128, text: no colon after "geben." M. 130, b. 1, l.h.: chord missing; dots on the spaces for A and g. Mm. 130 and 141, b. 2, l.h.: middle note (e) missing in second chord. M. 135, text: no comma after "alle." M. 141, b. 1, l.h.: chord missing; dots on the spaces for A and b. M. 142, b. 2, r.h.: no slash on 8th-note ornament. M. 144, r.h.: notes 5–6 engraved an octave lower with *8va*.

[2.] DER SCHWERMÜTIGE

The irregular beaming in mm. 2, 5, 6, 37, 40, and 41 appears to convey nuances of interpretation and has been retained; chords with measured-tremolo slashes have been realized with standard beaming. M. 3, b. 3, voice: no slash on 8th-note ornament. M. 4, text: no comma after "prangen." M. 5, voice: note 2 has handwritten ♮. M. 9, text: no comma after "Heil'genschein." M. 11, r.h., note 5: c' (compare m. 46). M. 13, r.h., note 3: c' (compare m. 48). M. 16, b. 3 through m. 23, r.h.: notes engraved using both staves; edition moves them to treble staff and adds change to bass clef. M. 20, text: no period after "ein." M. 23, r.h., last rest: 16th rest. M. 27, r.h.: ♮ is on c′ (moved to a in edition). Mm. 29–31, r.h., written in two parts: upper part consists of a single line and is notated with measured-tremolo slashes (except for m. 30, notes 5–6); lower part consists of dyads and uses measured-tremolo half notes in mm. 29–30, and in m. 31, bb. 1–2 are beamed together. M. 29, text: no comma after "vergangen." Mm. 31–32, text: no exclamation mark after "Heil'genschein." Mm. 32–33, r.h.: notes engraved using both staves; edition moves them to treble staff and adds change to bass clef. M. 35, voice: whole rest missing. M. 37, l.h.: chord lacks augmentation dots. Mm. 38–39, text: no comma after "verbangen." M. 41, text: colon after "mein." M. 42, text: "Allverlangen" is one word, capitalized. M. 51, text: comma after "Pein." M. 51, b. 3 through m. 59, r.h.: notes engraved using both staves; edition moves them to treble staff and adds change to bass clef. M. 53, r.h., note 1: f♮. M. 57, text: no period after "mein." M. 58, r.h., chord 3: 8th notes. M. 59, l.h.: source lacks second 16th-note A and additional tie to half note.

[3.] Der Liebewütige

Mm. 1 and 18, text: no quotation marks. Mm. 2–3, text: lowercase "verschmähet!" M. 4, text: lowercase "wer." Mm. 4, 23, 42, 61, and 95, pn.: single accent between staves (applied to both hands in edition). Mm. 7–14, r.h.: notes engraved using both staves; edition moves them to treble staff and continues to use the source bass clef for m. 6. Mm. 25–33, 44–52, 63–71, and 97–105, r.h.: notes engraved using both staves; edition moves them to treble staff and adds change to bass clef. M. 32, r.h., notes 2, 5, 8, and 11 (middle notes of triplets): all d′. M. 34, l.h., note 1: cautionary ♭. M. 38, voice: whole rest missing. M. 43, text: comma after "stumm." Mm. 49–52, r.h.: two slurs, one for m. 49, the other for mm. 50–52; in edition, the slurs are placed on mm. 49–50 and 51–52 to match parallel cases (compare to e.g., mm. 11–14). M. 50, text: comma after "sinnig." M. 52, text: no comma after "wallt." M. 56, text: no quotation marks. Mm. 58–59, text: no quotation marks. M. 59, text: lowercase "sie." M. 60, text: comma after "Regel." Mm. 61–62, text: no period after "Gezerr." Mm. 63 and 64, text: lowercase "ihr." Mm. 63 and 67, text: no quotation marks. M. 68, r.h., note 10: g. Mm. 74–75, text: no quotation marks. M. 75, l.h., note 1: E (ledger line missing). Mm. 75 and 91, text: no quotation marks. Mm. 78–79, text: comma after "heran." Mm. 84–85, r.h.: all 16 notes slurred together. Mm. 86–87, text: comma after "bereut." M. 88, text: lowercase "sie." Mm. 90–91, text: period after "gescheut." M. 97, text: capitalized "Da." M. 111, r.h.: *pp* below note 5 (moved to note 3 in edition).

[4.] Der Gleichmütige

Mm. 5–6, text: no semicolon after "unerträglich." M. 7, text: capitalized "Treibt." M. 7, b. 2, text: "eine" [*sic*]. M. 11, text: capitalized "Ruhig." M. 12, r.h., chord 1: quarter notes. M. 13, r.h.: chord 1 missing; dots on the spaces for a′ and c″. M. 14 has *Fine* indication. V. 2, l. 5: no comma after "matt." V. 3, l. 2: no semicolon after "Essen." V. 3, l. 4: comma after "vergessen." V. 4, l. 2: no comma after "Wandern." V. 4, l. 3: extra "man" between "gern" and "thut." V. 4, l. 4: semicolon after "Andern." V. 4, l. 6: no comma after "an." V. 5, l. 2: period after "Laufen." V. 5, ll. 5 and 6: no commas after "ein" and "Mondenschein." V. 6, l. 2: comma after "küssen." V. 6, l. 3: no comma after "Höllenlast." V. 6, l. 4: semicolon after "müssen." V. 7, l. 4: semicolon after "lästern." V. 7, ll. 5 and 7: no quotation marks. V. 8, l. 4: comma after "bequemlich." V. 8, l. 5: no comma after "lau."

Notes to Performers

Strophic Settings and Declamation

Good strophic settings with careful attention to proper declamation were admired in the early nineteenth century, yet the more striking a melody and the more closely it portrays the first verse, the less easily it fits subsequent verses. For example, Wineberger's dramatic setting of "Die Sonnenblume" works well for the first verse, with rising dotted figures on "majestätisch" (majestically) and a long, held note on "Fülle" (fullness) descending to a *piano* close; in subsequent verses, however, the rising dotted figures fall on "sehnend" (sighing) and the descent to a *piano* close delivers "Gewalt" (might). Not surprisingly, through-composed forms gained prominence at the same time music began to challenge poetry's primacy.

Imperfect declamation is often less noticeable, however, in later verses, because repeated melodies tend to become increasingly less prominent as new words attract attention. Also, in carefully crafted songs, subsequent verses can refer back to earlier verses to add meaning or irony through melodic recall; in other words, a verse that seems not to fit well in isolation sometimes fits well in context. When choosing which verses to include, performers may want to check not only content and verse order, but also context, declamation, subtle internal references, and the cumulative effect of singing several verses. Weber's "Der Gleichmütige," for example, is the shortest in that cycle, but has by far the most verses. The verses seem to overwhelm the tiny song, and that is precisely the point: each performer must discover how many verses he has to sing for his audience to grasp the humor without singing so many as to bore them, and still tell the story.

Below, problematic declamation has been noted and suggestions offered; the merely awkward has been left to performers to solve.

Ornaments

Appoggiaturas should be played on the beat. Variable appoggiaturas last, as they usually indicate, half the duration of the following note, or two thirds the duration in compound meters; invariable appoggiaturas are played as a quick "snap," their duration subtracting very little from the following note. There is, unfortunately, no distinction in notation between variable and invariable appoggiaturas in these sources. Performers must make their own decisions according to their knowledge of the style. Occasionally, a composer will notate a variable appoggiatura shorter than half the duration of the following note, the most common being one quarter the duration (an eighth note appoggiatura preceding a half note, for example); durations should be adjusted accordingly in performance. Most, but not all, grace notes should be played before the beat. A brief summary of each composer's use and notation of ornaments precedes the notes of each cycle, and suggestions for performance are provided for individual songs.

Dynamic and Articulation Marks

In the absence of dynamic indications, performers may assume *mezzo* or *mezzo piano*, indications that were rarely indicated; in these sources, most dynamics mark special events. Composers provided few marks in vocal parts; those that are provided should receive special consideration. Vocalists should take cues from and interact with the piano part, an efficient system for a time when one person both sang and accompanied. The exception, of course, is the piano's *piano* when the voice enters: at that point, the voice assumes the primary role, picking up the piano's dynamic from the prelude as the piano recedes into a supporting role. When shifting between dynamic levels, the voice often begins the new dynamic on upbeats preceding its notation in the piano accompaniment, so singers need to look ahead. Also, while the piano part tends to shift between dynamic levels, the voice has more latitude for surging within and between levels.

The sources contain no indications of a sustaining pedal; it should be used as little as possible, if at all. In fact, a rapid decay is essential to many gestures in these sources, and details of voicing, such as those in mm. 33–34 of Wineberger's "Die Wasser-Lilie," would be buried by a sustaining pedal.

Composers generally set the text of the first verse most carefully, and often employed a notational shorthand, here called initial markings, whereby the markings in the first occurrence of a passage established its character. Composers expected performers to apply those markings wherever appropriate, an inherently subjective decision. In subsequent verses, performers should exercise their option of altering rhythms, articulations, dynamics, and ornaments to suit themselves as well as the texts; improvised embellishments were still very much a part of the style.

Markings often change at cadence points; such changes should not be regarded simply as discrepancies, but as signaling the close.

Die zwölf Monate

Bornhardt's ornaments have no slurs and are divided almost equally between those one-half the duration of the main note and those of the same duration. In "December," four ornaments are one-quarter the duration of the main note (two in voice [m. 27] and two in piano [m. 29]) and two are slashed (in piano, mm. 8 and 20); one other, in piano (m. 38), though unslashed, is similar in function to the slashed ornaments. Ornaments should be played on the beat.

[1.] Januar

Mm. 1–4 present the two faces of Janus, which performers should emphasize, and which Bornhardt underscored by changing clefs with each character: *forte* in bass clef, *piano* in treble. Compare mm. 16–17: "Schmeichelei'n" is obsequious flattery and calls for a more *legato* delivery than "Wünsche plappern" (prattling best wishes).

[2.] Februar

Note the awkward harmony in mm. 16–17 and 21–22, which outlines G minor (ii) rather than F minor (i); perhaps these are examples of the musical world becoming foolish.

[4.] April

Considering April's "moody" character, dynamics are surprisingly few, particularly as the music seems to demand dramatic contrasts; performers should add them as appropriate. The beginning measures here are a prime example of initial markings: there should be aural space between the sixteenth triplets and the following eighth note throughout. In m. 23, the slur is new in this third statement of the figure; it underscores both "gar zu sehr" (entirely too much), the turning point of the text, and the slur (pun intended) on the female character.

[5.] Mai

Con and *senza sordino* should be played *una corda* and *tre corda*. Compare the l.h. slurring in mm. 11 and 13; no slur in m. 13 may be owing to the text's "frischer Jugend."

[6.] Junius

"Junius" and "Mai" have several similar gestures, most notably the motive of three eighth-note upbeats leading into a *legato* sigh (all in the piano). Throughout "Junius," however, the three eighth-note upbeats are not slurred. Performers must decide whether the motive recalls "Mai," and therefore should be slurred likewise, or comments on "Mai," and therefore should be varied.

[9.] September

Note the several levels of juxtaposition: in the tale (the hunter versus the doe); in the text ("will entwischen" [wishes to escape] versus "da trifft's" [strikes it (the doe)]); in the articulation (*staccato* versus *legato*); in the range (wide-ranging arpeggios versus narrow conjunct figures); and in the dynamics (*fortissimo* versus *pianissimo*). In fact, dynamics are an integral part of this song's message: the juxtaposition between *piano* and *forte* underscores that between doe and hunter. Note that the *fortissimo* in m. 26 is not the result of a crescendo but a sudden burst representing the hunter's shot, just as the ensuing fermatas and *pianissimo* chords represent the demise of the doe.

Note also the disjunction between the ways text and music relate the storyline. The doe is shot in m. 23 in the text, but in m. 26 in the music: the voice completes the tale first, giving the audience the opportunity to "experience" the musical shot. This disjunction also allows the doe to die appropriately at the end of the tale (mm. 27–28), in the silence of the pause, giving the audience time to grieve and perhaps shed a mental tear before receiving the allegory's explanation in the second half.

In m. 19, the disjunction in articulation between voice and piano reveals not only the hunter's dominance but also Bornhardt's sarcastic pity for the "poor little doe," placing him squarely on the hunter's side of the conflict.

In the second half, the singer abandons a neutral narrative position with "Ihr lieben Frauen" (you dear ladies), and sides with the hunters, singing in rhythm with the piano's relentless left hand eighth notes, while the wounded "poor little doe" attempts to flee in falling triplet arpeggios, eventually succumbing in m. 41. Rhythmic disjunction (see m. 35) underscores the textual: the vocalist/hunter sings a dotted-eighth to sixteenth note rhythm against (i.e., in conflict with) the piano's/doe's triplets.

The appoggiaturas in m. 37 probably play with the lower octave of the right hand, creating a dissonance. The dissonance is a poignant setting of "Eure Tugend" (your virtue) and contrasts sharply with the sweet, "pure" initial statement (m. 29), suggesting that hunting ladies' virtue, such as it is, is perhaps not so terrible a thing.

Die Jahreszeiten

Schneider uses surprisingly few ornaments, only seven for the entire cycle. All except one are half the value of the following note and without slurs or slashes. The exception, in "Weinberg," m. 1, r.h., is slashed and of the same value as the following note, i.e., a grace note and played before the beat. The only ornament for voice, in "Herbstöde," m. 7, and the remaining five, in "Frühlingserde," mm. 11, 12, and 14, for the piano, should be played on the beat.

I. Winter

2. Winterruhe

Mm. 3–4: v. 1 uses the notes with upward stems (g♯'–d♯''–b'–g♯'–a♯'–b'); vv. 2–3 use those with downward stems (g♯'–g♯'–b'–d♯''–a♯'–b').

II. Frühling

2. Frühlingserde

Mm. 9–10 (see original notation in critical notes): vv. 1–2 use notes with upward stems; v. 3 uses notes with downward stems. Heinroth's poem contains three stanzas of four lines, alternating nine and eight syllables. Schneider set five lines, constructing an extra eleven-syllable line from the previous two lines. The source provides the fifth line for only v. 1. Fifth lines for vv. 2 and 3 have been provided for convenience; performers should feel free to construct their own.

IV. Herbst

1. Garten

M. 3, text: "Lilie" here has two, not the usual three, syllables. Mm. 16–17, l.h.: source indicates tied notes, but the ending sounds better if the low A_1 is reiterated.

2. Weinberg

The opening provides the only grace note in this cycle; it is played quickly, before the beat.

Die Farben

Individual songs can be excerpted or the set reordered to suit the performer or occasion; as explained above, the cycle appeared in several different versions and at least one song was published separately.

Hůrka uses ornaments sparingly—only seventeen scattered among six songs; Himmel is more generous, using eight in his one song. All are notated without slurs or slashes and as half the duration of the main note. Also, almost all ornaments are for the voice: the piano ornaments in tandem with the voice only twice (mm. 11 and 13 of "Lob der grünen Farbe"), and the piano ornaments alone five times (also m. 11 of "Lob der grünen Farbe" and mm. 1–2 of "Lob der blauen Farbe"). Ornaments should be played on the beat.

Gradual dynamic changes (*crescendo* and *decrescendo*) are not notated in this music, even where the music seems to demand them; performers should add them as necessary.

[2.] Lob der roten Farbe

As reported in the critical notes, in m. 15, note 8 of r.h. is b♭' in the Simrock edition. The Oehmigke edition has g', however, and this has been used in the present edition. B-flat, although conceivably part of a ii$^6_5$ chord in B-flat major, which is the chord printed in the guitar part (e♭' + b♭' + c''), causes a cross-relation with B-natural (see note 9 of r.h.), which does not appear in the guitar part. Although the cross-relation could be dismissed as a surface-level passing tone from b♭ to c' in the alto part, the awkward voice leading caused by b♭' cannot be dismissed so easily: b♭' appears out of context and emphasizes the dissonant seventh of the chord with a *sforzando*, while g' leads from and to f', providing smooth contrary motion to the I$^6_4$ chord on b. 1 of m. 16. Additionally, g' supports the voice's arpeggio while b♭' creates a dissonance with the voice's c'' and awkwardly anticipates the voice's resolution in m. 16.

[3.] Lob der blauen Farbe

The Oehmigke edition has no ornamentation in mm. 1–2. Note that mm. 5–6 do not repeat the ornaments; performers can opt to omit the ornaments altogether, use the initial ornaments for mm. 5–6, or add their own. Notice also that Hůrka has reinforced the 'alla Polacca' rhythm with his beaming; the rhythm is an important part of the song's style.

Sechszehn Blumen

In setting these poems, Wineberger relies on the topic to unify the songs, so individual songs can be excerpted or the set reordered to suit performers and occasions. Wineberger focuses on portraying each flower's character: note the florid aria style of the rose, the almost saccharine lullaby of the poppy, the undulating waves of the water lily, the excessive trills of the lavender, etc. As usual in strophic writing, Wineberger avoids word-painting and line-by-line depiction, striving instead to capture the overall character of each poem and to create a "natural," graceful scansion. Notation often suits the first verse best; performers should alter dynamics and articulations to suit subsequent verses.

Wineberger notates ornaments inconsistently. By far, most ornaments are half the duration of the main note, but a couple are the same and another few, one-quarter the duration. None are slashed, but they are almost equally divided between slurred and unslurred. Differences in notation apparently offer no differences in meaning; nonetheless, ornaments remain exactly as in the source for study purposes, except that their slurs have been omitted. In performance, ornaments for the voice should be sung on the beat except as discussed below under "[11.] Die Wasser-Lilie." Ornaments for the piano can be played either on or before the beat, at the performer's discretion.

[4.] Die Nelke

In m. 8 in the original, the *fz* lies between bb. 1 and 2, but probably pertains to b. 2, where it has been moved in the edition.

[5.] Die Nachtviole

Wineberger provided no dynamics, possibly because the song, like a lullaby, waxes and wanes within the mezzo range. Note the unusual beaming in m. 13, which highlights overlapping chromatic lines in the bass (a♭–a♮) and alto (g♭′–g♮′) leading into the cadence.

[6.] Die Lilie

This song reveals some painful lapses in compositional technique. Note the awkward harmony in m. 11, in which the F-sharp triad is set up as a pivot between tonic and dominant regions but loses that function since it is altered into major. None of the verses offers a reason for the alteration.

Besides the awkward melisma in v. 3 on the third syllable of "Könige," l. 5, note the unusually poor text setting for l. 6, where a rest falls in the middle of "Bourboniden" (Bourbons). In mm. 17–20, for voice 1, try adding b′ on b. 2 of m. 18 using the rhythm below (this rhythm can be adapted to voice 2 as well, adding e′ on b. 4 of m. 17):

[8.] Die Rose

The leap of a tenth in the voice part of m. 7 suits vv. 1, 3, 4, 5, and 6, but is less fortunate on v. 2's "Mund" (mouth) and especially unfortunate on v. 7's bowing down to "Erde" (earth). In the voice part of m. 9, b. 2, the rest interrupts "Möglichkeiten" (possibilities) in v. 4 and "Hyperion" (Hyperion) in v. 5. Performers may wish to omit the rest and add a dot to the eighth note.

[11.] Die Wasser-Lilie

Wineberger provides no dynamics, possibly because the light, $\frac{6}{8}$ *allegretto* song remains within a *mezzo* to *mezzo piano* range. The ornaments in mm. 3–4 should be played as notated, before the downbeats. Slurring and a break in beaming signal the beginning of new phrases in mm. 12 and 22.

[12.] Die Hyazinthe

The D-sharps in m. 10, which appear in a descending line and do not resolve, provide only transitory color, as there is no modulation. In m. 12, the break in beaming signals the beginning of the second half. In m. 16, the voice's sustained e′ option suits vv. 4 and 6 particularly well ("erhalten" and "Vereine," respectively), the rising melisma, vv. 2 and 3 ("heben" and "Wellen," respectively); see also the relevant critical note. "Proteus" in l. 1 of v. 4 (m. 5) must be two syllables, not the usual three. Rests mid-word in l. 2 of vv. 6 and 7 (m. 11) can be avoided by lengthening the sixteenth note into an eighth.

[13.] Die Mohn-Blume

The opening line, made even more prominent by its recurrence from no. 10, "Die Kornblume," recalls Goethe's "Kennst du das Land?" Scholz's reference would have been easily grasped: Goethe's poem was published in his novel *Wilhelm Meisters Lehrjahre* (1795), which was widely read in the early decades of the nineteenth century and was followed by *Wilhelm Meisters Wanderjahre* in 1821. "Kennst du das Land?" was set to music numerous times and appropriated for a wide variety of uses, from parlor games, to concert lieder, to the theater. Its recall in this text's escapist journey on drugs would have been appreciated. The *piano* prelude, unusual for Himmel, sets up the dreamlike, quasi-hallucinogenic trance maintained throughout. The unusual beaming across the beat in m. 21 is probably intentional; the two chords echo the vocal cadence. For l. 3 of v. 4 (m. 11), a rest in the middle of "kos'te" can be avoided by dotting the eighth (note 4).

[16.] Der Lavendel

In m. 15, the voice does sing a B-natural against the piano's B-flat.

Die Blumen und der Schmetterling

For these songs to work as a cycle, nos. 1, 9, and 10 must be included and the songs must be sung in order. The music was written "with accompaniment by piano and an optional violoncello."

Himmel liberally uses a wide variety of ornaments. His favorites are appoggiaturas, trills, and *coulades* or slides. In general, he notates appoggiaturas without slurs or slashes (the one slash is in m. 27 of "Zueignung and Deutschlands Töchter"), and the vast majority are notated as half the duration of the main note. Ornaments should begin on the beat and trills on the note above. When the trill's note is identical to the previous note, the two are tied; m. 7 of "Das Veilchen," for example, would sound as follows:

Himmel frequently gives an ornament to only one of two parts in unison (see, for example, m. 26 of "Zueignung an Deutschlands Töchter"); the resulting dissonance is intentional and should not be eliminated by adding the ornament to the other part.

[1.] Zueignung an Deutschlands Töchter

Notice the heterophonic relationship between voice and piano in mm. 20, 26, and 27; unusually, here it is the piano that adds ornaments. To accommodate the extra syllable in v. 2, l. 5 (mm. 20–22), try adding a b♭' with the following rhythm:

To avoid a rest in the middle of "Pfirsichwange" in l. 1 of v. 3 (m. 11), b. 2 becomes a quarter note.

[2.] Das Schneeglöckchen

M. 22, b. 1, r.h.: The editorial trill, added to match m. 21, should begin on e♭".

[4.] Die Myrte

L. 6 of vv. 2 and 3 (see mm. 21–24) will read better with an altered distribution of syllables:

v. 2, l. 6: -den Knos- pen ____ zu schmük- ken.
v. 3, l. 6: all- mäch- tig ____ Di- o- ne.

[5.] Die Narzisse

Notice the "decay" decrescendos prevalent throughout the song; they are significant both musically and symbolically, as is the "echo" of the final line (mm. 11–13). Mm. 13–15, r.h.: The appoggiaturas are played on the beat; the harsh dissonance they create against c" is intentional.

[6.] Das Vergissmeinnicht

M. 8, b. 1, voice: The appoggiatura should be sung in unison with the piano.

[7.] Die Palme

The extra syllable in l. 1 of v. 3 (m. 5) changes bb. 3–4 to a quarter note followed by two eighths.

[8.] Die Rose

The thirty-second note run in the voice part at the end of m. 9, although a musically cogent variation for the repetition of the last line of each verse, is nonetheless awkward in performance. For some of the verses, the line reads more smoothly with the syllable change on the final two thirty-second notes, a more common scansion pattern in German.

[9.] Wechselgesang der Blumen

This is the only part-song in the cycle, written for three treble parts in close harmony, for female chorus, for all seven soloists from the previous songs, or for the three soloists whose songs are not reprised ("Das Schneeglöckchen," "Die Narzisse," and "Die Palme"). The choral beginning and end enclose four reprises in their original keys and meters, linked only by brief, occasionally awkward modulations. Himmel was inconsistent with his dynamics and articulation marks; performers should compare their previous solos with their reprises and decide whether to reconcile the two or to retain the discrepancies for new effect.

The *fz* in m. 108, lying between notes 2 and 3 of the r.h. in the source but moved to note 2 in the edition, initially seems odd, but notice that the modulation to B-flat major is still tenuous at this point and that the emphasis cues the voice's entrance on F, the new dominant. The *fz*, an emphasis rather than a true *sforzando*, begins an anacrusis into m. 109 and pertains to the r.h. alone. Performers who find the *fz* awkward or the cue unnecessary should omit it rather than shift it back onto the downbeat of m. 108.

[10.] Das Schmetterling

M. 16, voice and piano: Ornaments begin on the tied note (bb. 2 and 5 of the ⁶⁄₈ meter); more important than when they begin, however, is that voice and piano ornament cleanly in tandem. Performers can choose whether to add a second ornament to the voice part.

Irregularities in beaming convey nuances of interpretation and have been retained, except as noted in critical notes.

Die Temperamente bei dem Verluste der Geliebten

Although these songs are delightful on their own, for their full effect, they must be sung as a group and in the order given.

The rejected lovers present distinct styles textually as well as musically. The text for "Der Leichtmütige" is written in the comic Hanswürst meter (-ᴗ-ᴗ-ᴗ-) in ten-line stanzas; "Der Schwermütige" contemplates suicide in short (four-line), square, trochaic (-ᴗ-ᴗ-ᴗ-ᴗ) stanzas; "Der Liebewütige" rages through his dramatic ballad in a riding eight-line dactyl (ᴗ-ᴗᴗ-), only to vent his rage on a little rabbit; and "Der Gleichmütige," unable even to maintain a consistent meter, rambles through abbreviated lines in irregular, seven-line stanzas.

Weber notated ornaments without slurs, mostly with slashes, and in eighth notes, regardless of the durations of the main notes and without distinguishing between variable appoggiaturas, invariable appoggiaturas, or grace notes. Consequently, all ornaments in this cycle appear as modern slashed grace notes; suggestions for performance are discussed under individual songs. As one might guess, "Der Leichtmütige" has numerous ornaments, "Der Schwermütige," a fair number, "Der Liebewütige," none at all (he is too angry to be "grace-ful"), and "Der Gleichmütige," only one miserly grace note tucked in at the end (he hasn't the energy for dissonance).

Weber wrote out most of the verses. There are numerous discrepancies between verses; performers need to decide whether the discrepancies are significant or should be reconciled.

[1.] Der Leichtmütige

The rapid alternation between *legato* and *staccato* is central to this flighty character, and performers should make the most of it. The accents in mm. 1–2, added editorially to mm. 68–69, replicate the downbeats at the corresponding places in v. 3 (mm. 35–36) and v. 5 (mm. 102–3).

Almost all of this cycle's discrepancies in ornaments occur in this one song. The discrepancies may be no more than inconsistencies or errors, but intriguingly, five of the "missing" slashes occur in the same place in four of the five verses. On closer inspection, the discrepancies may suggest a distinction between ornaments played before the beat and those played on the beat. In vv. 1 and 2, ornaments in mm. 6, 7, 8, and mm. 30, 31, 32 are in the piano part alone and appear to be played before the beat. These remain consistent in all five verses, the one exception being m. 142 in v. 5, where the lack of a slash may be an error. All other "missing" slashes are in m. 11 of vv. 1 and 2 and its corresponding place in subsequent verses: in m. 11, the slash is missing in the r.h. but is present in the voice, while in m. 45 (v. 3) and m. 78 (v. 4), the slash is missing in both voice and r.h. In all these cases, the voice and piano ornament together and playing on the beat would be not only more appropriate musically but easier to coordinate as well. Unfortunately, such an interpretation creates its own discrepancies, as the slashes that are present on eighth-note ornaments in m. 11, b. 1, voice, and those in m. 112, b. 1, voice and r.h., would then be considered errors. Similarly, the slashes on the eighth notes ornamenting the voice's "zu mir!" (to me!) in the coda, mm. 137–39, which almost certainly should be sung on the beat, would also be errors. To summarize, in performance, ornaments in the voice part alone or in the voice and piano parts together should be played on the beat, while those in the piano part alone should be played before the beat.

[2.] Der Schwermütige

Ornaments, all in the voice, should be sung on the beat. In m. 25, the clashes between the voice's G-flat and the piano's A-natural "resolving" to the voice's F-natural against the piano's E-flat, an apt portrayal of "zerklangen," is correct.

[3.] Der Liebewütige

Vv. 1–4 and 6 are written out to accommodate subtle modifications, such as the syncopation on "spionieret" in m. 40, the declamatory mm. 14–16 and 33–35, or the staccato emphasis in m. 17. In mm. 63–67, notice that m. 62's "Gezerr" and Don Marco's exclamations suggest a *forte*, but the piano's *pianissimo* reveals a fierce whisper that Klara overhears. There are no staccatos in m. 72 as there were in corresponding measures (mm. 15, 34, and 53): a new voice has entered. Klara's entrance (mm. 74ff.) and the tempo change to *grazioso* call for a new dynamic, but Weber supplies none, possibly because she speaks in a well modulated *mezzo*, in contrast to Don Marco's *fortissimos* and *pianissimos*.

[4.] Der Gleichmütige

Significantly, Weber provided no dynamics: the song is sung almost in a monotone, the only concession a subtle accent in m. 12. The sole ornament in m. 12, voice, should be sung on the beat and should not be rushed.

Recent Researches in the Music of the Nineteenth and
Early Twentieth Centuries
Rufus Hallmark, general editor

Vol.	Composer: Title
1–2	Jan Ladislav Dussek: *Selected Piano Works*
3–4	Johann Nepomuk Hummel: *Piano Concerto, Opus 113*
5	*One Hundred Years of Eichendorff Songs*
6	Etienne-Nicolas Méhul: *Symphony No. 1 in G Minor*
7–8	*Embellished Opera Arias*
9	*The Nineteenth-Century Piano Ballade: An Anthology*
10	*Famous Poets, Neglected Composers: Songs to Lyrics by Goethe, Heine, Mörike, and Others*
11	Charles-Marie Widor: *The Symphonies for Organ: Symphonie I*
12	Charles-Marie Widor: *The Symphonies for Organ: Symphonie II*
13	Charles-Marie Widor: *The Symphonies for Organ: Symphonie III*
14	Charles-Marie Widor: *The Symphonies for Organ: Symphonie IV*
15	Charles-Marie Widor: *The Symphonies for Organ: Symphonie V*
16	Charles-Marie Widor: *The Symphonies for Organ: Symphonie VI*
17	Charles-Marie Widor: *The Symphonies for Organ: Symphonie VII*
18	Charles-Marie Widor: *The Symphonies for Organ: Symphonie VIII*
19	Charles-Marie Widor: *The Symphonies for Organ: Symphonie gothique*
20	Charles-Marie Widor: *The Symphonies for Organ: Symphonie romane*
21	Archduke Rudolph of Austria: *Forty Variations on a Theme by Beethoven for Piano; Sonata in F Minor for Violin and Piano*
22	Fanny Hensel: *Songs for Pianoforte, 1836–1837*
23	*Anthology of Goethe Songs*
24	Walter Rabl: *Complete Instrumental Chamber Works*
25	Stefano Pavesi: *Dies irae concertato*
26	Franz Liszt: *St. Stanislaus: Scene 1, Two Polonaises, Scene 4*
27	George Frederick Pinto: *Three Sonatas for Pianoforte with Violin*
28	Felix Mendelssohn: *Concerto for Two Pianos and Orchestra in E Major (1823): Original Version of the First Movement*
29	Johann Nepomuk Hummel: Mozart's *Haffner* and *Linz* Symphonies
30–31	Gustav Mahler: *Die drei Pintos: Based on Sketches and Original Music of Carl Maria von Weber*
32	Niels W. Gade: *St. Hans' Evening Play Overture*
33	Charles-Marie Widor: *Symphonie pour orgue et orchestre, opus 42bis*
34	Edvard Grieg: *The Unfinished Chamber Music*

35   Johann Nepomuk Hummel: *Twelve Select Overtures*
36   *Motets for One Voice by Franck, Gounod, and Saint-Saëns*
37   *Topical Song Cycles of the Early Nineteenth Century*